Pay No Heed to the Rockets

Pay No Heed to the Rockets

Life *in* Contemporary Palestine

MARCELLO DI CINTIO

COUNTERPOINT
Berkeley, California

Library of Congress Cataloging-in-Publication Data
Names: Di Cintio, Marcello, 1973– author
Title: Pay no heed to the rockets : Palestine in the present tense / Marcello Di Cintio.
Description: First Counterpoint hardcover edition. | Berkeley, California :
    Counterpoint, [2018]
Identifiers: LCCN 2018007702 | ISBN 9781640090811
Subjects: LCSH: Arabic literature—Palestine—History and criticism. | Literature
    and society—West Bank. | Literature and society—Gaza. | Palestinian Arabs—
    West Bank—Intellectual life. | Palestinian Arabs—Gaza—Intellectual life. |
    Palestinian Arabs in literature. | Arab-Israeli conflict—Literature and the conflict. |
    Di Cintio, Marcello, 1973– —Travel. | West Bank—Social conditions. | Gaza—
    Social conditions.
Classification: LCC PJ8190 .D53 2018 | DDC 956.9405/5—dc23
LC record available at https://lccn.loc.gov/2018007702

Jacket designed by Nicole Caputo
Book designed by Jordan Koluch

COUNTERPOINT
2560 Ninth Street, Suite 318
Berkeley, CA 94710
www.counterpointpress.com

Printed in the United States of America
Distributed by Publishers Group West

10 9 8 7 6 5 4 3 2 1

For the people of Gaza

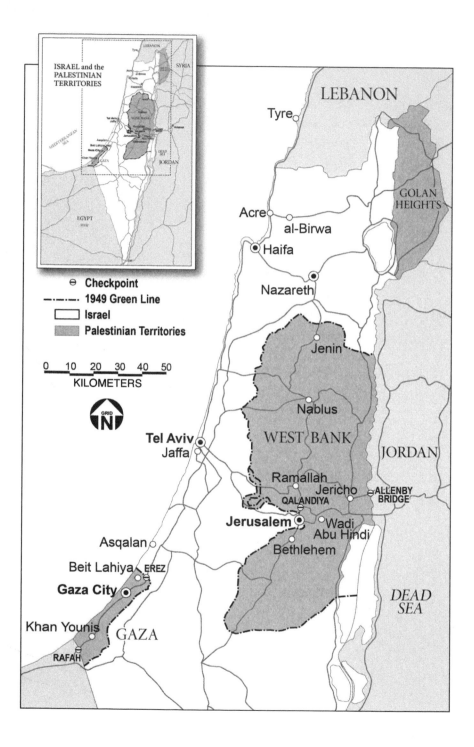

ISRAEL and the
PALESTINIAN
TERRITORIES

MEDITERRANEAN
SEA

EGYPT
SINAI

⊖ Checkpoint
-··-··-··- 1949 Green Line
☐ Israel
▨ Palestinian Territories

0   10   20   30   40   50
KILOMETERS

GRID
N

LEBANON

Tyre

GOLAN
HEIGHTS

Acre
al-Birwa
Haifa

Nazareth

Jenin

Nablus

WEST BANK

JORDAN

Tel Aviv
Jaffa

Ramallah
Jericho   ALLENBY
QALANDIYA   BRIDGE

Jerusalem   Wadi
Abu Hindi
Bethlehem

Asqalan

Beit Lahiya   EREZ

Gaza City

DEAD
SEA

Khan Younis   GAZA

RAFAH

CONTENTS

Pay No Heed to the Rockets

The Girl in the Green Dress

In 1996, Mourid Barghouti sat in a waiting room on the Jordanian side of the Allenby Bridge. He passed the time leafing through the manuscript pages of what would become his ninth book of poetry. But anxiety about the quality of his poems—a typical writer's doubt—compelled him to return the manuscript to his bag. Instead, he reflected on the first poem he ever published, "Apology to a Faraway Soldier," which came out on the first day of 1967's Six-Day War. The Arab armies fell to the Israelis by the sixth day, and the river Barghouti now waited to cross became a border. Barghouti once joked, "I wonder if the Arabs were defeated and Palestine was lost because I wrote a poem."

In his memoir *I Saw Ramallah*, Barghouti described stepping out of the waiting room and glancing west across the bridge at the land of Palestine after three decades of exile:

Who would dare make it into an abstraction now that it has declared its physical self to the senses?

It is no longer "the beloved" in the poetry of resistance, or an item on a political party program, it is not an argument or a metaphor. It stretches before me, as touchable as a scorpion, a bird, a well; visible as a field of chalk, as the prints of shoes.

I asked myself, what is so special about it except that we have lost it?

Eventually, a Jordanian soldier told Barghouti he could cross the bridge. He walked with a small bag on his left shoulder and the bridge's "prohibited wooden planks" creaking beneath his feet. "Behind me the world," he wrote, "ahead of me my world."

Nineteen years later, I sat in the same waiting room as Barghouti, or one just like it, and waited for my chance to cross the same bridge. I'd traveled to Israel and Palestine many times since millennial madness first drew me to Jerusalem in the final days of 1999, but I'd only ever arrived at Ben Gurion Airport near Tel Aviv. The last time was in 2012. I'd signed on as the writer-in-residence at the Palestine Writing Workshop and ran a creative nonfiction course in a beautiful old stone house in Birzeit. Over the course of a month, I instructed nine writers to craft stories from their own lives. Before the residency began, I wondered how many would write about their experience of the Israeli-Palestinian conflict. How many would recount memories of their grandfather's lost olive trees or pen narratives of humiliations at the hands of checkpoint soldiers? I was curious to see if they would write the sort of stories I'd grown accustomed to hearing from Palestine.

They didn't. One woman wrote about the day her little brother wandered off during Friday prayers at Jerusalem's al-Aqsa Mosque. Another wrote a charming piece about eating ice cream in the winter as a child, a mild rebellion that shocked her classmates. "Very few things fail to surprise Catholic schoolgirls," she wrote. There were many family stories. Some made me laugh aloud, like one writer's teasing of her mother's vanity or another's recollection of her parents' bizarre indecision around naming their children. Others were disturbing. One young woman wrote a chilling account of the night she quarreled with her domineering father who, enraged, commanded his wife to fetch a knife so he could kill their daughter.

Each of the nearly thirty stories the women wrote in the workshop was uniquely Palestinian, but almost none addressed the conflict—at least not directly. My students' assignments provided my first glimpses of a complete Palestinian life. Until then, I'd only viewed Palestinians through the lens of the struggle: through journalism, activism, and political discourse. After reading my students' stories, I started to see the regular humanity of the Palestinian experience. The conflict complicated their lives, surely, but so did strict schoolteachers, threatening fathers, lost brothers, and mothers who needed help coloring the gray out of their hair. My students' stories revealed individual Palestinian lives that existed alongside the greater collective struggle.

My departure from Palestine after the residency abruptly disconnected me from these human narratives. My diet of Palestinian stories came instead from newspaper reports, press releases, the rambling of politicians, and the coverage of war. Five months after I left Palestine, the Israeli military exchanged rockets with militants in Gaza in a weeklong war that killed at least a hundred Gazan civilians, dozens of them children, and four Israeli civilians. The following year brought the relatively banal news of failed peace talks, demolished homes, and detained children. Israeli soldiers shot to death fifteen Palestinian civilians in 2013, and the occasional rocket fizzled out of Gaza. Numbed by all of this, I almost forgot what I learned from my writing students in Birzeit: there is more to Palestine than the cruel accounting of death and despair.

Then, in the hot summer of 2014, I saw the girl in the green dress. Israel had launched Operation Protective Edge against militants in the Gaza Strip. During a brief lull in the bombing, a series of four photos emerged of a young Gazan girl sifting through the wreckage of a destroyed building. The girl—around ten years old—wore a green dress and pink leggings, and her long hair was tied back in a neat ponytail. She pulled books from beneath shattered concrete and cinder blocks and stacked them in her arms. The books were tattered and filthy, their covers dangling from their bindings. But in the last photograph, the girl walked away smiling.

I'd seen countless photos from the war. Images of wailing women. Bloodied men on stretchers. Funeral processions. Gray and yellow corpses. Few, though, had as profound an effect on me as these four photos of the girl and her broken books. I was tempted to reduce her to an abstraction. In Barghouti's "poetry of resistance," this girl could represent all of "beloved" Palestine. Her thin frame might embody the more than five hundred Gazan children who were killed during the fifty days of Protective Edge. She could have been one of them, for all I knew. The shattered building around her might be a convenient symbol of loss, her smile a symbol of Palestinian resilience, her youth a symbol of hope.

But just like the land Barghouti saw from across the bridge in 1996, this girl is neither an argument nor a metaphor. She, too, has a physical self to declare. She is loved not as a line of verse but as a daughter. A sister. A schoolmate. I wanted to see her like I wanted to see Palestine: not as an enduring and unsolvable political problem but as something physical that exists in the present tense. And I wanted to see Palestinians as a people unto themselves, not merely as one half of a warring binary. Not in opposition but in situ.

Most of all, though, the girl in the photos made me long for beauty. All we think we know of Palestine is its ugliness. Palestine is a place of despairing gray broken only by the red of blood and flame. But the girl in Gaza was beautiful in the way all children are beautiful, and more beautiful still for the unexpected flash of her green dress against the gray rubble. So I traveled to Palestine to find beauty. I wanted to touch the bird and the well, not just the scorpion.

Nothing is more beautiful than a story. And nothing is more human. To weave the snarled strands of a life, either real or imagined, into literature is a form of blessed alchemy. Twists of plot and turns of phrase mirror the messy details of human existence. We are nothing more or less than the stories we tell. But the only story most outsiders ever hear about Palestine is a thin volume of enduring conflict. The character of the Palestinian is either a furious militant throwing stones with a keffiyeh wrapped around his face or an old woman in a hijab wailing in front of her destroyed home. This single Sisyphean narrative of anger and deprivation holds the Palestinians hostage, and little beauty is to be found in such a plot.

Inspired by the girl and the books she rescued from the detritus of war, and by my students' stories, I decided to seek out the brokers of grace itself: the poets and writers of Palestine. They gather the fragments of their existence onto their pages, verse by verse and line by line, and bare the beauty of a place known mostly for its opposite. Certainly, the writers, and those who keep and sell their books, would have different stories to tell than the one I'd grown weary and despondent of hearing. Surely, they could reveal what made Palestine special, other than the fact that it has been lost.

I never got the chance to meet Barghouti himself. The best I could do was to follow his footsteps across the border. And so, after I'd waited in the Jordanian departure salon for an hour with a group of Arab families, a border soldier returned our passports and led us outside. The wooden bridge Barghouti walked across was no longer in use. This disappointed me. I wanted to retrace Barghouti's footfalls on Allenby's "prohibited wooden planks." The new paved crossing robbed the journey of its pedestrian poetry. Instead, we boarded a bus already nearly full of travelers from other waiting rooms. We drove for a few meters before stopping behind a line of identical buses stretching from the Jordanian border to the customs post on the other side. When our driver realized the buses were not moving, he pulled ours out of the line and roared past the unmoving vehicles to the front, where he talked his way past the official at the checkpoint. Then he edged the bus into a space in front of the Israeli border post. Some of the passengers applauded. Half of them passed Jordanian banknotes to the driver as a tip. Uncertain of the protocol, I did neither.

We waited inside the bus for another quarter hour before being allowed to exit into the chaos of the checkpoint. Hundreds of people, mostly Palestinian families, fought to navigate the gauntlet of Israeli security. Mustached men wrestled heavy suitcases through the crowd while their headscarved wives clutched crying children. Many of the Arabs were returning from *umrah* pilgrimages to Mecca and carried large plastic vessels of water with them, a sacred liquid souvenir from the holy Zamzam well in the Great Mosque.

Each arrival pressed through the mob under the disinterested gaze of young Israel Defense Forces soldiers. The border soldiers always looked bored to me, whether here on the bridge, on the smooth tiles of Ben

Gurion Airport, or at the West Bank checkpoints. I never knew whether their indifferent calm was somehow part of their uniform—a way to mask a trained alertness, say—or if the borders simply bored them. Barghouti noticed this, too. When he passed through here, he looked at the face of one of these soldiers. "For a moment he seemed a mere employee," Barghouti wrote. "At least his gun is very shiny. His gun is my personal history. It is the history of my estrangement. His gun took from us the land of the poem and left us with the poem of the land."

I merged into the current of bodies as best I could and followed the lead of those in front of me. I pushed my way to a counter where I showed my passport to an Israeli soldier in exchange for tags for my backpack. Then I squeezed out of the queue and toward a conveyor belt that swept my bag somewhere inside the building. Finally, I joined three successive lines in front of three different glass booths to show my documents to three different officials. The last, a woman of about twenty years, asked me where I planned on staying and what I planned on doing. She interrupted me when I started to list the Palestinian writers I wanted to meet. "Don't say Palestine," she said. "This is Israel. Stop saying Palestine."

The Homeland Is Where
None of This Can Happen

I once read a story about a time when the late poet Mahmoud Darwish crossed the Allenby Bridge into Palestine. His Israeli interrogator recognized him and, starstruck, asked Darwish to recite some of his poetry. Darwish refused. "A prisoner does not sing to his prison warden," he said.

I can understand the border soldier's admiration for Darwish. Of all the writers of Palestine, he is the most beloved. Darwish's poetry is recited, remembered, and loved by readers around the world. His portrait hangs in Palestine's cafés and is spray-painted on its walls. My intention was to seek out living literary culture, not the august figures of Palestine's past, but Darwish hovered over nearly every conversation. Following his ghost meant beginning to know this place.

Mahmoud Darwish was seven years old in May 1948. He was living in al-Birwa, a hilltop village overlooking the junction where the highway to the Mediterranean coast at Acre met the road from Nazareth, when a group of weary refugees arrived on foot seeking a night's respite. They were Palestinians from Haifa, they said, and were on their way to Lebanon. When the village mukhtar asked the refugees why they'd left

Haifa, they said that Jewish soldiers were shooting the men and raping the women who stayed behind.

The previous year, the war-weary British declared an end to their quarter-century mandate over the land of Palestine. The newly formed United Nations drew up and voted for a partition plan that divided the territory into separate Jewish and Arab states. Most of the region's Jews accepted the partition. Palestine's Arabs, who made up two-thirds of the population but were granted less than half of the territory, rejected it outright. A civil war began immediately after the UN passed the partition resolution in November 1947. This escalated into all-out war between Israeli forces and a coalition of Arab militaries on May 15, 1948—the day after British soldiers left the region and Israel declared itself an independent state, and a few days before the refugees reached al-Birwa.

More and more refugees passed through al-Birwa in the days that followed as they fled the fighting along the coast. All told stories of chaos and violence. No one in al-Birwa could be sure what was true, what was exaggeration, and what was propaganda. Still, the news rattled the villagers. They'd heard rumors of a massacre in the coastal village of Tantura where unarmed men were lined up and shot by Israeli soldiers. Farmers harvesting corn began to spot Israeli tanks and armored vehicles on the far edges of their farmland. Once news broke that the Israelis had occupied Acre, some of al-Birwa's families, fearing a night raid on the village, decided it was safer to sleep in their fields than in their houses.

At the time, and for centuries beforehand, almost everyone in al-Birwa was a farmer. Water from freshwater springs irrigated melons, cucumbers, tomatoes, and eggplants. Cows and goats wandered among the olive and mulberry trees. Neighbors shared whatever they had with those who were lacking. "We were very happy with the life we had at the time," Abu Ahmed Sa'ad told me. "All of us were connected together."

I'd reached out to Abu Ahmed because I wanted to learn about the fate of the village he shared with Mahmoud Darwish. He invited me to his home in Jadeidi-Makr, an Arab town near Acre. Abu Ahmed was enviably robust for a man of eighty years. Only his snowy hair and the slight curve of his back betrayed his age. It was a warm April morning, and we sat on a table in front of his home while a younger woman—perhaps a granddaughter—brought out sweetened Arabic coffee in a blue pot. Abu Ahmed insisted on pouring my cup himself.

No two families in al-Birwa were connected as closely as the Darwishes and the Sa'ads. The Sa'ad family home stood across the road from the Darwish family's. "We were always at their house," Abu Ahmed said. His mother and Mahmoud's mother were cousins, and both came from the nearby village of Dimoon. Abu Ahmed would eventually marry the daughter of Hassan Darwish, the village mukhtar and Mahmoud's great-uncle. Abu Ahmed's sister married Mahmoud Darwish's brother. The two families even shared a private cemetery in al-Birwa. "We were more or less the same family," Abu Ahmed said. "Two names, one family."

Abu Ahmed told me what happened in the spring of 1948, his family's version of a story I'd hear over and over during my time in Palestine. Despite the soldiers edging al-Birwa, the Sa'ad and Darwish families refused to leave the village. They changed their minds, though, when soldiers shot Mohammad Asham, a man both families knew. Mahmoud and Abu Ahmed's fathers instructed their wives to flee with the children and the other women to Shaab, a village a few kilometers to the east, where they were to stay with relatives until the fighting ended and al-Birwa was safe. Abu Ahmed walked with Mahmoud Darwish and his family along the dirt road to Shaab. They were the last families to leave al-Birwa, and they took nothing with them. Darwish later wrote: "We left everything as it was—the horse, the lamb, the open doors, the hot dinner, the call to the evening prayer, the one radio set continuing, perhaps to this day, its broadcast of the news of our victory."

The soldiers reached al-Birwa on June 11. Most of the villagers had left by then. The few women and children who remained took refuge in the village church, while a small group of villagers, armed with what Abu Ahmed called "old-fashioned rifles," clashed with Israeli troops. The soldiers quickly overwhelmed al-Birwa's defenders, who fled to the surrounding villages. Two weeks later, the villagers decided to return to al-Birwa to harvest their crops before they spoiled. Two hundred men and women marched on al-Birwa. Half carried rifles; the others wielded shovels, axes, and sticks. They surprised the occupying Jewish soldiers and forced them out of al-Birwa. "They liberated it at nightfall," Darwish wrote, "drank the conqueror's hot tea, and spent their first night of victory in sleep." The villagers harvested their fields for a couple of days before soldiers from the Arab Liberation Army, a collection of volunteer soldiers from nearby Arab countries, convinced them to entrust the protection of the village to them.

The ALA failed to hold al-Birwa. Israeli forces routed the Arab soldiers a day later and occupied the village for a second time. While clashes continued on the outskirts of al-Birwa, some of the exiled villagers managed to enter to gather their possessions. Abu Ahmed's father snuck in to retrieve olive oil and wheat from the family larder. By mid-July, though, al-Birwa was lost.

Shaab's villagers ridiculed al-Birwa for surrendering to the Israelis. "They said the people from al-Birwa were cowards," Abu Ahmed told me. "They said they would fight the Jewish soldiers and not give up as the people in al-Birwa had done. They said, 'In Shaab, we are not afraid.'" In spite of their insults, the determination of Shaab's residents heartened the Sa'ad and Darwish families and the other refugees from al-Birwa. But their confidence in their hosts crumbled when Israeli forces occupied a hilltop in the neighboring village of Mi'ar and began firing on Shaab's resistance fighters.

The Sa'ads fled east to the village of Majd al-Krum while the Darwish family headed north to Lebanon. "We slept one night by the filthy Rmesh pool, next to pigs and cows," Darwish wrote. "The following morning, we moved north. I picked mulberries in Tyre. Then our journey ended in Jizzine. I had never seen snow before. Jizzine was a snow farm, and it had a waterfall. I had never seen a waterfall before. And I had never known that apples hung from branches, I used to think they grew in boxes."

Abu Ahmed's family continued east in an attempt to stay ahead of the advancing Israeli soldiers. "It was summer, and we were very hot and thirsty," he told me. "All the children were crying." They arrived first in Deir al-Assad and then camped around a freshwater spring near Nahf before the Nahf villagers invited them to take refuge in their homes. The Sa'ads thought they were safe in Nahf until a Jewish soldier was killed in fighting near Majd al-Krum. Vengeful Israelis entered Nahf, lined four young men up against a wall, and shot them dead. Abu Ahmed watched their execution, and he still remembers their names: Youssef Taha, Salim Khashan, Showis Shaleh, and Kassem Aieshi. "When I saw them shot, I was totally convinced that what I'd heard before about the shooting and killings was true," Abu Ahmed said. "It was not propaganda or rumors." The family fled Nahf for villages named Yarka and Kafr Youssef, but these were already overcrowded with refugees. Eventually, Abu Ahmed and his family found safety in a village called Joolis.

The war would last fourteen months. By the time the final armistice agreement was signed in July 1949, Israel had seized control of all of the land promised to them by the partition plan, plus half of the land allocated for the Arabs. Seventy-eight percent of the British Mandate territory of Palestine became part of the State of Israel, while Egypt administered the Gaza Strip and Jordan annexed the West Bank. Israel had effectively erased over four hundred Palestinian villages from the map, and between seven hundred thousand and nine hundred thousand Palestinian Arabs were expelled or fled from their homes. Most never returned. The refugees and their descendants, many still residing in refugee camps, now number in the millions. For Israelis, May 15 is Independence Day. Palestinians call it the Nakba, or "catastrophe."

The Darwish family lived in a Lebanese refugee camp for about a year before a guide smuggled them back across the border. By then, the Israelis had destroyed al-Birwa. Darwish discovered he was now both homeless and stateless. Because they had been absent during the new Israeli government's first census of Arabs in 1949, the Darwish family were considered infiltrators. "Our legal status according to Israeli law was 'present absentee,' meaning that we were physically present, but without papers," Darwish said in a 2005 interview. "Our lands were taken and we lived as refugees." The family settled in a village in northern Galilee near Haifa and, like all Arabs in Israel, lived under Israeli military rule.

Darwish would later write that living in a state of internal displacement, a refugee in his own country, drove him to hate the second half of his childhood. "Everything here is proof of loss and lack," he wrote. "Everything here is a painful reminder of what had once been there. What wounds you most is that 'there' is so close to 'here.' A neighbor forbidden to visit." Darwish's father found work at a quarry but struggled financially. One afternoon, he summoned his three sons and told them that he could not pay for all of their educations. He asked for one of them to volunteer to quit school and join him at the quarry to help support the family. In unison, all three boys said, "I will." Their father started to weep. This was the first time Darwish had ever seen him cry. Then he said, suddenly, "No, none of you." They would somehow get by.

As a boy, Darwish found solace in reading and writing, in "escaping the mire into an imagined world, ink on paper." When he was twelve years old, village officials invited Darwish to write and recite a poem marking Israel's Independence Day. Darwish would enrage them. Instead of rejoicing in Israel's founding as a nation, Darwish's poem reflected on how Arabs were forced to celebrate the anniversary of their own occupation. "You can play in the sun as you please, and have your toys, but I cannot," wrote the boy poet. "You have a house, while I have none. You have celebrations, while I have none." The military governor of Galilee called Darwish into his office to scold him and warned that if he continued writing such poems, the governor would have Darwish's father fired from his quarry job. "In a sense he was my first literary critic," Darwish later said. "The incident made me wonder: the strong and mighty state of Israel gets upset by a poem I wrote! That must mean that poetry is serious business. My deliberate act of writing the truth as I deeply and honestly felt it was a dangerous activity."

Darwish finished his schooling in Haifa before beginning a journalism career as a translator and editor for two communist newsletters. He published his first book of poetry, *Birds Without Wings*, in 1960. Darwish was under a confinement order and had to register twice a day at the local police station. One night, during a literary festival in Haifa, Darwish stood up and excused himself from a dinner with his fellow writers, saying he had to check in with the police. This outraged Dalya Rabikovitz, an Israeli poet, who shouted, "Don't give us your Arab propaganda! In our country, we don't have people who have to check in with the police twice a day!" Darwish invited Rabikovitz to accompany him to the station. She did, and when she discovered Darwish was not lying, she scolded the policeman on duty.

Like other present absentees, Darwish also required a permit to travel throughout Israel. He often flouted this law and was imprisoned five times during the 1960s for the crime of leaving Haifa without permission. Police once arrested Darwish in Jerusalem as he came offstage from reciting poems at a poetry evening held in his honor. Darwish wrote of one of his prison sentences in his memoir *In the Presence of Absence*:

> The expanse of the earth here is two meters, with a permanently shut iron door. The stocky sound of shoes bringing you lentil soup cooked with weevils. . . . You do not know if a new war has erupted, or if the old one has ended. You do not know if your clothes have stopped giving off their smell, or if your sense of smell has dulled.

At the same time the Darwish and Sa'ad families were escaping al-Birwa, another future lion of Palestinian literature, Ghassan Kanafani, was also in flight. Both writers' stories begin with frightened boys fleeing a war. Both follow Palestine's frayed plotlines. And both stories end with a detonation.

Kanafani was twelve years old and living in Acre when the city fell to Israeli forces. Like Darwish, Kanafani fled with his family to southern Lebanon—the two future writers may well have followed the same route across the border during the same merciless nights. Unlike Darwish, though, Kanafani never returned to what had become the State of Israel. His family moved from Lebanon to a UN-run refugee camp in Syria. Living as desperate refugees shocked the Kanafanis. The family had been well-off in Acre. Ghassan's father worked as a lawyer, and young Ghassan studied in first-rate schools run by French missionaries. He read very little literature in Arabic at those schools, and even though he was still a boy, Kanafani realized he lacked a connection to the language and writings of his people. When he broke his leg jumping on boulders with his friends, Kanafani spent his six-month convalescence studying Arabic literature.

After graduating from high school, where he wrote some of his first stories, Kanafani began a course of study in Arabic literature at Damascus University. His political awakening occurred after he met George Habash, who led the Arab Nationalist Movement, a group of socialist activists committed to promoting unity among the region's Arab states.

Kanafani traveled to Kuwait in 1955 to take a teaching job in a government school, and in 1960 he moved to Beirut to join the editorial staff of *Al-Hurriya* (*Independence*), a political magazine Habash had started.

As a Palestinian, Kanafani could not legally take the magazine job. He needed to be a member of the writers' union to work as an editor, and he could not join the union because he was not a Lebanese citizen. Eventually, Kanafani managed to leverage the fact that his grandmother was Lebanese and obtained a passport. Until then, he was forced to live and work in secret. He wrote his first novella, *Men in the Sun*, while in hiding. The book told the story of three exiled Palestinians being smuggled into Kuwait inside the empty tank of a water truck. *Men in the Sun* earned much praise in Lebanon and elsewhere after its publication in 1962, and established Kanafani as one of the Arab world's newest literary talents.

I traveled to Beirut to meet Kanafani's widow, Anni. Her office shares a street with a Lebanese government minister, which means military checkpoints blocked the road at both ends. The soldier at the security booth demanded my passport and asked me whom I wanted to see. He didn't recognize Anni's name. I called her on my cell phone and held the phone out to the guard. He refused to touch the phone, took a half step backward, and said Anni would have to come to the checkpoint herself before he would let me pass.

Anni walked up the street from her office to meet me. She is in her seventies now, small and a little hunched from age. I felt guilty for compelling her to hike up the hill, but she didn't seem bothered. We went up to her office on the tenth floor, where she made Arabic coffee and served me little date cookies. We sat at a sunny table and talked about her husband.

Kanafani met and married Anni in 1961. She was a teacher from the Netherlands with a soft spot for political reactionaries—her own father spent five years resisting the German occupation of Czechoslovakia. The sixties proved productive for Kanafani. He became editor in chief of a daily newspaper that included a weekly supplement called *Filastine*. Then, in 1967, Kanafani started the newsletter for the Popular Front for the Liberation of Palestine, a Marxist organization dedicated to Palestinian statehood that morphed out of the Arab Nationalist Movement. He also acted as the PFLP's spokesman.

Kanafani somehow found time to edit an anthology titled *Poetry of Resistance in Occupied Palestine*, which introduced a young Mahmoud Darwish to the greater Arab literary scene. Kanafani also contributed journalism and editorials to several publications. "He had a sharp and satirical pen," Anni said. "He used that sharp pen in many ways." Kanafani wrote a regular political satire column under the pseudonym Faris Faris, a character who would often "argue" with Kanafani in print. Kanafani's sense of humor frequently shocked those who considered him a sober political thinker. "We had foreign visitors and journalists in our home, and one evening a man said he couldn't believe we were the same people who were so serious and so strong in the office," Anni said. "Ghassan told him you need to get rid of some of that seriousness or you wouldn't survive."

With his days filled with politics and journalism, Kanafani wrote his short stories and novellas in the evenings once he returned home from work. "He was a very fast writer. Incredibly fast," Anni said. "And his manuscripts would need very few corrections." After the critical success of *Men in the Sun*, Kanafani's friends encouraged him to abandon political journalism altogether and focus on his stories. But Kanafani refused to limit himself to fiction. In a 1962 letter, he wrote:

> Now the advice from my friends to pay less attention to journalism is growing stronger. In the end, as they put it, journalism will destroy my artistic ability to write stories. In truth I don't understand this logic. . . . I want to say something. Sometimes I can say it in the official news of the morning, sometimes fashioned into an editorial, or into a small piece on the society page. Sometimes I can't say what I want to say in anything but a story.

Kanafani saw no disconnect between his literary impulses and his political activism. But Anni told me he considered himself a fiction writer first. Kanafani himself once said, "My political position springs from my being a novelist. Insofar as I am concerned, politics and the novel are an indivisible case, and I can categorically state that I became politically committed because I am a novelist, not the opposite."

Returning to Haifa, published in 1969, may be Kanafani's most beloved work. I remember sitting in a café in Haifa with a Palestinian who wept as he described the novella's plot. The story begins in the wake of 1967's Six-Day War, when Israel defeated armies from Egypt, Syria, and Jordan. The Israeli army captured East Jerusalem and the West Bank from the Jordanians, the Sinai and Gaza from Egypt, and the Golan Heights from Syria—all territories populated mainly by Palestinians. Arab governments were humiliated. Palestinians were despondent. Israel would eventually return the Sinai to Egypt, but its occupation of the rest of the territory seized in 1967 is ongoing.

In the aftermath of the war, with boundaries blurred by the occupation, Palestinians from the West Bank and Gaza were permitted to travel to Israel for the first time since the Nakba. In *Returning to Haifa*, a Palestinian couple from Ramallah—Said and Safiyya—make their way to Haifa to see what has become of their former home. As they drive, Safiyya recalls the scene in Haifa in the spring of 1948, when Jewish forces advanced on the city. Haifa's Arab population panicked and fled toward the sea, where British boats waited to transfer them out of Haifa. The streets were chaos. Eyewitnesses described children and the elderly being trampled in the stampede to the port. In Kanafani's novella, Safiyya sees the fire of war approaching from the hills behind her neighborhood. Leaving her five-year-old son, Khaldun, in his crib, Safiyya rushes down to the main street to look for Said and ask the crowds what is going on. "Suddenly she found herself in the middle of a wave of people pushing her as they themselves were being pushed from all over the city in a massive, unstoppable, powerful stream," Kanafani writes. "She was carried along like a twig of straw." Saffiya and Said somehow find each other in the confusion but are unable to escape the "flood of humanity" surging toward the port. They end up on a boat to Acre. Khaldun is left behind. For twenty years, silenced by sadness and guilt, Safiyya and Said never even utter Khaldun's name. "The few times they had spoken of the child they always said 'him,'" Kanafani writes.

Miriam, a Jewish woman from Poland who lost her father in Auschwitz, answers the door of Safiyya and Said's old house in Haifa. She invites them inside and serves them coffee and biscuits from a tin. Then she reveals that she and her husband adopted Khaldun in 1948. They named him Dov. "I don't know what his name used to be, nor if it even matters to you," Miriam tells them, "but he looks a lot like you. . . ."

When Khaldun, or Dov, returns home, Said is shocked to see the young man, his lost son, in the uniform of an Israeli soldier. Dov treats Said and Safiyya roughly. He declares that Said is "on the other side" and the true nature of his parentage does not change anything. He scolds them for leaving him behind in his crib twenty years earlier. "Perhaps none of that would have happened if you'd behaved the way a civilized and careful man should behave," he tells Said and calls him weak and backward. "I belong here, and this woman is my mother," he says. "I don't know the two of you, and I don't feel anything special towards you."

Before they stand to leave, Said turns to his weeping wife and says, "Do you know what the homeland is, Safiyya? The homeland is where none of this can happen." He thinks of their son in Ramallah—Khalid—who yearned to take up arms against the occupation, but Said wouldn't allow it. "We were mistaken when we thought the homeland was only the past," he tells Safiyya. "For Khalid, the homeland is the future." At the end of the story, as their car reaches the outskirts of Ramallah, Said hopes that Khalid has disobeyed him and joined the resistance. "I pray that Khalid will have gone—while we were away!"

Students throughout the Middle East still read and study *Returning to Haifa*. The book is considered a masterpiece of Arabic literature, and it inspired Susan Abulhawa's epic 2010 novel *Mornings in Jenin*. But of all Kanafani's work that I've read, a letter he wrote to his son, Fayez, during the 1967 war most affected me. Kanafani's letter describes overhearing Fayez, still a young boy, ask Anni: "Mama, am I a Palestinian?" When she tells him yes, he is silent for a while. Then he begins to cry. Kanafani believes his son's tears to be the pangs of his inevitable birth as a true Palestinian. "It was as if a blessed scalpel was cutting up your chest and putting there the heart that belongs to you," Kanafani wrote. "I knew that a distant homeland was being born again; hills, plains, olive groves, dead people, torn banners and folded ones, all cutting their way into a future of flesh and blood and being born in the heart of another child." A Palestinian boy does not grow into manhood. Instead, "he is born suddenly—a word, in a moment, penetrates his heart to a new throb. One scene can hurl him down from the ceiling of childhood onto the ruggedness of the road."

On the morning of July 8, 1972, just after fixing Fayez's electric train, Kanafani walked out of his house in Lebanon with his teenage niece, Lamis. Kanafani's five-year-old daughter, Leila, was sitting on the building's front steps. Kanafani bent down to give her a piece of chocolate and kiss her goodbye before walking with Lamis to his car. Lamis was visiting from Kuwait, and Kanafani had agreed to take her to visit her cousins in downtown Beirut.

Lamis adored her Uncle Ghassan. Every January, Kanafani would handwrite and illustrate a book for her on her birthday. He had long considered Lamis his muse. But the two had been quarreling that day. Kanafani's work with the PFLP meant Israeli agents continually pursued him. Kanafani stubbornly refused to travel with a bodyguard, and Lamis feared for his safety. She begged her uncle to cease his revolutionary actions and focus instead on writing fiction. "Your stories are beautiful," she'd told him the day before, hoping to flatter him away from his dangerous politics.

"Go back to writing stories? I write well because I believe in a cause, in principles," Kanafani told her. "The day I leave these principles, my stories will become empty. If I were to leave behind my principles, you yourself would not respect me."

When Kanafani turned his key in the ignition, the booby-trapped car exploded. The blast killed them both and scattered fragments of their bodies over the ground.

Anni frowned at me when I said I knew why the Israelis killed her husband. "What do you think you know?" she asked. I told her I'd read how the PFLP recruited members of the Japanese Red Army—a communist militant group founded in Lebanon—to attack the Lod Airport near Tel Aviv in May 1972. Three Red Army agents pulled Czech assault rifles and hand grenades from violin cases and murdered twenty-six people. Eighty more were injured. I'd also read that after the massacre a photo emerged of Kanafani with one of the Japanese terrorists. I thought Kanafani's assassination was retribution for his suspected role in planning the attack.

Anni scoffed. "The plan of the Zionists was to liquidate all the intellectuals. Ghassan's murder was ordered by Golda Meir herself," Anni said, referring to the Israeli prime minister who famously claimed there is "no such thing as a Palestinian people." Anni didn't know if a Mossad operative or a Lebanese collaborator killed Kanafani, only that his name appeared on a list of PFLP members to be eliminated. "He was very dangerous," Anni said. "He didn't carry a gun, but he carried a pen."

I don't know if Kanafani helped plan the airport attacks, or if he ever carried a gun, but he was unquestionably an influential member of an organization that bombed supermarkets and hijacked airplanes—the latter being something of a PFLP specialty at the time. Kanafani himself openly advocated "revolutionary violence" as a means to liberate the oppressed.

I've seen black-and-white photos of Kanafani playing with his children, of him tossing his infant daughter into the air with the same paternal danger I risk with my own son. Anni sold me a reproduction of *The Little Lantern*, the book Kanafani wrote for Lamis on her eighth birthday, about a young princess who must bring the sun inside the palace walls in order to claim the throne. I read the book to my son at bedtime. But I can't help but wonder if the man who wrote and illustrated that charming book, and the smiling mustached man in the photos I'd seen, could see a kind of victory in the spilling of innocent blood. Did beauty coexist with its opposite in Kanafani's hands?

I didn't ask Anni this. I am not sure why. Maybe I couldn't find a way to question a widow about her dead husband's cruelty as she served me coffee and biscuits. Or maybe I am just a coward. I am sure, though, that had the situation been reversed, Kanafani would have asked the question.

Darwish was in Beirut when Kanafani was assassinated. In the eulogy he wrote, Darwish revealed the two men had planned to meet the day of the bombing:

> My friend Ghassan! We did not eat our last lunch together, and you didn't even apologize for your lateness. I lifted the telephone to scold you as usual: "It's two o'clock and you're not here yet. Please rid yourself

of this bad habit." But then they told me—he already blew up. No man can live how he pleases. But we see you in every place. You live within us and for us, without even knowing it.

Later, Darwish would compose a poem full of sadness and fury for his friend. "Blessed is the heart that does not stop because of a bullet," Darwish wrote. "A bullet is not enough! They blew you up like they would a front, a base, a mountain, a capital, and they waged on you a war, like they were fighting an army." Darwish calls his friend a volcano, and in the end he pleads, "All I want to ask of you now is to allow me to cry a little, do you allow it? Do you forgive me?"

Darwish had gone to the Soviet Union two years earlier to study political economics at Moscow's Academy of Social Sciences, a move which had angered Kanafani and other Arab writers who considered his leaving Israel a betrayal of his role as a resistance poet. Kanafani wrote to Darwish, "We are in the midst of the stage of Return and Steadfastness, the stage of eternal exile has ended. Let us hope you will return to Israel . . . to prison, whatever the price may be."

The friction between the two men was mild and would not endure. When Darwish left Moscow for Cairo, Kanafani wrote glowingly of his friend in a weekly Egyptian newspaper. "His sharp poetry has placed him in confrontation with the enemy's authorities," Kanafani noted. "First he struggled for his livelihood, and then also for his freedom. He was distanced from his village, arrested, and from prison he wrote the best and most subversive of his poetry." Kanafani's introduction endeared Darwish to Cairo's literary society. He wrote for the newspaper *Al-Ahram* and attended salons alongside great Arabic writers such as Yusuf Idris, Tawfiq al-Hakim, and Nobel laureate Naguib Mahfouz.

After Cairo, Darwish moved to Beirut, where he founded the literary journal *Al-Karmel*. He lived in Beirut for a decade, enduring both the Lebanese Civil War and the 1982 Lebanon War between the Israelis and Lebanon-based Syrian and Palestinian forces. One of my favorite pieces of Darwish's writing comes from a long meditation about brewing coffee during Israel's siege of Beirut in the summer of 1982:

Gently place one spoonful of the ground coffee, electrified with the aroma of cardamom, on the rippling surface of the hot water, then stir slowly, first clockwise, then up and down. Add the second spoonful and stir up and down, then counterclockwise. Now add the third. Between spoonfuls, take the pot away from the fire and bring it back. For the final touch, dip the spoon in the melting powder, fill and raise it a little over the pot, then let it drop back. Repeat this several times until the water boils again and a small mass of the blond coffee remains on the surface, rippling and ready to sink. Don't let it sink. Turn off the heat, and pay no heed to the rockets.

Darwish could not ignore the rockets for long and left Lebanon. In 1985—after stints in Damascus, Tripoli, and Tunis—Darwish reached Paris. He considered the city his birthplace as a poet. "I cherish my poetry that I wrote in Paris during the eighties and beyond," Darwish said. Paris afforded him the time and freedom to write undisturbed by gunfire and bomb blasts. He also avoided the social distractions of the Paris cafés, preferring instead to work in his apartment, where he would read for ten hours a day and write for four. Being far from Palestine also granted Darwish a healthy perspective. "There, I had the opportunity to reflect and look at the homeland and the world and things from a distance—the distance of light. When you see from a distance, you see better, and see the scene entirely." Exile, "a misunderstanding between existence and borders," both saddened and inspired him.

Like Kanafani, Darwish involved himself in official Palestinian politics. He joined the Palestinian Liberation Organization in 1973. At the time, the organization advocated violence and armed struggle as tools to advance the Palestinian cause. Darwish's PLO membership resulted in his being banned from returning to Israel. He joined the PLO's executive committee in 1987 and penned the Palestinian Declaration of Independence the following year. Still, Darwish never felt comfortable with party politics and resigned after the PLO and Israel signed the Oslo Accords in 1993.

The accords were intended to be an interim agreement that would, after five years, lead to the end of the conflict. In exchange for the PLO's recognition of Israel and renouncing of terrorism, Israel agreed to accept the PLO as the legitimate representative of the Palestinian people and withdraw its military forces from Palestinian territories. The accords created the Palestinian Authority and granted the PA limited governance over the West Bank and Gaza. Some credit Oslo for bringing an end to the First Intifada, a violent uprising against the Israeli occupation that had raged since 1987.

The Oslo Accords won Yasser Arafat, Yitzhak Rabin, and Shimon Peres a Nobel Peace Prize, but most Palestinians consider the agreement a shameful surrender. Today, the PA governs less than 20 percent of the West Bank territory, which is divided into eight noncontiguous areas. Israel maintains exclusive control over 60 percent. (The rest falls under joint Israeli-Palestinian jurisdiction.) Israeli settlements divide Palestinian towns and villages. Military checkpoints control Palestinian roads while settlers speed along on highways built exclusively for them. Today the dream of a viable Palestinian state is more distant than in 1993.

Oslo's failure did not surprise Darwish. "I felt Oslo would pave the way for escalation," he said. "I hoped I was wrong. I'm very sad that I was right." Darwish's stance on Olso angered Yasser Arafat, who even demanded Darwish alter one of his most critical poems about the agreement. Darwish complied, changing the line "Like a handful of dust this peace will leave us" to "Like a handful of dust this journey will leave us." But Darwish remained outspoken against the accords. In his 2006 memoir, he wrote: "What cunning rule or language could formulate an agreement for peace and good neighborliness between a palace and a hut, between a guard and a prisoner?"

For all their failures, the accords did allow political exiles like Darwish to return to the West Bank and Gaza. Darwish moved to Ramallah in 1996—the same year Mourid Barghouti crossed over the Allenby Bridge. Darwish did not consider his return to Palestine the end of his expulsion. "Exile is not a geographic state," he said. "I carry it everywhere as I carry my homeland." And al-Birwa had long since been destroyed. Still, Darwish preferred his return to Palestine to the decades he spent wandering. In a poem, he wrote, "the house is more beautiful than the path to the house."

Darwish was an international literary star by then. Readers throughout the Arabic-speaking world read and memorized his poems, and he became the bestselling poet in France. At a 1987 poetry reading in Rabat, five thousand fans crowded into a theater hall to listen to Darwish while loudspeakers broadcast the reading to forty thousand others listening in the streets outside. A reading in Tunisia in 1994 drew a throng of sixteen thousand. Twenty-five thousand fans filled a Beirut soccer stadium to hear him recite his poems. In 2007, he read from atop a bridge in Macedonia to thousands of fans on the riverbanks below. Boats crowded the river, and fireworks burst overhead in his honor.

For Palestinians, Darwish was more than just a poet. He was their champion, the eloquent voice of their struggle. Darwish never desired this role, but nor did he resist it. He first began composing poems as a means of self-expression, he wrote, "but my individual case, the great uprooting from place, was the story of an entire people. So, the people found in my individual voice their individual and collective voices." Even Darwish's poem about a prisoner's quiet longing for his mother's coffee became a rallying cry.

But the Palestinian adoration for Darwish sometimes manifested as possession. His readers felt that he belonged to them. They expected poetic nationalism from Darwish, often demanding he recite his most famous "resistance" poems during readings, and judged him harshly when he deviated from his role as his nation's voice. While in Cairo, Darwish wrote an article titled "Am I Free to Marry a Woman?" that expressed his desire to take a sabbatical from politics and focus on his personal life. This outraged his critics, who considered such trivialities beneath a man who had more important things to do. Then, in 1998, Darwish produced a book of love poems called *A Bed for the Stranger*. His critics felt it vain and shallow for a Palestinian poet, especially Darwish, to write about love while under occupation. They felt the book amounted to Darwish abandoning his people. His friend author Anton Shammas accused Darwish of sending the message: "To hell with Palestine—now I'm on my own!"

In response to Shammas, Darwish wrote: "I am waiting for the moment when I shall be able to say 'to hell with Palestine.' But this will not come before Palestine is free. I can't achieve my private freedom before the freedom of my country. When it's free, I can curse it."

Darwish believed that Palestinian literature needed to explore metaphysical themes like love and death and liberate itself from an airless preoccupation with politics and oppression. "The Palestinian cannot just be defined as terrorist or freedom fighter," Darwish said. "Any trite, routine image ends up reducing and usurping the humanity of the Palestinian and renders him unable to be seen as merely human. He becomes either the hero or the victim—not just a human being. Therefore, I very seriously advocate our right to be frivolous." According to Darwish, Palestinians should not shackle themselves to the solitary idea of political liberation. "This is a prison," he said. "We're human, we love, we fear death, we enjoy the first flowers of spring. So to express this is resistance against having our subject dictated to us. If I write love poems, I resist the conditions that don't allow me to write love poems."

I would have disappointed Darwish. I had been as guilty as anyone of anticipating politics in the Palestinian writing I'd read. I found it difficult not to see the conflict lurking between each line of verse and hiding behind each metaphor. Every mother in every poem stood for the land of Palestine. Each description of red anemones blooming on a hillside represented the blood of martyrs. I couldn't see beauty for beauty's sake. Darwish felt that Palestinian literature was under attack by readers like me. "It is as if the text is expected to adhere to previous expectations, as if there is a reading that precedes the poem," he wrote. "It is essentially a siege of reading."

Darwish lived quietly in Ramallah, preferring solitude to the noisy cafés or the social obligations his celebrity might have demanded. "No artistic work can be done without isolation," he said. "You must be alone, plucking your thorns with your hands." Darwish was not religious but he had his rituals. He woke each morning at eight and opened his bedside dictionary to a random word to conduct "cerebral calisthenics": memorizing lines of poetry that corresponded to the various meanings of his chosen word. He would drink a glass of cold orange juice then brew his coffee according to "strict ritual and the teachings of the roaster of cardamom." Before he sat at his desk to write, Darwish dressed in proper clothes and elegant black shoes, treating his writing time with the same formal respect as any other professional. Then he entered his office. "Your cup of coffee is on the left side of the desk and on the right side is a box of pens, next to a pot of black ink. In the middle, there is white paper full of white writing. It calls to you and you call to it. It holds and hides the memories of predecessors. Alone, without assistance or assurance, you try to find your own line in this white thicket that stretches between writing and speech. You no longer ask, What will I write? but rather, How will I write?"

The power of Darwish's poetry to portray Palestinian identity bred fierce opposition against it. In 2000, the Israeli education minister decided to include some of Darwish's poems in an optional multicultural school curriculum. Considering Darwish's birthplace and global recognition, the inclusion of his work in such a book seems obvious. But the move enraged right-wing members of the Knesset, the Israeli parliament. "Only a society that wants to commit suicide would put Darwish's poetry on its curriculum," one MK seethed. When members of the ruling coalition threatened to oust then prime minister Ehud Barak over the matter with a vote of nonconfidence, Barak backed down, claiming that Israelis were "not ready" for Darwish. The fury of the debate amused the poet, who said, "Israelis do not want to teach students that there is a love story between an Arab poet and this land." The education ministry eventually relented and allowed Jewish schools in Israel the option of studying Darwish, but it wasn't until 2012 that the ministry approved the inclusion of Darwish in the curriculum of Arab schools.

Darwish's work remains controversial in Israel. In 2016, Israel's Army Radio broadcast a Hebrew recitation of Darwish's "Identity Card." The poem, written in 1964, is Darwish's most famous and most requested. "Identity Card" accuses Israel of stealing Palestine's orchards and farmland, leaving "nothing for us / Except for these rocks." The poem includes the notorious lines:

> Write down on the top of the first page:
> I do not hate people
> And I do not steal from anyone
> But if I starve
> I will eat my oppressor's flesh
> Beware, beware of my starving
> And my rage.

Defense minister Avigdor Leiberman accused Darwish of calling "in his poetry for the expulsion of the Jewish people from the State of Israel," and compared his work to Hitler's *Mein Kampf.* Evidently, no one told Leiberman that one of Darwish's poems, "Think of the Other Person," is taught in Arab high schools in Israel as part of a unit on the Holocaust.

Not all Palestinians adored Darwish, either. "One shouldn't forget that there are many who detest me," he told a journalist in 2007, "both poets and those who consider themselves poets." Some Palestinians felt he was too close to Arafat and Fatah, the political party he led. Others labeled his participation with Israeli institutions "normalization": activities hardliners equate with treason. Darwish's reluctance to praise the martyrs of the Second Intifada also angered many Palestinians, especially conservative Islamic leaders. But Darwish never saw heroism in those who killed themselves to kill others. He believed a martyr, or *shahid*, acts out of misery and desperation, not out of a desire for paradise. A martyr's death was a tragedy to mourn rather than a sacrifice to celebrate. Darwish wrote:

> The martyr explains: I have not searched beyond the distance
> For eternity's virgins, I love life
> On Earth, among the pines and figs,
> But I had no access to it.
> I've searched for it, using every last thing I own:
> Blood in a body of azure.

Kanafani perished in a car-bomb blast, but Darwish died from another sort of detonation. "I am carrying a small explosive charge in my heart, which could go off at any moment," he once told a friend. Darwish suffered a heart attack in Vienna in 1984 and another in Belgium in 1998. He quit smoking and drank less of his beloved coffee. Then, in 2008, he traveled to Houston for a third surgery. He felt anxious about the complicated operation, and his mother pleaded with him not to go. Darwish didn't survive. He offered no eloquent farewell to befit a poet of his stature. Instead, he died as he lived: quiet, modest, and private.

Years earlier, while he brewed coffee beneath the rockets in Beirut,

Darwish imagined his own funeral. He wrote that he wanted a "well-organized" memorial, wreaths of red and yellow roses, and "a radio announcer who's not a chatterer, whose voice is not too throaty, and who can put on a convincing show of sadness." Darwish wanted an elegant coffin from which he could eavesdrop on the mourners as they gossiped about his womanizing, his dandy's taste in clothes, his Swiss bank account, and the rugs in his house that are "so plush you sink into them up to your knees." He wrote: "I'll smile in my coffin and try to say, 'Enough!' I'll try to come back to life, but I won't be able."

I wonder what Darwish would have thought of his actual funeral. The ruler of the United Arab Emirates arranged for Darwish's body to be flown from the United States to Jordan, where bereaved readers gathered for a ceremony at the Marika military airport. There, the PLO representative in the Arab League called him "the moon of the Arabs." Then a Jordanian helicopter carried Darwish to Ramallah. Palestinian president Mahmoud Abbas declared three days of mourning followed by a state funeral, an honor only ever before bestowed on Yasser Arafat—and not bestowed since. Abbas also delivered the first eulogy. Tens of thousands gathered beneath an August sun to line the streets of Darwish's funeral procession. Left-wing members of the Israeli Knesset also attended. Darwish's elder brother and their mother, eighty-five years old and wheelchair-bound, arrived at the ceremony in an Israeli ambulance hired by the family. The two lived in Upper Galilee, and as Arabs with Israeli citizenship they needed special documents to attend. Mourners circulated a petition demanding permission to bury Darwish in the Galilee, close to al-Birwa. His family, however, wanted him to be buried in a place where all Palestinians could visit him. "I realize, of course, that he is no longer just my son," his mother said, "but the son of the entire Palestinian people."

They buried Darwish on a hilltop in Ramallah. I visited his tomb each time I traveled there. Darwish's wide white gravestone resembles the blank pages of an open notebook. A recording of Darwish reciting his poems plays in a repeating loop inside the adjacent museum, which holds a collection of his personal effects: his desk, his pens and eyeglasses, his car keys and cigarette lighter, and white coffee cups. "Dark-colored cups spoil the freedom of the coffee," he once wrote.

Mahmoud Darwish is as close to a saint as the Palestinians have ever had. Each time I climbed the hill to his tomb felt like an act of pilgrimage. Still, I felt Darwish was out of place here. He always considered Ramallah just another place of exile. The city was not his home. I wanted to see what he had left behind in 1948. So I asked Abu Ahmed to take me to al-Birwa, or at least to what remains.

Abu Ahmed drives like a proper octogenarian: erratic and a bit too slow. Once we stepped out at al-Birwa, though, he showed a stubborn sure-footedness that belied his age. The houses and cattle barns of an Israeli kibbutz and moshav now stand on much of al-Birwa's land, but Abu Ahmed showed me a stretch of nearly buried cobblestone road and a hedge of unruly cactus that testify to the Palestinians who lived here. He led me to an old and overgrown Muslim cemetery where his grandfathers are buried. Not, however, his father, who was so shattered by the destruction of al-Birwa that his health started to fail. When he died, Abu Ahmed could not bury him in al-Birwa. He lies in a Nazareth cemetery now.

Abu Ahmed pointed to a hilltop. "There were houses there, and from them you could see Haifa, Acre, Nahariya, and the sea," he said. "But they destroyed the houses and bulldozed the land. The hills were higher before." Gone are al-Birwa's beehives and sunflowers. The jasmine and carob and orange trees, the basil his ancestors grew, the strawberries: These survive only in Darwish's verses now—and in the fading memories of old men.

Afterward, I followed Abu Ahmed through a patch of tall grass to a one-room stone schoolhouse—al-Birwa's last standing building. A locked steel door and bars across the window frames prevented us from entering, but we could see through the windows into the classroom. Two cracked blackboards, still dusty with chalk, remain fixed to one wall. Plaster had fallen off the ceiling to expose a skeleton of rusting rebar. Abu Ahmed pointed to the place where his desk used to be and to where his favorite classmates sat. "Mohammed used to sit there. He is in Jordan now. And there was Abdullah Aishan, who died a few years ago."

Darwish studied here, too. "White letters on a blackboard inspire the awe of dawn in the countryside," he once wrote. Darwish couldn't have spent more than a year in this classroom. He was only seven years old when he fled the village with Abu Ahmed, but I knew he was already writing poetry by then. As I peered into the dilapidated stone schoolhouse, I wanted to believe that Darwish first learned to love language here. I imagined his eyes widening as his teacher read poetry to the class. I imagined young Mahmoud penning his first lines of verse—marked by simple end rhymes, no doubt—in front of those old blackboards. I wanted to believe that Darwish was thinking about this schoolhouse when he later wrote:

> What a game! What magic! The world is gradually born out of words. In this way, school becomes a playground for the imagination . . . and you run to it with the joy of one who is promised the gift of a discovery. Not only to memorize the lesson, but also to rely on the skill of naming things. Whatever is distant becomes near. Whatever is sealed opens up. If you do not misspell "river," the river will flow through your notebook. The sky, too, becomes one of your personal belongings if you do not misspell it.

I wanted to believe that I stood where Darwish, the poet, began.

I glanced over at Abu Ahmed as he stared into the classroom. His eyes were shining. He'd told me earlier that he visits the village often, sometimes to tend to his grandfathers' graves or just to walk among the roads he once knew. He used to come alone, but he doesn't feel safe here anymore. The sons and grandsons of the moshavim are "radical and provocative," he said. "Their fathers were less violent." Now he comes with visitors like me to show them where the olive trees used to grow and point out the stables that stand where his father's house stood. He likes to tell al-Birwa's story. But in those silent moments at the schoolhouse window, I felt that Abu Ahmed had forgotten I was there at all. He'd disappeared into his schoolboy memories. He'd lost himself in all that he'd lost.

After a few moments, though, I interrupted him. I needed to know something else. "When did you realize that you would never live here again?" I asked.

Abu Ahmed looked at the ground. "I still hope to return."

2

Whenever My Sore Heart Gets Hungry

Palestinians wish each other a *sabah al-khair*, or "morning of good-ness," and respond with *sabah al-noor*, or "morning of light." The greeting bears a warmth and poetry my cold English "good morning" lacks. In Palestine, this morning light shifts the olive leaves to green from silver, and dyes Ramallah's limestone buildings the color of cream. The morning also sharpens the fragrance of orange blossoms and of the jasmine growing in the courtyard of the library near my guesthouse. Though I could not see them over the garden wall, I could smell the flowers as I passed by.

During my days in Ramallah, I'd buy breakfast provisions from the shops a little up the road from my guesthouse. Plastic tubs of hummus and labneh, and tiny bags of *za'atar*—a salty blend of thyme, sumac, and sesame I ate with pita warmed over my stove's gas burners. Sometimes I'd walk to the center of town for morning falafel or to stock up on Arabic coffee so freshly roasted the bag was nearly too hot to hold. Men gathered in the barbershops, mobile phone stores, or on the plastic chairs lining the sidewalks in front of cafés while their wives, sisters, and daughters shopped in the main market. Vendors hawked watermelon, muskmelon, and pale pumpkins. They splashed water on mounds of mint and declared the virtues of tiny eggplants and blooming zucchini. I bought cucumbers and tomatoes and tiny bulbs of baby fennel here. Green chickpeas encased in stubborn pods. Apricots. Ramallah is not the most beautiful of cities, but for all of this.

Barghouti found beauty here, too. He wrote of the "swinging slopes" of Ramallah's hills and "the green that speaks in twenty languages of beauty." He thought Ramallah an odd place, never masculine or solemn, and always "first to catch on to some new craze." Barghouti watched the traditional Palestinian *dabke* dances in Ramallah, but he also danced the tango. He played snooker and grew to love movies. Barghouti's cinemas are all gone now, but boys still crowd the downtown billiards halls. And Ramallah remains on trend. Now that tango is passé, a Mexican restaurant offers rooftop salsa dancing on Tuesday nights. Women wearing Western fashions drink mojitos at slick cocktail bars, their hair loose on their shoulders. Twice a week, Vintage Café serves fresh sushi—spicy tuna rolls, California maki, and something called Finding Nemo Soup. A youth center houses Palestine's first skateboard park. Yoga classes abound.

Ramallah's gravitational pull on Palestine's literary class has also endured. In the years following Oslo, the city was where exiled writers like Darwish and Barghouti came to reassemble their fragmented identities into poems, stories, and songs. Ramallah granted them desks to write at, stages to read from, and cafés to gather in. A quarter-century later, Ramallah remains the center of Palestinian artistic expression and home to a new generation of authors. Many of the writers I wanted to meet live, or have lived, in Ramallah. So I found a place to stay, hung around Ramallah's cafés, and made a few friends.

The A. M. Qattan Foundation, a Palestinian cultural center housed in a beautiful old stone mansion, occupies one of Ramallah's hilltops. Qattan's managers allowed me to stay in the simple one-room guesthouse they reserve for visiting artists. I once returned to the guesthouse after three days away to find my bathroom crawling with hundreds of fat winged ants. Mahmoud Abu Hashhash, Qattan's director of culture and arts programming, told me, "It is because of the hot dry wind from the south. It is called *khamsin*." Mahmoud was less able to explain the sudden appearance of a tiny black-headed kukri snake next to my toilet a few days earlier. But I didn't meet with Mahmoud to talk about my bathroom menagerie. I wanted to talk about the poetry scene in Palestine, and in Ramallah in particular, following the death of Darwish.

"The passing of Mahmoud Darwish changed the scene dramatically," Mahmoud told me. "He used to have a big shadow on the literary scene in Palestine, especially the poetry scene. Writers used to struggle to get out of his shadow." The entire literary community, in Palestine and throughout the Arab world, focused on every new collection Darwish published, while other writers starved for attention. "Now it is different," Mahmoud said. "I don't want to sound as if Darwish's passing was an advantage, but I try to track how things have changed. It is really great to rediscover the importance of other poets. This gives us a sense of diversity that we could not see before because whenever we talked about the poetry scene, we talked about Darwish, Darwish, Darwish."

The local poetry community experienced a different shift a decade earlier, in the wake of the Oslo Accords. Poets like Darwish who had been living in exile returned to Palestine and worked with the new cultural institutions. The newly formed House of Poetry committed to seeking out Palestine's young poets, Mahmoud among them, and introducing them to the world. It was the first such manifesto since Ghassan Kanafani decided to present his "writers of resistance" back in the 1960s. "But we were not resistance writers," Mahmoud said. "We were, in a sense, calling for the normal presentation of the Palestinian. Not the hero. Not the victim. We'd had enough of these labels. *Khalas.*"

Until Oslo, most Palestinian writers engaged in a collective national project. They considered writing a political act, part of the effort toward achieving dreams of independence and justice. Their work traded in blunt patriotic symbols like tricolor Palestinian flags, keffiyehs, Kalashnikovs, and the keys to village houses lost in the Nakba. The writing during the First Intifada, in particular, presented Palestine and the resistance as proud, unified, and strong. The literature glorified casualties of war. Every young man was fearless, every child pure, and every poem a stone hurled at the enemy.

But Oslo betrayed the poets' resistance. Palestinian writers, and artists in general, realized committing their art to the political cause had achieved nothing. They had wasted their time and talents waving the flag, only to have politicians sign away their country. So Mahmoud and his poet friends scrapped the clichés and began to use their work to express their personal lives rather than national aspirations. "The political discourse changed, and in a sense, people's tastes changed," Mahmoud said. Any art that traded in old nationalist symbols, whether on the page or canvas, "was not valued under the reality of Oslo."

I've heard people say that this was a new style of Palestinian writing that emerged only in the 1990s, but Mahmoud disagrees. Diaspora Palestinians started writing about their internal lives more than a decade earlier. Darwish, after all, devoted pages and pages of verse to the brewing of coffee in Beirut in 1982. But the poets who remained in Palestine had no idea. Before Oslo and the return of writers like Darwish—and before the internet changed everything—Palestine's poets had little access to this poetry. They didn't know what their exiled icons were writing about.

The Palestinian poetry scene blossomed when these writers returned, especially in Ramallah. Mahmoud and his fellow poets used to take pages to the Ministry of Culture, Birzeit University, or the House of Poetry to be critiqued by poets like Ghassan Zaqtan, Zakaria Mohammed, and Hussein Barghouti. This was the first time emerging poets could interact with the well-established exiles whose work, and lives, they so admired. "It was a very exciting time," Mahmoud said. "They were really our mentors. We were very close to them. Sometimes they would invite Darwish to come and speak to us."

Mahmoud was especially grateful for the tutelage of Hussein Barghouti, an intellectual and writer who studied abroad in Hungary and the United States before returning to Ramallah. Al-Barghouti wrote poems, novels, and essays—and translated *Romeo and Juliet* into Arabic—but Mahmoud knows him best for his mentoring of the new generation of poets. Al-Barghouti used to hold court for hours with young writers at Birzeit University. Mahmoud remembers bringing him a stack of fifteen poems to read. Mahmoud sat in his office as al-Barghouti read each of them. Occasionally al-Barghouti would look up from the text and comment, "I will remember you from this poem" or "This is something really new." "He was the most generous cultural figure," Mahmoud said. "He would give you whatever knowledge he had and spend as much time with us as he could. He would stay talking for ten hours. He was great." Al-Barghouti's death in 2002 dealt a serious blow to the local literary scene.

The cultural supplement in *Al-Ayyam* newspaper also served as a boon to Ramallah's young poets. "It was very important for us to find a space to be published in *Al-Ayyam* because it was one of the only chances to be published locally, the only chance to be able to write a poem or a text and have it be read by people," Mahmoud said. "Now it is less significant. You can just write on your Facebook page."

The House of Poetry named this new generation of Palestinian poets, somewhat melodramatically, the Everlasting Guests of Fire and published an anthology of their work in the mid-1990s. They used to gather at Ziryab, a café-restaurant on Ramallah's main street. The owner let the poets linger until two or three in the morning drinking beer and debating literature. Palestinian poets used to come from as far away as Haifa to spend nights there. But the Everlasting Guests proved to be less than everlasting. Time fractured the group. Some poets moved away. Most stopped writing. Rada Shafeh, a promising poet and a favorite of Darwish, disappeared altogether. "There was a mystery about her," Mahmoud said. "Some say she became a Sufi mystic. Others say she married a strict Muslim and they moved to Afghanistan. No one knows."

As for today's poets, Mahmoud sees a continuation of the post-Oslo mood in which the personal dominates the political. "Everybody wants to figure out his own life," Mahmoud said. "The writers address the national failure but not in a direct way. They talk about their own failures. Their own supplications. The failure of the national project makes their writing take another direction."

Writer Maya Abu-Alhayyat met me at the traffic circle in the center of town and led me to Café Ramallah. "I hope you don't mind smoky cafés," she said. It was early evening, and the ground floor was full of men wearing blazers over collared shirts, drinking tea and tiny coffees and pulling long drags on their nargileh pipes. I could see a few framed portraits of Darwish, Kanafani, and other Palestinian authors through the haze at the back of the room.

The Middle East is full of cafés like this. Rows of water pipes on a shelf. Glass jars filled with mint or sage for tea. Tiny coffee cups that get rinsed rather than washed between customers. Often a television will hang from a ceiling bracket, usually broadcasting news in Arabic or one of the Saudi movie channels, but unless an important football match is happening the customers tend to ignore it. There is no Wi-Fi here either, though I usually managed to hijack the signal from Ziryab Café next door—where the Everlasting Guests of Fire used to meet. People come, instead, to talk. To discuss politics, sports, or family matters while they blacken their lungs with tobacco and yellow their teeth with coffee.

I've read travelers' accounts that liken these cafés to Western-style pubs, but I believe the comparison demeans them. The old Arab cafés are for thinkers. There is no wine to dull the intellect or beer to soften the tongue. Conversation, highbrow or otherwise, remains unslurred. Tempers, if they flare, do so unaided by alcohol's muffling of inhibition. And no lonely drunks slump on back corner tables. The café is not the place to chase oblivion.

Such places are usually the preserves of men, but Maya was clearly a regular here. After we found a quiet table on the second floor, a young waiter approached with Maya's usual—a nargileh loaded with lemon-mint tobacco. I ordered one of the same, and we chatted beneath a poster of Elvis Presley.

Maya started writing poems and stories when she was a child. "Writing was the way I could express things, and people would hug me. I wrote so my teachers would give me love." Maya was born in Lebanon in 1980 to a Lebanese mother and a Palestinian father, Mohammad al-Nabulsi, a high-ranking official with the PLO. Maya told me he forced her mother to marry him and that their marriage did not last long. The pair divorced when Maya was only a year old. Her father retained custody of Maya and sent her to live with his sister in Jordan while he worked for the PLO in Beirut. Maya assumed her aunt was her mother until she was six years old, and she wouldn't see her actual mother again until she took a trip to Jordan when she was twenty-one. Her father didn't approve of the visit, even after so many years. "We had the system of not talking about my mother," Maya said.

If Maya's mother was a distant and unknowable factor of her childhood, so too was Palestine. "I was the child of a PLO fighter," she said. "Palestine was a place for my father, not for me." Maya lived with her father in Lebanon and Tunis but never in the land he struggled for, the land she was supposed to desire. Maya didn't understand the idea of returning to a place she'd never been. "I only knew Palestine from what I saw on television," she said, "and what I read in the poems of Mahmoud Darwish." She never imagined Palestine as some sort of lost paradise. For her, Palestine was a place where there were no cities, where people lived in tents, and where "everything is about children throwing stones."

In 1993, after the Oslo Accords, Maya and her father moved from Tunis to Jordan, then crossed into Palestine and settled in Nablus in 1995. Maya was sixteen years old. "I felt that Tunisia kicked us out," she said, "but my father didn't feel this way. He told me, 'I just want to live in a dump in Nablus.'" All Maya's father ever wanted, all he ever fought for, was the opportunity to return home. "He was really happy," Maya said. "He just wanted to sit in his flat in Nablus and do nothing. Just be a Palestinian in Palestine." For the teenage Maya, settling in Nablus marked the end of an exhausting nomadic existence. "I loved living in Palestine. I loved the feeling of not having to think of leaving again."

Maya finished her secondary schooling in Nablus before enrolling in a civil engineering program at An-Najah National University. Then, on the first day of the Second Intifada in 2000, Israeli forces shot Maya's boyfriend at a demonstration in Nablus. He died of his wounds later that day in the hospital. Because of a curfew enforced by the Israel Defense Forces, Maya could not go to the hospital to say goodbye. "It was a big shock for me," Maya said. "One of those things that break you very hard."

Her boyfriend's death was followed by the perverse violence of the Second Intifada. Just as the Oslo Accords might be credited for the end of the First Intifada, the failure of the accords to bring about positive changes for Palestinians could be blamed for the second. The five-year surge of Palestinian terror attacks and Israeli military reprisals left three thousand Palestinians and one thousand Israelis dead. Nablus, considered a wellspring of Palestinian suicide bombers, became one of the Second

Intifada's bloodiest battlegrounds. Hundreds of Israeli soldiers, tanks, and armored vehicles entered the city in the spring of 2002 to engage with militants. Much of the fighting took place in the twisted alleyways of the Old City where buildings, some dating back to Byzantine times, were shelled by tanks, leveled by rockets, and flattened by Israeli bulldozers. More than seventy Nablusi died during the four-day siege. Maya was nearly one of them. She recalls looking out of her bedroom window one day at a gunfight happening on the street below. Just as she turned away from the window to answer her phone, a volley of bullets slammed into her room. Had she still been standing in the window, she would have been shot.

The sorrow of her lost love and the greater conflict exploding around her was nearly too much for Maya to bear. "I needed to believe in something," she said. So Maya put on the veil and sought comfort in the strictures of conservative Islam. She prayed five times a day, attended Friday prayers at the mosque, and refused to shake the hands of men who were not related to her. Maya's father disapproved. He was traditional, Maya says, but hardly devout, and he didn't like Maya's newfound piety. Maya also stopped writing for the first time in her life.

After two years of self-imposed devotion, Maya realized that religion was not comforting her. She'd found little solace in the mosque or under her hijab. So she started writing again. Maya penned her first book in between her college studies. She based the novel, *Grains of Sugar*, on her lost boyfriend. Maya discovered that writing granted her everything religion had failed to provide. She found meaning while crafting stories and developing characters. "I survived by writing this novel," she told me. Maya abandoned her hijab and her prayers when the book was finished and moved from conservative Nablus to the more secular environs of Ramallah. She kept the book a secret from her father until after it was published. "He didn't like writers and artists," Maya said, and he believed the best way to raise his daughters was to keep them out of the public eye. Keeping her writing a secret also granted Maya a certain freedom on the page. "I could write without being conscious of who around me would read it."

Maya's father passed away before she wrote her most recent novel, *Bloodtype*. He would not have liked it. The novel challenges the notion of the infallible mother and father common in Palestinian culture. The society expects children to revere their parents, but the mother and father in Maya's novel are deeply flawed. "I don't know if it was their mistakes or history's mistakes," Maya said, "but we all have mental disease because of everything that happened in our history as Palestinians. The whole thing makes us ill."

Maya's novel centers on a family that closely resembles her own. A father in the PLO who longs to return to Nablus. A forced marriage and early divorce. A girl who discovers that writing poetry can earn the affection of the adults she loves. A daughter sent to live with her aunt in Jordan. A move to Tunis. Maya, though, insisted the book is fictional and bristled at my clumsy questions about whether certain events in the novel happened in real life. Was her father part of Black September, the Jordanian civil war of 1970, like the father in the book? Did he really threaten to blow up a soccer stadium or put a gun to her mother's head? "I don't know why you ask these kinds of questions, which I really hate and don't enjoy answering," she scolded.

Maya said she lacked the courage to write such a personal novel while her father was still alive. "Otherwise it would have been a disaster for me," she laughed. She did not, however, consider her mother's reaction. Since Maya did not grow up with her mother, she was less protective of her feelings. "Besides, I didn't expect her to read it," she said, laughing. Maya's mother felt the novel revealed too many family secrets. The flawed character of the mother in the book also disturbed her, though Maya insists most readers sympathize with the character in spite of her imperfections. Maya's mother hadn't spoken to her since the novel came out.

A few years ago, Maya married an "IT guy" and moved to East Jerusalem, where he is from. "We don't have some great love story," she said, but she enjoys a degree of independence not common in Palestinian marriages. They have three young children, nine-year-old twins—a boy and a girl—and a six-year-old daughter. Since they were born in Jerusalem, the children all have blue Israeli identity cards. "But mine is green," Maya said.

Maya started writing for children soon after her twins were born. Even though her children's books have earned accolades in the Arabic-speaking world, Maya finds the genre challenging. "It takes a lot of courage to write for children," she said. In one of her books, a child longs for his father, who, unbeknownst to him, is serving a sentence in an Israeli prison. His mother suggests the child write a letter to his father to ask him to come home. He does this, but the father does not return. Then his mother suggests he pray for his father's return, but God does not bring his father back, either. "It is a Palestinian story," Maya said.

Maya derives more joy from working with kids than from writing books for them. She pays regular visits to rural villages and refugee camps where she gives storytelling workshops to children. "I feel sorry for them," she said. Palestinian children believe their parents and teachers want them to behave like adults and participate in the struggle. "To throw stones. To fight. To be a hero." The refugee children want to tell stories about people they know who were killed at a checkpoint. "It is heartbreaking," she said. "These are their stories. This is what they know."

I remembered how Kanafani wrote that a Palestinian child is "born suddenly" and "one scene can hurl him down from the ceiling of childhood on to the ruggedness of the road." Maya's workshops grant these otherwise serious children a respite from this ruggedness. Maya coaxes silliness out of them, if only for a little while.

Maya and her husband do their best to shield their own children from politics, lest the occupation toughen them like the refugee camp kids she works with. They also keep their children away from religion. Maya never returned to the veil she abandoned after writing her first novel, and neither she nor her husband are practicing Muslims. Too often, Palestinian governments use religion as "an excuse not to change things," Maya said. "They don't provide you what you need, but they point you to God." If you are good Muslims, the men in charge suggest, all we deny you in this life will be granted to you in the next.

I confessed to Maya my habit of trying to find the conflict in everything I read by Palestinian authors. She said that this is not necessarily wrong. "There is always something political, even in the small details of life," Maya said. "My whole life story gives me depth. And I don't write as a victim. I always write as a person. I am a person struggling all her life. I am a very strong woman. And I am Palestinian." Maya's comment reminded me of my favorite poem of hers, simply titled "Children." The poem portrays the fears all parents everywhere have for their children's safety, but at the same time, it remains undeniably rooted in Palestine:

Whenever I see an image of a child's hand
Sticking out of the rubble of a collapsed building
I check the hands of my three children
I count the fingers of their hands, the toes on their feet,
I check the numbers of teeth in their mouths, every
Last hair in each finely marked wee eyebrow

Whenever a child goes silent in Al Yarmuk Camp
I turn up the volume on the TV, the songs on the radio,
I pinch my three children
To make them cry and squirm with life

Whenever my sore heart gets hungry
At Qalandia checkpoint
I comfort-eat, I
Emotionally overeat, craving excessive salt
As if I could then somehow say: enough, block out
The salt spark of the tears everyone around me is crying.

Being a female writer in Palestine means following a unique set of rules and being "nice" to the men who control the cultural life. "Especially," Maya said with some modesty, "if you are a little bit beautiful." Her male colleagues didn't take her seriously at first. Then they wanted to take credit for "discovering" her. "But mostly the men want you to clap for them." Maya believes the major difference between male and female writing in the Arab world, and in Palestine in particular, is that men focus on big issues while women are interested in the intricacies of life. Also, men "can't write about weakness. Not even their own weakness. Even if they are not heroes, they will not portray themselves as weak. They will remain strong."

Maya took a long pull from her pipe and leaned back in her chair. She feels more comfortable in Ramallah than she does in East Jerusalem. Maya comes to Ramallah—a trip that can take up to three hours depending on the crowds at the checkpoint—just to spend thirty minutes smoking nargileh at Café Ramallah before returning home. She doesn't have a network of friends in Jerusalem. "I feel free in Ramallah," she said. "I can be with people I know and love." Jerusalem boasts a vibrant cultural scene, "but it is not for me," Maya said. "In Jerusalem, the life you want to live is for Israelis. Not for Palestinians. We feel we are living in the enemy's culture."

Israelis rarely appear in Maya's stories and poems for the simple fact that she doesn't know them. "For me, they are aliens," she said. Maya cannot speak Hebrew, for one thing, but the anxiety of the conflict erects higher barriers than language. "Living in Jerusalem is different than living in other cities," Maya said. "It is full of fear for us Arabs." She rarely sees any Israelis in East Jerusalem, and she always feels uncomfortable in the predominantly Israeli west.

Maya illustrates this estrangement near the end of *Bloodtype*. As her character Jumana rides the city's light-rail train, a Jewish woman asks her something in Hebrew. Jumana confesses in English that she doesn't understand. And when her phone rings on the train, she answers it in English rather than Arabic. Jumana does not want to be identified as Palestinian:

> Whenever I board the train, I worry about being found out. If anyone I know sees me—especially Laila or any of her Jerusalem-ID friends—they'll simply brand me a normalizer and probably lecture me on how I should boycott the light-rail system because it's designed to help expand the settlements. . . . If, on the other hand, Israelis realized I was Arab, I'd be subjected to all kinds of unseemly staring, and the security guard would ask to see my ID. . . . That's why I practice sitting in the most neutral and least terroristic way every time I use the train.

Maya wishes she knew Israelis well enough to write them as more than nameless faces on a train. Her work focuses on the realistic stories of everyday life, and she considers it important to have contact with the Israelis. She admires the bravery of her fellow Palestinian writers who are able to write Israelis as fully formed characters rather than one-dimensional villains. "I don't want to write in clichés," she said. "Israelis are humans. And if you want to write about them, you have to know their motivations."

Once our tobacco had burned black, Maya invited me to join her and her friends at a nearby bar for a drink. Everyone on Ramallah's main street, men and women both, turned to look at Maya when she passed. She had to stop several times to return their various greetings. "You see I am famous," she laughed. These fans recognized her from television, especially for her acting roles in the popular monthlong television soap operas that run each year during Ramadan.

Maya said she had always wanted to be an actress, but her father prohibited it. After he died, a producer saw Maya interviewed on television talking about her writing. He liked her look and her energy and offered her a role on a television show. Since then, she has appeared regularly in movies and commercials—including an ad for a mobile phone company I kept seeing over and over. She also starred in a film comedy called *Love, Theft and Other Entanglements*, in which a bumbling petty thief named Musa unwittingly steals a car with a kidnapped Israeli soldier in the trunk. Maya plays Musa's married girlfriend. The film screened at both the Seattle Film Festival and Berlin Biennale. "I went and walked the red carpet," she said, beaming. "I was living the Hollywood dream."

The bar was the antithesis of Café Ramallah—the sort of slick but generic cocktail bar that could exist anywhere in the world. Three young women were waiting for Maya at a table inside. One was Dalia Taha, a poet and playwright whose play *Fireworks* had been staged in London earlier that year. I recognized Dalia from a story the *Guardian* published about her, in which she scolded her interviewer for his preoccupation with politics. "I hate these questions," she told him. "It's always like this for artists or writers who come from places with conflicts and wars. You expect us to make a political statement, to tell the story of our suffering." I told Dalia I would like to speak with her about her work and that after reading the *Guardian* piece I considered myself warned. In the end, she opted not to meet with me. She never told me why. I suspect she didn't trust I could see anything but politics in her work.

Another one of Maya's friends gave me a second warning. Upon hearing of my interest in Palestinian literature, she asked me flat out how I would "avoid being Orientalist." The question startled me. I didn't have a good answer for her. As we left the bar, she apologized for putting me on the spot, adding, "A lot of foreigners are coming here to write about Palestinians. They weren't interested in us when we were blowing ourselves up."

After my meeting with Maya, I visited Café Ramallah nearly every day to smoke nargileh, drink coffee, and write in my notebook. One afternoon, a man with a reddish beard, a fedora, and a gray T-shirt printed with the image of the Persian poet Rumi walked in. He borrowed a tube of Krazy Glue from the owner at the desk, then scanned the room for a place to sit. The only empty chair was at my table. The man sat down and, without looking at me, plucked his eyeglasses from his face and dabbed tiny blobs of glue on the broken frames. He noticed my notebook and told me in growly imperfect English that he was also a writer. He introduced himself as Moheeb Barghouti.

While Moheeb returned his attention to his eyeglass frames, I googled his name on my phone. Moheeb used to be a photojournalist who covered political demonstrations. I found a Facebook page with a photo of Moheeb lying in a hospital bed showing off the bullet wounds in his legs he suffered during a protest. Another article told a story of Moheeb suffering injuries during a different demonstration. The story included photos of Moheeb smiling in spite of the blood streaming down his face from a wound on his head.

I held up my phone to Moheeb and showed him the photos. "Is this you?" I asked.

He slipped his glasses back on his face and squinted at the screen. "Yes," he said. "But I don't cover protests anymore. Nothing new is happening." Now Moheeb writes poems.

Moheeb was at Café Ramallah, sitting amid the smoke and gossip, nearly every time I came in. I'd sit with him and we'd talk about his favorite books, his former life as a Trotskyist, and the years he spent in Jordanian, Syrian, and Iraqi prisons. He told me that until he read Charles Bukowski he didn't know that Americans did anything "except kill people with guns." Mostly, he would talk about the philosophy that fuels his own poetry. "My darkness is my best friend," he'd say. Or, "I don't believe Sartre that hell is other people. Hell is in the mirror." Or, "I want to write poems that change myself. Not change the world. Fuck the world. The world is not my problem."

Later, I'd find a couple of Moheeb's poems translated to English in a British literary journal, and at the end of a poem called "Death Squad," I find Café Ramallah:

> Hey short story writers, poets and novelists of either sex,
> kick me out of your gatherings, and pour oil on my memory,
> for the likes of me are good for nothing but homelessness and leftovers.
> You deserve Kundera, Georges Bataille, Rimbaud, and Sartre.
> My thoughts are sinful, my waters sewage
> and my room is smaller than Your Excellencies' bathrooms . . .
> Oh, friends of cookery,
> do as you wish;
> use every weapon of torture and destruction to inflict pain on me, to
>   turn me into ruins,
> and use every kind of technology to drag my memory through the
>   streets;
> yet I beg of Your Excellencies and I crave from Your Honours;
> leave me Café Ramallah
> and go wherever you wish, even to hell.

"I like to believe I was born in 1954," poet Ghassan Zaqtan told me, but he doesn't know for sure. After the Nakba and the scattering of Palestinians from their homes, official records were often lost. Ghassan chose 1954 because it is the Year of the Horse according to the Chinese zodiac. "Nineteen fifty-five was the goat and 1956 was the monkey, but I like horses better," Ghassan said. "This is the only reason." The bass and timbre of Ghassan's voice reminded me of an Arab Leonard Cohen. His rumbling laugh resonated below the screech of the espresso grinder at Zamn, a café that opted for a polished aesthetic more akin to Starbucks than the smoky masculinity of Café Ramallah.

Ghassan's family came from Zakariyya, a village named for the father of John the Baptist. The Zaqtans fled Zakariyya in 1948 and settled in Beit Jala, where Ghassan was born. His father worked for the Red Cross during the Nakba then found a job as a schoolmaster in the Dheisheh refugee camp near Bethlehem, where he started the camp's first school for girls. This placed him at odds with some of his more conservative colleagues and led the family to leave Beit Jala in 1961. The loss of his childhood home figures in an achingly sad poem Ghassan would write decades later called "A Picture of the House in Beit Jala":

He has to return to shut that window,
it isn't entirely clear
whether this is what he must do,
things are no longer clear
since he lost them,
and it seems a hole somewhere within him has opened up . . .

. . . he must return to shut that window
the upper-story window which he often forgets
at the end of the stairway that leads to the roof
Since he lost them
he aimlessly walks
and the day's small
purposes are also no longer clear.

Ghassan's family settled in Jordan's Karameh refugee camp, but not for too long. Karameh grew into a center of Palestinian resistance in the 1960s, and the Israel Defense Forces razed the entire camp to the ground in 1968. As a young refugee in Jordan, sports interested Ghassan more than poetry or politics. He played amateur basketball before quitting to become a coach and phys ed teacher. "If I had been five centimeters taller my life would've been very different," he said. Ghassan started to write poetry in between classes and basketball practices. One of his poems won a prize from the Jordanian Writers Union. Ghassan's attendance at the award ceremony was cause enough for the Jordanian authorities, who had no love for the union's leftist tendencies, to arrest and imprison him for three months. Ghassan hesitated to tell me this. Compared to the long and multiple sentences so many Palestinian men serve, Ghassan considers his three-month turn insignificant. He felt embarrassed to even mention it.

Still, three months was enough time for Ghassan to decide to commit himself to both poetry and politics. Upon his release from prison, Ghassan left his teaching job, sold his car, and prepared to move to Beirut. "It was 1979," he said. "Beirut was the center of the revolution. The PLO was there. So were many of my leftist friends." Ghassan delayed telling his father his Beirut plans as he was certain his father would disapprove. "I prepared myself for a clash," Ghassan said, but his father gave him his blessing. Looking back, Ghassan figures that his father regretted not joining the resistance himself as a young man and so supported Ghassan's decision.

Ghassan was living in Beirut during the 1982 Lebanon War. His poetry collection *Old Reasons* had been published a few days before the Israeli invasion. As Darwish stirred coffee elsewhere in the city and tried to "pay no heed to the rockets," Ghassan had no such luxury. An Israeli missile struck Ghassan's third-floor apartment while he was out on an errand and incinerated everything inside, including his fifteen author copies of *Old Reasons*. Then a fire broke out in the warehouse where boxes of his new book were being stored. They all burned. Only about a hundred copies of *Old Reasons* that his publisher sent out in advance, and the two copies Ghassan had on his person at the time, survived the Lebanon War.

Like Maya's father and other PLO activists of the time, Ghassan traveled constantly. He spent a few months in the Soviet Union, where he frequented a library full of nineteenth-century Russian novels translated into Arabic. There he met a Jew from Odesa with whom he debated literature and politics and who inspired him to be a reader as well as a writer. Although they were an odd pair—a Russian communist Jew and a Palestinian poet from the PLO—the two grew close. "He was a good teacher," Ghassan said. He returned to Beirut from the USSR and then bounced back and forth between Damascus, Tunis, Cyprus, and Gaza.

Ghassan is often compared to Mahmoud Darwish. The two poets became friends in Tunis in 1988 after Ghassan published his book *The Heroism of Things*. Once Darwish read the book, he instructed his writer friends: "Bring Zaqtan to me." Duly summoned, Ghassan visited Darwish at his home in the early evening, a few hours before Darwish was scheduled to meet with the Algerian foreign minister. He and Ghassan talked until four in the morning, and Darwish missed his meeting altogether. I asked Ghassan what they talked about. "*He* talked. I listened," Ghassan corrected me. "We talked about my book."

"For ten hours?" I asked.

"There may have been some alcohol involved," Ghassan said.

The two poets grew closer once they'd both moved to Ramallah after Oslo. "He was a good leader," Ghassan said. "He was my teacher, but not as a poet. As a thinker. He had a very wide knowledge, especially in the Hebrew language and in Hebrew literature. And he was very generous with his knowledge." Ghassan said Darwish possessed a great sense of humor and a quick wit, but he protected his privacy. "There were rumors about him," Ghassan said, whispers about women and money problems. "But not facts." Darwish also generously shouldered the Palestinian cause. With a global audience focused on Darwish as the Palestinian flag-bearer, writers like Ghassan could focus on their own work. Darwish used to joke with Ghassan about his bad luck ending up as the mouthpiece for his people while everyone else could just be a poet.

Another of Darwish's contributions to Palestinian poetry, according to Ghassan, was his unique ability to portray Israelis as individual humans rather than a uniform collective of villainous ghosts. In an essay titled "We Were Born in the Houses of Storytellers," Ghassan argues:

> It is easy to defeat a ghost, to burden it with the causes and excuses of loss, to achieve a desired heroism through ignorance and exaggeration. But it is difficult, to the extent it is realistic, to confront an "enemy" who contains contradictions and human tendencies with all their attendant implications.

The occupation—for all its cruelties—allows Palestinians to come into daily contact with Israelis. "Quotidian life," Ghassan writes, enables Palestinians to humanize the Israeli and "grant him nuance without excusing him for the basic condition under which the 'relationship' has come about, the occupation."

Darwish was particularly adept at this, Ghassan says. His poetry

managed to express his Palestinian identity while simultaneously revealing the individual humanity of his Israeli characters "as if uncovering
cracks in a wall." Ghassan presents Darwish's famous poem "Rita and the
Rifle" as an example. The poem—inspired by Darwish's own romance
with a Jewish dancer named Tamar Ben Ami—describes a forbidden love
affair between the poet and an Israeli soldier. Rita's name was a feast in
the poet's mouth, her body a wedding in his blood. But in spite of her
"honey-colored eyes" and her "loveliest of braids," Rita always remains a
soldier of the enemy. "Between Rita and my eyes," Darwish writes, "there
is a rifle."

In 2013, Canada's Griffin Trust shortlisted Ghassan's book *Like a
Straw Bird It Follows Me, and Other Poems* for the Griffin Poetry Prize.
The prize committee invited Ghassan to attend the award ceremony, but
the Canadian diplomatic office in Ramallah denied his visa request. In
its rejection letter, the office stated that the $65,000 award, one of the
world's richest poetry prizes, provided "insufficient grounds for a visa." It
also expressed "uncertainty" about both Ghassan's financial situation and
his "true desire to return home."

The irony of the visa official questioning a Palestinian refugee's desire
to return to Palestine was not lost on Ghassan, but the Canadian decision
neither offended nor surprised him. The previous year, Ghassan canceled
a two-month book tour to the United States because of visa delays. "It is a
policy against the Palestinians, and not only in Canada and the US. Even
in the Arab world. We have this problem everywhere. It is not personal.
I am sure about that."

Barred from Canada, Ghassan traveled to Turkey instead, where he
gave readings at Istanbul University. Then he got a call from his wife. The
Canadian visa office had changed its mind and approved Ghassan's application. Ghassan figured it was too late. He told the Canadian office that
he was traveling and would not return to Ramallah in time to pick up the
visa. When Ghassan mentioned he was en route to Jordan from Turkey,
the Canadians offered to send his visa to their office in Amman. "So I
went there. I waited twenty minutes, and then they gave me the visa." Six
hours later, he was on a plane to Toronto. Ghassan was more surprised
at the lengths to which the Canadians went to eventually deliver his visa
than he was at being rejected in the first place.

Ghassan won the Griffin. One of the judges, Chinese poet Wang Ping, wrote of Ghassan's book:

> What does poetry do? Nothing and everything, like air, water, soil, like birds, fish, trees, like love, spirit, our daily words. . . . It lives with us, in and outside us, everywhere, all the time, and yet, we are too often oblivious of this gift. It's a poet's job to bring this gift out and back, this gift that makes us human again. And Mr. Zaqtan has done it.

Many in the poetry world have bestowed Darwish's "Poet of Palestine" mantle onto Ghassan. Darwish himself christened Ghassan the most important Palestinian poet living today. But Ghassan doesn't believe that Palestinians need a poet-spokesperson anymore, and believes that poetry's importance to Palestinian society has diminished. Besides, "politics corrodes and constrains poetry," Ghassan said. He feels the poet needs to "clear his body from political speeches. From political statements. It is time to clean it."

Ghassan suspected I would not like this idea. He figured that I, as a foreigner, would prefer to hear that his work advanced Palestine's national cause. Maybe he was right. I admitted to Ghassan that I reflexively sought politics lurking between his stanzas and behind his metaphors—and in all Palestinian writing—even if there is none. "That is *your* problem," he said bluntly. "You can interpret what you like." Ghassan doesn't want to speak on behalf of his people. He prefers to "walk behind the demonstrations and see what falls and catch the evidence. The handkerchief. The child's backpack. The purse." Ghassan believes Palestinians need to stop seeking inspiration from their leaders of the past, however iconic, and instead look to those who populate their daily lives. "The taxi driver. The physical therapist. These are our heroes now."

The Khalil Sakakini Cultural Center occupies another gorgeous stone mansion a little down the hill from the Qattan Foundation. Since its establishment in 1996, the center has hosted and promoted events such as art exhibits, film screenings, and author readings. The building also held the offices of *Al-Karmel*, the literary quarterly Mahmoud Darwish edited until his death.

The center has preserved Darwish's office as he left it before he died. Writers dream of such a workspace. Large windows allow sunlight to reflect off the polished stone tile floors. A simple sofa and coffee table sit in one corner where Darwish used to entertain visitors. The caretaker told me Darwish's desk remains exactly how he left it. I am not so sure. The clutter seemed staged to me, the pile of letters and envelopes on his desk blotter too artfully messy. Still, I felt a sort of thrill in seeing his leather-bound phone book and 1970s-era pen holders—and sadness for his unflipped desk calendar.

In 2002, only days after Darwish and an international cadre of writers, including Wole Soyinka, José Saramago, and Russell Banks, gave a reading in Ramallah's Al-Kasaba Theatre, the Israel Defense Forces launched Operation Defensive Shield. The goal of the massive military operation into the West Bank—the largest such incursion since 1967's Six-Day War—was to root out the terrorist factions responsible for a plague of bloody suicide bombings in Israel. During their three-week occupation of Ramallah, IDF soldiers used explosives to blast their way into the Sakakini Center. They ransacked rooms, broke sculptures, and trashed Darwish's second-floor office. The soldiers pulled Darwish's books and manuscripts from their shelves and trampled them. They left shattered glass all over the floor and a bullet hole in a window.

Palestinians could not see any security justification for the invasion of Sakakini. They wondered how an institution that sponsors concerts, art exhibits, and poetry readings could be a target for the Israeli military. But Darwish knew. When he heard news of the soldiers ransacking his office, he said: "They wanted to give us a message that nobody is immune, including cultural life. I took the message personally. I know they're strong and can invade and kill anyone. But they can't break or occupy my words."

Many consider the Israelis' action at the center part of an ongoing "cultural cleansing" of Palestine. Just as the Knesset opposed the idea of allowing Israeli children to read Darwish's "love story" for the hills of Palestine, the trashing of the center aimed to obliterate evidence of Palestinian presence on the land. "Israelis never wanted Palestinians to express themselves in a creative way," Mahmoud Abu Hashhash once said. "Because, to Israel, the most dangerous thing is to start seeing the Palestinians as artists who can express and convey the spirit of the times."

Adila Laïdi, the center's director at the time, was more blunt: "I guess our art is very dangerous if you don't want us to exist at all."

I was in Ramallah for the beginning of Ramadan, the monthlong fast when observant Muslims are forbidden to eat, drink, or smoke during daylight hours—and when Maya Abu-Alhayyat appears on every television on the Ramadan soap operas. The day before the fast began, Moheeb reassured me that Café Ramallah would remain open during the day, even during fasting hours. "The front door will be locked," he said, "but you can come around the back." I loved how Ramadan transformed my local café into an Arab speakeasy with a secret entrance.

I'd planned to meet Dr. Sharif Kanaana one morning at Rukab's Ice Cream shop so we could talk about Palestinian folktales over breakfast sundaes. The shop, of course, was closed, so I led Sharif across the street to Café Ramallah. Metal shutters had been pulled down over the front door and windows, just as Moheeb predicted, but I told Sharif we could enter through the back. He was skeptical. He followed me slowly behind the building but paused before entering the back door. "Are you sure?" he asked.

We stepped past the washrooms into a café filled with men cheating on their fast. Because the windows and doors were closed, the place was dark and hazy with unventilated smoke. The proprietor nodded at me, and Sharif and I found a table beneath the television. Sharif doesn't hear well, so he sat close to me and spoke softly through his thick white mustache.

Sharif told me about the fading tradition of Palestinian storytelling, or *hikaye*. During the winter months, when there was less work to do in the fields and people had more time to receive guests, Palestinians would gather after dinner to hear storytellers recite their favorite folktales from memory. *Hikaye* was predominantly a female art form. Boys might be encouraged to recite stories for their younger siblings, but once they reached puberty, boys typically stopped telling tales for fear of seeming womanly. Such stories often involve magic or the fictional quarrels between female family members—tales considered too frivolous for serious men. Participating in the *hikaye* could earn a man the unflattering label of *niswanji*: a man who prefers the company of women.

Individual storytellers embellished the tales as they told them, and the best *hikaye* tellers had their own distinctive styles. The tradition, though, allowed for no significant improvisation. Just as Cinderella's fantasy ends at midnight in every retelling, *hikaye* narratives remain the same. Some stories are famous. "Half-a-Halfling," a tale about the adventures of a tiny boy hero, and "Little Piece of Cheese," about a girl with skin as perfectly white as cheese, are as familiar to most Palestinians as Disney's versions of Grimm's fairy tales would be to people in the West.

But the days of gathering in the salon to listen to Grandmother tell old stories are over. Sharif believes that the tradition waned after 1948, when Jewish immigrants from Europe introduced radios, and then televisions, to the Palestinian population. These devices replaced the storytellers. But the emotional impact of the Nakba also played a part in *hikaye*'s decline. "The whole mood changed," Sharif said. "The whole life was something different." The Nakba displaced half of the Palestinian population. No family was unscathed. Sharif's mother, for example, lost her own mother and sister to exile in Lebanon. Families lost touch with each other. They feared the soldiers in the streets. They rationed food and struggled to survive in an upended society. Among all that the Palestinians lost during those years was the inclination to tell amusing stories.

Sharif knew he could not save the storytelling tradition, but he could at least rescue the stories themselves. In his work as an anthropologist during the late 1970s, Sharif collected about fifteen hundred of these old folktales, mostly from women. He and his colleague Ibrahim Muhawi published forty-five of the stories in a book called *Speak Bird, Speak Again: Palestinian Arab Folktales*. The Institute for Palestine Studies in Beirut distributed three thousand copies to school libraries throughout Palestine in 2001.

The book drew controversy in 2006 after Hamas, a militant nationalist-Islamist movement known for violent resistance against Israel, won a slim majority of seats in the Palestinian parliamentary elections. Many viewed Hamas's victory as a rejection of the incumbent Fatah party that had dominated Palestinian politics for decades and was widely seen as ineffectual and corrupt. The Hamas government turned out to be short-lived. Violence between Hamas and Fatah in Gaza compelled President Abbas to dismiss the Hamas-led cabinet the following year. At the time, though, many Palestinians and outside observers wondered how a parliament guided by fundamentalist Islam would govern.

They did not have to wonder long. Hamas's newly appointed minister of education, Nasser al-Din al-Shaer, promptly sent a notice calling for the removal of *Speak Bird, Speak Again* from school shelves because of content that "insulted the common sense of decent people." Hamas wasn't satisfied with simply culling *Speak Bird*. It wanted the books burned. "The memo said that the school principal should be present when the books were pulled to ensure that they were properly destroyed," Sharif told me.

For those who feared Hamas planned to impose its strict interpretation of Islam on Palestinians, the action against *Speak Bird* represented the canary in the coal mine. The call to destroy the books spurred street protests in Ramallah, though Sharif believes party politics inspired the protesters more than any notions of cultural freedom. "Most of the demonstrators were from Fatah, of course," Sharif said. Then the international news media descended. Sharif remembers coming home one evening to find a reporter and cameraman waiting for him in his salon, another group of reporters in his kitchen, and a third waiting outside his front door. Sharif knew the journalists cared little about Palestinian education or literature. They wanted a story that criticized Hamas and the party's members in the new unity government. "Had the minister not belonged to Hamas, it would have not gotten so much attention," Sharif said. He refused to publicly condemn Hamas for the reporters crowding his home.

Sharif thought the ban was more personal than religious anyway. Sharif and Minister al-Shaer had their own troubled history. Al-Shaer had led a religious student group at An-Najah National University years earlier when Sharif was the university's president. After al-Shaer's group brawled with a nationalist student group on campus, Sharif suspended both leaders. Sharif figured al-Shaer's call for the destruction of his book was merely an act of delayed vengeance.

Still, *Speak Bird* contains plenty of material a conservative parent, or a Hamas education minister, might object to. The text is peppered with obscenities. "There were words like 'son of a whore.' Or 'your mother is a this-or-that,'" Sharif said. "I collected them because this is the way the stories sounded." Sharif figured two stories in particular troubled the minister. One was "The Little Bird," a truly bizarre tale in which the sultan's son shoots, plucks, cooks, and swallows a female bird who manages to sing throughout each step of her ordeal. At the end, after the sultan's son "got up and shat her," the bird continued to sing:

"Ho! Ho! I saw the prince's hole,
It's red, red like a burning coal."

Another story is titled, bluntly, "The Woman Who Married Her Son." In this tale, a mother is so jealous of her daughter-in-law's beauty that she throws her out of the house while her son is on hajj. The mother disguises herself as her daughter-in-law, sleeps with her son when he returns from Mecca, and becomes pregnant. While on an errand to fetch sour grapes—pregnant Palestinian women crave sour grapes the same way Western women crave pickles—the son discovers his mother's deception. He then sets a bundle of wood on fire and burns his mother to death. "Hamas thought this story was very terrible," Sharif said.

The education minister reversed the ban on *Speak Bird* after a few weeks. "Al-Shaer sent around an order saying we should keep the book, but he did not admit he was wrong," Sharif said. "Things went back to normal." The only lasting effect of the ban was, unsurprisingly, to boost the book's popularity. The Institute for Palestine Studies had to print hundreds more copies to meet the new demand.

A decade later, government authorities pulled another title from Palestinian bookshelves. In 2017, the attorney general of the Palestinian Authority, now back under the control of Fatah, sent police to raid a Ramallah bookshop and seize copies of Abbad Yahya's novel *Crime in Ramallah*. The attorney general also ordered the confiscation of all one thousand copies of the book from libraries and bookstores across the West Bank and summoned Yahya for questioning. Hamas issued a statement condemning the book, too, and calls for Yahya's lynching started appearing on his Facebook page. A Nablus book club canceled a planned discussion of *Crime in Ramallah* after receiving its own storm of death threats. Yahya was visiting Qatar at the time. "I don't know what to do," he said in an email. "If I go back, I will be arrested, and if I stay here, I will be far from my home and family."

Crime in Ramallah focuses on three young men connected to the murder of a woman outside a Ramallah bar. The police arrest one of the men. He is eventually cleared and released but not before officers savagely beat him when they learn he is gay. The second man works at the bar where the murder took place. His conservative family shuns him for serving alcohol, and he becomes an Islamic extremist. The third man, the boyfriend of the murdered woman, kills himself.

The attorney general claimed *Crime in Ramallah* "contained indecent texts and terms that threaten morality and public decency, which could affect the population, in particular minors." The book's sexually explicit language included references to homosexuality, masturbation, and this particularly icky description of a Yasser Arafat poster:

> When I came out of school, I was facing a poster of Arafat in army fatigues. He was clutching a rifle, which looked like a giant penis . . . The cheap white glue they used to stick the posters to the gate was dripping from the edge of the paper toward the mouth of the barrel. The scene was perfect. A white liquid trickling from the rifle.

Palestine's writers didn't believe the ban had anything to do with morality. Other sexually explicit novels by Arab authors and foreigners such as Henry Miller remained available in Palestinian bookstores and libraries. And the child protection laws the attorney general invoked would not apply to a book like Yahya's, which was clearly written for adults. Instead, most observers believed Fatah banned the novel for disrespecting Arafat, revered by Fatah as the godfather of the Palestinian cause. Worst of all, the book painted a bleak picture of contemporary life in Ramallah under the Palestinian Authority. The government based its decision on politics rather than ethics.

The Independent Commission for Human Rights, an agency within the PA itself, opposed the decision. Even the Palestinian minister of culture, Ehab Bseiso, demanded that the attorney general revoke the ban and cheekily announced he would immediately start reading the book.

Nearly one hundred Palestinian authors, artists, and intellectuals signed a statement protesting the government action.

Yahya has not returned to Palestine. He accepted an invitation by the German PEN Center, which offered him a scholarship and a yearlong "writers-in-exile" fellowship. I reached him the day after his arrival in Germany. He told me his wife would join him but that their future remained uncertain. "I'm already confused about my stay, my wife's status, and my work," he wrote. "I can't think clearly about what I want to do after the fellowship ends."

Even in Ramallah, at the font of Palestinian artistic expression, writers can find themselves besieged by those who strive to restrict and suppress their work. And the Israeli occupation does not always reign as the primary bogeyman. Political feuds and personal grudges, sensitive mothers and disapproving fathers, religion, tradition, and gender: all throw up their own barriers before the authors of Palestine, who must find their way over, under, or around them.

While Café Ramallah remained my daytime haunt, I'd take nightly coffee, beer, and nargileh at Café La Vie, a lovely garden café not far from the guesthouse at Qattan. An American woman named Morgan runs the café with her Palestinian husband. When I walked into La Vie on the first night of my last trip to Ramallah, Morgan beamed. "I guess our nargileh sales are going to go up," she said. It felt good to be recognized, but Morgan was pregnant at the time and avoided my table when I was smoking. I would read and write beneath the tiny spring figs on La Vie's trees and watch groups of young Palestinian women wave fiercely at the slow-moving waiters. Eventually, the alcohol, caffeine, and nicotine would collude to swirl away my attention. Then I'd return to my guesthouse a little light-headed and rubber-legged.

Morgan occasionally hosts author readings at La Vie, and I performed at one of these a few years earlier when I was writer-in-residence. Accustomed to Canada's poorly attended literary readings, I was unprepared for La Vie's crowd. The staff had moved nearly every chair from the inside of the café outside for the reading, and each of these was full. (Only a few chairs remained indoors for the handful of customers wanting to watch a high-stakes European Cup match. Poetry trumps soccer at La Vie.) Fairy lights hung from the trees and wrapped around the tree trunks. Thick clouds of citrus-scented smoke tumbled out of the mouths of the nargileh smokers. Lemon-mint was the preferred flavor that spring, though I was more partial to watermelon.

Several foreigners sat among the crowd, young activist types wearing keffiyehs and speaking tortured Arabic with European accents. Most of the audience, though, were Palestinians of varying ages. I shared the night with a couple of local poets, the visiting Palestinian-American poet Hala Alyan, and a fabulous local guitarist. The main draw, though, was Kifah Fanni, a local poet in his fifties. During his reading, Morgan whispered to me that Fanni rarely reads in public, and his appearance at La Vie was an extraordinary occasion. Fanni, suitably bohemian in his beard and beret, recited soft Arabic verses from loose pages while the audience sat still and respectful.

When it was my turn at the microphone, I decided not to read anything I'd written about Palestine. The idea of reflecting my outsider's experiences of the struggle back to those who live it every day struck me as arrogant. More than this, though, I didn't want to darken such a night with bleak politics. Despite the foreign activists, their keffiyehs broadcasting solidarity with the Palestinian cause, this was a venue for art.

I recited a magazine piece I wrote years earlier about becoming a father. It is a story about love—and beauty. I don't know how many in the garden fully understood my reading. English was a first language for very few. But the audience was quiet and attentive. I could sense, in a tiny way and only for a moment, what Darwish meant when he said writing about love liberated his humanity. To stand in Palestine and read aloud about something other than the familiar narrative—to speak not of the Nakba or the checkpoints or the fallen olive trees—felt both subversive and profoundly human. I read from the same story back home several times, but nowhere did the experience feel as visceral as that night at La Vie. Nowhere did it mean as much to me.

My map of Palestine is a mess of barriers and forbidden space. A pox of red X's denote military checkpoints. Red lines indicating Israel's "separation barrier" lacerate the edges of Palestine's border and slash inward to embrace the blue blotches of Israeli settlements. Purple tangles show where stretches of new walls will rise.

Israel started its wall project in the fall of 2002, during the bloodiest days of the Second Intifada. More than six hundred and fifty Israeli civilians had been killed by suicide attacks since the outbreak of violence in 2000. Palestinian terrorists blew themselves up in restaurants, cafés, and buses. The checkpoints and military incursions into the West Bank were not working, and the terrified Israeli populace demanded a different response from their government. Israel began to erect a seven-hundred-kilometer-long system of security barriers around the West Bank. For most of its route the barrier is a three-meter-high fence equipped with barbed wire, electronic sensors, and night-vision cameras. Smooth strips of sand next to the fence reveal the footprints of anyone who makes it over. Red signs in Hebrew, Arabic, and English threaten "mortal danger" and warn "any person who passes or damages the fence endangers his life."

Alongside the larger Palestinian centers, the barrier is more wall than fence. Great gray slabs of concrete rise out of the ground, bound so tightly together not even a thread of sunlight can infiltrate. Floodlights and security cameras mark the length on top of the wall, and cylindrical watchtowers pose like vertical cannons along the route. I'd passed through the wall's checkpoint dozens of times, but I was always struck by the barrier's concrete brashness, its proud rejection of nuance and grace.

Only a tenth of the wall follows the Green Line, the armistice boundary drawn in 1949 and the internationally accepted border between Israel and the West Bank. Most of the barrier creeps east of the Green Line and inside Palestinian territory. In some areas, the barrier plunges deep into the West Bank, swinging wide around Jewish settlements in order to keep them, and much of the land surrounding them, on the Israeli side. The barrier also divides Palestinian villages from both their farmland and neighboring towns, and annexes a tenth of Palestinian land in the West Bank to Israel. The International Court of Justice declared the wall illegal in 2004, and while proponents claim the barrier saves lives, officials in Israel's own intelligence agency concede the barrier does not play a major role in reducing terrorist attacks. If the wall can be admired at all, it must be for its audacity.

As soon as the wall rose, artists from around the world came to the West Bank to use it as a canvas. Graffiti art covers the gray concrete throughout the West Bank but most famously in Bethlehem, where ironic murals by reclusive graffiti artist Banksy are a boon to local taxi drivers who offer "Banksy tours" to visitors. In 2017, Banksy opened the Walled Off Hotel in Bethlehem, which includes a shop—called Wall Mart—that rents ladders, sells spray paint, and offers stencil tutorials. "Your one-stop shop for decorating the wall," the website declares. Most of the Palestinians I spoke to, however, despise the decorations. They feel the art lends permanence to a structure they hope will one day come down. More than this, though, they don't want anyone to make the wall beautiful.

In his collected diaries, *A River Dies of Thirst*, Mahmoud Darwish describes the wall as a "snake eager to lay its eggs between our inhalations and exhalations so that we say, for once, because we are nearly choking to death, 'We are the strangers.'" But the wall is not a place for metaphors, I don't think, compelling as they are. Just as Barghouti's glance across the bridge transformed Palestine from an argument and a metaphor into something "touchable," the wall casts the idea of the occupation into a literal concrete reality. For the Palestinians who live in the wall's shadow— those the wall was built to enclose and exclude—the wall is not a snake or a symbol. The wall is a wall.

Barghouti knew this. He describes seeing the wall for the first time in *I Was Born There, I Was Born Here* and rages against the barrier in a single continuous paragraph that spans more than two pages. He writes:

This wall disfigures the sky itself. It disfigures the clouds that pass above it. It disfigures the rain that falls upon it. It disfigures the moonlight that touches it and the rays of the sun that fall next to it. . . . This wall has been designed to imprison an entire human community. To imprison a morning greeting between neighbors. To imprison a grandfather's dancing at his grandson's wedding. To imprison the handshakes exchanged at a ceremony of mourning for the death of a relative. To imprison the hand of a mother and prevent it from holding her daughter's when she gives birth. To separate the olive tree from the one who planted it, the student from his school, the patient from his doctor, the believer from his prayers at the mosque. It imprisons dates between teenagers. The Wall makes you long for colors. It makes you feel that you are living in a stage set, not in real life. It imprisons time within place.

The wall cuts such a compelling line across the landscape that I felt tempted to define the hills of Palestine by their desecration rather than their beauty. I wanted to see more than this, so I went to see Raja Shehadeh. I learned about Raja after reading his remarkable book *Palestinian Walks: Forays into a Vanishing Landscape*. The book recounts his hikes through the hills of Palestine and reveals how the land has changed over decades of occupation and the rapid expansion of Israeli settlements. "It was as though the tectonic movements that had occurred over thousands of years were now happening in a matter of months, entirely redrawing the map," Raja writes. "The Palestine I knew, the land I thought of as mine, was quickly being transformed before my eyes."

I wanted Raja to take me on one of these walks, but he said he hikes very little these days. He used to be able to descend into the valley from his house and quickly escape the city. Now Ramallah has spread so wide there are no nearby trailheads, and Raja has to drive in order to find a place to walk. The settlements and security apparatus also make it difficult to locate an easy route. And there are wild boars. Over the last few years, boars have wandered down the valley from the Galilee. Raja thinks the garbage created by the city attracts them. They are not dangerous, he insists, "but they are off-putting for hikers." So instead of walking we sat in his garden amid olive trees, lavender, and hibiscus. We drank Shepherds beer and ate pistachios from a tray his wife, Penny, brought out to us.

Raja's father's family fled Jaffa in 1948. When his family used to stand on Ramallah's hills and look west toward Jaffa, they never even glanced at the landscape that stood between them and the coastal city they'd lost. In his memoir, *Strangers in the House*, Raja wrote: "My life then was shaped by the contrast between the meagerness of life in Ramallah and the opulence of life in the city across the hills. There were daily reminders of that cataclysmic fall from grace." His grandmother would show young Raja the son of a rich landowner who now peddled used clothes from a cart. Or the Salman brothers, once owners of a prestigious women's clothing store in Jaffa, reduced to hawking needles and thread. The primacy of Jaffa rings out in one of the most heartbreaking passages in *Stranger*. For years, his family would point at the lights along the distant Mediterranean and say, with longing, "There is Jaffa." Years later, they realized that the lights were actually from Tel Aviv and that they could not see Jaffa at all.

Raja's father, Aziz Shehadeh, worked as a lawyer in an office in Ramallah. In the wake of the 1967 war, Aziz worked out a detailed peace plan that would establish a Palestinian state next to Israel. The memorandum, which a young Raja typed out for his father on a manual typewriter, countered the view of most Arab leaders that there should be no compromise with Israel. Aziz, though, did not see any value in continuing a policy that had failed Palestinians since 1948. "My father dared to utter the unspeakable: recognition of Israel," Raja wrote. The reaction to Aziz's transgression was swift. In 1968, Raja heard a message broadcast from a Palestinian radio station in Damascus that addressed Aziz directly:

A.S., you are a traitor, a despicable collaborator. You want to surrender and sell our birthright. We know how to deal with the likes of you. A.S., you will pay for your treason. We shall eliminate you. Silence you forever. Make an example of you for others. Traitor. Collaborator. Quisling.

Raja realized that referring to Aziz only by his initials was significant. His revolutionary brethren in Damascus refused to acknowledge his existence in the same way they refused to use the word *Israel*. His father had become a pariah, but he continued his legal practice in spite of the threats.

By way of heartbreaking irony, a Palestinian informant working for the Israeli security services—an *actual* collaborator—stabbed Aziz to death in 1985. The killer was never punished for the crime but died of gunshot wounds in a drive-by shooting in 1994. Raja would have to wait until 2006 before receiving confirmation this man was indeed his father's murderer. A British historian friend of Raja's heard it from an Israeli cabinet minister who had access to the security service's secret files.

While a student at Birzeit junior college, Raja sent stories to the *Jeru-*

salem Post, an English-language Israeli newspaper that had a youth page. "I saw that people my own age were sending writing, so I thought I might as well try." Aziz praised Raja's writing but showed little enthusiasm for his literary ambitions. Raja's grandfather had been a poet, and the last thing his father wanted was for Raja to take after him. "He wanted to make me a man of the world," Raja wrote. "That meant being a lawyer, not a writer."

Aziz succeeded in convincing Raja to enroll in law school after he'd graduated from an English literature program at the American University of Beirut. Raja traveled to London to devote himself to two pursuits. The first was to fulfill his father's wishes and study law. The second was to embrace his belief in "personal freedom, in free love, in living outside society" and become a "nonconformist in the world of letters." When he returned to Ramallah in 1976, he was the first Western-educated lawyer to come back to the West Bank since 1948.

Raja spent the first two and a half years learning about the legal situation of Palestinians under the first decade of the Israeli occupation. He spent his days in the courts, in his father's law office, and, eventually, in the offices of Al-Haq, a non-governmental organization devoted to protecting human rights and the rule of law that Raja cofounded in 1979. In his role as lawyer, Raja came into regular contact with the suffering of his fellow Palestinians. He knew militants who endured torture and prison sentences and activists who were denied visas and work permits. Most Palestinians, though, suffered chronic but less acute indignities like "underdevelopment, land confiscation, collective punishment, and general despair that made life so intolerable."

All that Raja witnessed lay heavily on him. What saved him from his own despair was what he called his "divided allegiance: lawyer by day, writer by night." Writing forced Raja to remain aloof and not be completely absorbed by the darkness of his daylight hours. His father did not understand this detachment from the law, but Raja believes it protected him from misery.

Raja spent a month in the United States at the end of 1979. He recalls an evening in Houston when his American Palestinian friends, after much food and drink, asked him about the situation in the homeland. Raja knew what they wanted to hear: "an inflamed passionate denunciation of the Zionist enemy as the source of all our troubles." Raja, though, could not oblige. "Only later did I realize that to do so would have been a betrayal of my own existence. To simplify my life and paint it in black-and-white terms was to deny my own reality, which I mainly experienced in tones of gray," Raja wrote. "If my countrymen really cared about me they had to see me as a human being, one who did not exist only in those heroic moments of struggle against the occupation, as they liked to imagine. They had to realize that I was like them; my society had an integrity of its own that was not derived from the negation of the Zionist enemy." While his colleagues listened politely for a while, this was not what they wanted to hear from him. "I almost felt that I needed to apologize for the lack of tragedy in my life," Raja wrote.

His listeners wanted tales of Palestinian heroism, and they wanted them in the shape of daring acts against the oppressor. Grand gestures of bravery. They did not understand, as Raja did, that for the majority of Palestinians heroism is a synonym for perseverance. The Palestinians have a word for this: *sumud*, or steadfastness. To wake each day and endure the small harassments and obstructions without flinching. "Our heroism lay in our determination to stay, not in our acts of daring or even in military operations taken in resistance to the occupation," Raja wrote. "The majority was resisting through staying put. This was the truth about life under occupation and this did not make for very exciting news or a narrative that could hold the attention even of the most ardent listeners."

Raja found, too, that his friends' view of Israel was one-dimensional. "In their view everything about Israel was evil. There were no gradations, no exceptions. All the Israelis were wicked people. But of course this is not true. There were aspects of Israel that I admired. But the moment I opened my mouth to speak of these, I was silenced. My listener would look at me with pity. I could imagine him thinking that the occupation forces must have terrorized me into losing my senses."

I suspect this is why I so enjoy speaking with Raja and reading his books. Even though the bulk of Raja's life's work, whether in the courts or on the page, serves to both reveal and challenge the injustices of the occupation, he expresses nuance beyond the ideas of good-versus-evil and us-versus-them. And he sees, just as his father did, the folly of pretending Israel does not exist or that the occupation will suddenly vanish. I would meet other Palestinians who believed that the end of the occupation, and of the State of Israel itself, was both inevitable and impending. They believed a century of political Zionism would conclude as if such a project had a natural hundred-year expiry date. "There will always be Jews here," one man would tell me, "but there will be no Israel anymore."

Such conversations always troubled me. I didn't want to argue about Palestine with Palestinians, but talk of the end of Israel was truly absurd. Nothing I'd seen during my travels suggested anything temporary about the State of Israel. Nothing I learned would support the idea that the Palestinians could simply run out the clock on the occupation. This felt completely unrealistic to me and, I think, to Raja, too. He finds reasons to be optimistic for Palestine. He sees potential in the actions of the Boycott, Divestment, Sanctions movement, which calls on the world to put economic pressure on Israel to end the occupation, and he envisions a time when world leaders "stop allowing Israel to do what it pleases." He also believes Israelis may finally "learn what sort of nation they'd become."

Israel, though, will remain. At the end of his book *Language of War, Language of Peace*, Raja writes what some Palestinians might consider sacrilege. "If there is to be peace in our region the Palestinians also need to come to terms with the existence of Israel and accept that its people are here to stay. What we should seek is not the destruction of Israeli society, but ways to forge a new relationship that would make it possible for both of us to have a full life based on justice and equality in this beautiful but tortured land which we share, for both of us—Palestinian Arabs and Israeli Jews—live here."

In the meantime, Raja believes Palestinians should actually experience the land at the heart of the struggle. Al-Haq's work on cases against the Israeli expropriation of Palestinian land led Raja into the hills and fields to map and measure thousands of square kilometers. Seeing the land in nature rather than as an entry in a court document—or a line on a map—revealed the beauty of the place to Raja. He believes the best way for Palestinians to counter the claustrophobia they feel in the shadow of checkpoints and borders and walls is to focus on the physical expanse of land. "There is a particular point after you leave Jerusalem and you are approaching Jericho when you see the Dead Sea for the first time," he said. "And you enter into that area where there is a wall of hills on one side and another wall on the other side, and an expanse between. This is the only place you can really extend your view. Here one can imagine the land extending all the way from southern Turkey, where the Rift Valley begins, to Lake Tiberius, the Dead Sea and beyond."

West Bank Palestinians cross this space all the time on their way to and from Jerusalem and the border post at the Allenby Bridge. But because of the "nastiness of crossing the bridge, and the complications and worries," they do not appreciate the long view of the valley. "And I think of the difference between what the Israelis are trying to make us feel, and what we can feel if we forget all of that and just look with that vision," Raja said. "It is so liberating. And it always does this to me." Not all Palestinians make the effort to see this. "You have to learn to see. Everybody had passed through this expanse into the Jordan Valley. But if you don't look, you don't see it."

Raja believes that most Palestinians don't perceive the land this way. Each March, Palestinians commemorate Land Day, the anniversary of a 1976 protest against Israeli plans to expropriate Palestinian land. "Every year, you have all these posters of farmers digging into the land," Raja said. "In the past, every villager knew about the land, about cultivation, planting, and so on. Now they have no idea." Many rural Palestinians have left their fields to become laborers in Palestinian cities. "This idealized, romanticized image is so unrealistic." And those who do not view the land through the prism of an idealized rural past see it instead through the impassive lens of real estate. When his next-door neighbor speaks about his land, he speaks only in terms of its monetary value. "There is no point in which he tries to preserve the land. You see this all around Ramallah: the complete destruction of the land because there is no longer any feeling for it. It is just property. A means of making money." The hills of Palestine, then, represent either a lost romantic past or a future investment. The land lacks a present tense.

Raja believes that this emotional disconnect between Palestinians and their land led to a bizarre incident a few days before our meeting. Three young men who shared a flat in Ramallah phoned their families to tell them they were going away for a while. They tore up their ID cards, pitched their mobile phones in the trash, and disappeared. Their parents panicked and called the Palestinian police, who, in turn, alerted their contacts in Israel. The Israelis feared a terrorist plot had been set in motion. "Everyone started looking for them," Raja said. "Finally, they were found camping near a spring in a very nice area called Ein Lamun." They had backpacks filled with camping gear and a tent.

The police arrested and handcuffed the men then brought them into custody where, according to their lawyer, they were tortured by interrogators. Hamas agents in the West Bank were worried that the men planned to volunteer as informants for the Israelis. "Nobody cared to know why they had gone into the hills," Raja said. "Maybe it was an innocent thing. Maybe they just wanted to be alone in the woods."

Raja discussed the episode with his barber during a haircut. The barber told Raja he had already argued with his son, who thought the men simply wanted to be left alone for a little while. This infuriated the barber, who hoped that their arrest and beatings would act as a deterrent to his own son. "We are not in the West. We are in Palestine. These things cannot happen. They must not happen."

"Nobody I talked to about it was sympathetic with the idea you might want to be in the hills and hike and enjoy yourself and be rid of the identity card and all of it," Raja said. "No one saw it as a heroic thing or a romantic thing. I think this is very telling."

"Don't you think that destroying their IDs and leaving their phones behind sounds suspicious?" I asked.

"Why?" Raja asked. "Why not say that we've been so tied to these things, our phones and IDs, that we just want to leave them and go away? But the idea that anyone would dare to do that here seems so dangerous. It is preposterous. There is so much fear about the present that it is not lived."

After talking to Raja, I wanted to see the land as he saw it, not as a collage of plots to be bought, sold, or fought over but as a place of beauty and solace. Besides, I'd spent so much time drinking coffee and smoking nargileh with poets in Ramallah's cafés that I could feel my body starting to revolt. I joined a hiking group headed by a man named Suhail Hijazi, who led weekly excursions into the countryside. On one of these trips, the group followed Suhail into the hills of the northern West Bank near

Jenin. We began at the white stone church at Burqin where Jesus had paused to heal lepers on his own journey from Nazareth to Jerusalem, and then we continued into the Hashmiyet Mountains.

The land is generous with its loveliness. We passed pomegranate trees ablaze with scarlet blossoms and old olive trees bearing new fruit as small and green as peppercorns. Wild mustard grew on the roadside along with an herb called *fejum* that wards off both mosquitoes and djinn. Tender chickpeas grew in wide fields near lentils, tobacco, and Egyptian cucumber. We climbed al-Barud mountain, which overlooks the Jezreel Valley, rested in the shade of a carob tree, and drank tea made from *za'atar baladi*, the wild thyme our guide plucked en route. Then we chased the tea's medicinal bitterness with cups of sweet coffee.

On another hike, Suhail brought us to Wadi Qana. Thorny weeds pricked my ankles through my socks. The occasional turtle crossed our path, seeming out of place in the dryness. We descended into the valley, where wild mint grew on the banks of a thin stream. Palestinians have long tended olive and citrus trees in the wadi. We passed through an orange grove where branches full of fruit shaded the previous autumn's fallen oranges lying soft on the ground. We stopped for tea at a small stone farmhouse owned by the family of our guide, then continued along the valley floor. Palestinian families from the nearby village of Deir Istiya laid picnic blankets under the fig trees.

The pastoral ideal withers, though, when one raises one's eyes to the Israeli settlements that top each of the bulldozer-flattened hills surrounding the wadi: Yaqir and Nofim to the south, Immanuel and the sprawling Karnei Shomron to the north, and Alonei Shilo, El Matan, and Yair Farm. Palestinians have always lacked the equipment, wealth, and permission to build on the hilltops. In *Palestinian Walks*, Raja wrote: "Only the Israeli side had the means to turn a hill into a plain." So, unlike the settlers, who could restructure the land, the Palestinians "had to follow its contours, build along the lines of the hills. Their villages and their gardens were in harmony with the land, organic outgrowths that pleased the eye." Now the hilltops are beheaded, their gentle curves gouged and sliced. "Ideology and the bulldozers are the bane of this land," Raja wrote.

But the settlements are more than an aesthetic insult. Here in Wadi Qana, the settlers commandeer the bulk of the valley's water resources, reducing the output of the wadi's seven natural springs to a mere trickle. And until 2006, the settlements discharged their waste water directly into the wadi itself. The pollution forced fifty Palestinian families living in the wadi to abandon their homes in the 1990s. Now Palestinians face further pressure as the Israeli government attempts to transform the wadi, declared a nature reserve back in 1983, into a tourism site. The government claims that Palestinian farming damages the natural splendor of the area. In 2010, the Israel Nature and Parks Authority destroyed irrigation channels that fed the fruit trees. The INPA allows Palestinian farmers to tend their old orchards but forbids them from planting new trees. Since 2011, it's uprooted around a thousand saplings and issued orders for the destruction of thousands more. Suhail believes this will lead to the eventual exclusion of all Palestinians from the wadi and the conversion of the land from an agricultural valley into what a settlement council official once called "the front yard of Karnei Shomron."

Raja had told me about the difference between how the Palestinians and Israeli settlers see the land. During one of his walks he came across a group of settlers on a guided nature hike. Their leader pointed out the various plants and trees in an attempt to increase their knowledge of the place they were laying claim to. Raja realized that, for them, the land was something to be fetishized. "It is like pornography," he said. They have to learn to embrace the hills, valleys, and springs that are foreign to them.

Darwish wrote about this in "A Soldier Dreams of White Tulips" as a conversation with a young Israeli soldier at the end of the 1967 war:

And the land? *I don't know the land*, he said.
I don't feel it in my flesh and blood, as they say in the poems.
Suddenly I saw the land as one sees a grocery store, a street, newspapers.

I asked him, but don't you love the land? *My love is a picnic*, he said, *a glass of wine, a love affair.*
– *Would you die for the land?*
– *No!*

All my attachment to the land is no more than a story or a fiery speech!
They taught me to love it, but I never felt it in my heart.
I never knew its roots and branches, or the scent of its grass.

– And what about its love? Did it burn like suns and desire?
He looked straight at me and said: *I love it with my gun.*

The poem angered Palestinians and Israelis both. Palestinians criticized Darwish for portraying an enemy soldier with sympathy, while Israelis were offended that Darwish depicted the soldier as disillusioned by his role in Israel's victory. At the end of the poem, the soldier abandons the land altogether. He tells the poet that, for him, homeland "is to drink my mother's coffee, to return, safely at nightfall":

I dream of white tulips, streets of song, a house of light.
I need a kind heart, not a bullet.
I need a bright day, not a mad fascist moment of triumph.
I need a child to cherish a day of laughter, not a weapon of war.
I came to live for rising suns, not to witness their setting.

The poem reveals an optimism that feels naive in the shadows of those fortified hilltop settlements. And yet, Ghassan Zaqtan doubled down on Darwish's hopefulness decades later, in a 2003 poem titled "An Enemy Comes Down the Hill." Ghassan also writes of the settlers' fragile and tepid commitment to the lands they seized. The only place where "their feet will leave a print in the rocks, mud and water," is on the main roads where the soldiers stand at the checkpoints. The rest of the land will eventually be "abandoned without effort." Ghassan writes: "From the mountain edges, all the caves will appear peaceful / and the road will seem as it were."

On another hike I visited Mar Saba. The monastery clings to the cliffs of the Kidron Valley midway between Jerusalem and the salt-encrusted shore of the Dead Sea. A forty-two-year-old Russian monk with a long beard and dark robes waited for us in a small courtyard at the bottom of a flight of narrow stone stairs. We could smell the lingering aroma of fried potatoes from the monks' breakfast. Our man led us to a chapel where chandeliers and incense burners hung from a ceiling covered with painted icons, and where Saint Sabas's embalmed corpse lay in a glass box. The monk offered us coffee and candy and postcards. "No one wants to be a monk anymore," he told us with the tone of a clockmaker mourning the death of his profession. When I asked him how long he'd stay at the monastery, he shrugged and said, "Until the end." We left him to his study and prayer and descended into the valley, a bleak landscape colored only by the purple flowers of Syrian thistle, before climbing Tel Omar.

As the Kidron Valley snakes northward toward Jerusalem, it passes another valley, Wadi Abu Hindi. I'd read about a Bedouin girl who writes fairy tales in Wadi Abu Hindi, and I set out to find her a few weeks later. No public vehicles travel to the Bedouin encampment, so I took a service taxi from Ramallah to the nearby town of Abu Dis. Such taxis, usually seven-passenger minivans, ply the Palestinian highways that link the towns and villages of the West Bank. They are not permitted to travel along the highways the Israelis have constructed for the settlers. Raja had told me that the service taxis were the Facebook of the 1980s, full of gossip, laughter, sly jokes, and loud music. "Now they are silent," Raja said. "Nobody speaks to each other." The music and the small talk have been lost, and the radio is often tuned to recitations of the Koran. According to Raja, this is not out of piety but out of a sense of hopelessness.

The journey to Abu Dis took nearly an hour because IDF soldiers were deployed along the roadways to stop cars and check IDs. Earlier that morning, two Palestinian women carrying a knife, a syringe, and a suicide note approached IDF soldiers at a checkpoint near Ramallah. According to IDF sources, the women asked the soldiers for water before one lunged at them with a knife. She was shot and injured. The other woman fled and was quickly captured.

Once in Abu Dis, I waited for a car to be sent by Wadi Abu Hindi's mukhtar. We turned off the highway onto a gravel road into the wadi. Our car passed through a graffiti-adorned tunnel beneath a settler-only highway linking the Ma'ale Adumim settlement, which overlooks the wadi from the north, to the Keidar settlement, which overlooks the wadi from the south. The Bedouin camp of Wadi Abu Hindi occupies the barren valley between the two hilltop Israeli settlements.

The Bedouin archetype of nomads perched upon tall camels, living among dunes in black tents laid with rugs and fetching water from isolated desert wells, is mere Orientalist romance. In reality, the gravel road to Wadi Abu Hindi leads past a catchment pool full of sewage from nearby Abu Dis. The camp itself is a scattering of dwellings made of tents and repurposed shipping containers. Old tires stand in heaps. A broken car sat inert on cinder blocks next to a bulldozer with flattened tires. The Bedouin here live in dwellings more like sheds than proper houses. Most are repurposed zinc shipping containers with doors and windows cut into them. Drying laundry hangs from lines strung between leaning posts, while sagging chicken-wire fences catch wind-blown plastic bags and other trash. Goats and sheep crowd pens fashioned from scraps of metal, wood, and wire gathered from building sites and dumps.

Wadi Abu Hindi is one of Oslo's victims. The accords divided West Bank territory into three distinct administrative categories: Areas A, B, and C. The Palestinian Authority administers land designated as Area A and shares the management of Area B territory with Israeli officials. More than 60 percent of the West Bank, though, is deemed Area C and under complete Israeli control. Although the wadi's Bedouins have lived in the valley and grazed sheep and goats on the hillside since the 1950s, Israel has declared the wadi as part of Area C and forbids residents to build anything permanent here, hence the shipping-container houses and ad hoc animal pens. Even the primary school, constructed with the help of an Italian NGO in 2010, is a shipping container retrofitted with soil bricks and bamboo. The army demolished two previous schools because they were built to last out of concrete and stone.

For all its roughness, the camp inspired fantasy in a fourteen-year-old Bedouin girl named Salha Hamdeen. In 2012, she wrote a fairy tale about another Salha, a fictional version of herself, who also lived in Wadi Abu Hindi. In the story, Salha wakes to the sound of Israeli army target practice and yearns to flee the clamor of bullets. "I do not have a bicycle, I do not have a car, I do not have a plane either, but I have something to run away by," Salma says. "I have a flying sheep. His name is Hantoush; he is black with long ears and two wings that he hides under his fleece."

Salha flies atop Hantoush to Barcelona, where she meets the great Argentine soccer hero and Barcelona forward Lionel Messi. Salha and Messi play football together while Hantoush keeps goal, and Salha's soccer prowess so impresses Messi he invites her to join the Barcelona team. Salha declines: "We want to go back to Abu Hindi valley, for my ewes were waiting for me to milk them. There is nobody but me to take care of them because my father has been in jail for six years, and he has another nineteen years more to go." Messi goes to Abu Hindi with Salha. The two of them clear the valley of landmines and then build the world's largest stadium to host the 2014 World Cup. The story, titled *Hantoush*, won the international Hans Christian Andersen prize for best new fairy tale in 2012.

I wanted to meet Salha, but before I was introduced to her I sat with the camp mukhtar—and Salha's uncle—Mohammed Hamdeen. He was born in 1969, and he and his family are refugees from Beer Sheva. We sat on carpets in a shipping-container dwelling set up as a sort of community center while a teenage Bedouin boy brought us coffee and mint tea. Mohammed sprawled on cushions, black cords holding his white turban in place, and rubbed his bare feet while we spoke. In his role as mukhtar, Mohammed acts as the tribe's connection to the outside world. He moderates discussions between tribe members and the Palestinian Authority or the Israelis. Mohammed also mediates disagreements among the Bedouin themselves. "Clashes. Disputes about territory and water. Or something about women and honor. It could be anything." Mohammed does not receive any compensation for this role. "I have sheep," he said. "And my sons work."

"How many sons do you have?" I asked him.

"Thirteen. I have twenty-three children altogether. From two wives." Mohammed laughed at my shocked expression. "Most Bedouins have two, three, or even four wives," he said. "We believe if you love women then keep marrying them instead of going after them unmarried."

Mohammed told me about the challenges of living in Area C. "If someone's son wants to get married, he cannot build a house. He would receive an order from Israel stopping him from building. This creates a lot of stress." In addition to the prohibition on building permanent dwellings, the Bedouin of Abu Hindi are forbidden from connecting to the local power grid or the water system. The only electricity comes from generators, and drinking water must be trucked in from elsewhere.

The Israelis are currently discussing the possibility of relocating these Bedouin out of the wadi and into Area A territory, which the Palestinian Authority administers. Mohammed does not oppose relocation as a matter of principle. "We wouldn't mind if they suggested to relocate us to a place in the wilderness where we would be free," he said. "But they are offering us lands near big cities and towns on land that already belongs to other people. We don't want to live on other people's lands just because the state ordered us. We want to avoid all that." Besides, the territory offered to them thus far has been too small for the Bedouin to graze their sheep and goats. Mohammed soon grew weary of speaking. "I have diabetes and I am tired," he said and pointed toward another caravan where I was to wait to speak to Salha. This caravan was a donation from a European NGO and featured zinc walls filled with Styrofoam. A photograph of Salha receiving a medal from Mahmoud Abbas hung on the wall next to tapestries embroidered by Salha's mother.

Salha came in accompanied by her brother. She was eighteen and hardly resembled the picture on the wall. She'd covered her head with a burgundy headscarf, and a tangle of rubber bracelets circled each of her wrists. I recognized the colors of the Barcelona football club on one of them. Her dark skin and bright eyes reminded me of the girl in the green dress.

I asked Salha about *Hantoush*. "I got the idea from the reality Palestinians live in. Especially here. And I wanted to transmit this message," she said. "I wrote it for children but also for older people who could identify and understand what the Palestinians are living through here. The story is about reality."

"But it is also a fantasy, right? A fairy tale?"

"I used fantasy because there are things that are impossible for Palestinian children."

"Like flying sheep."

"I mean it is impossible for us to leave Palestine at all. To leave the country. To see the world and meet Messi." Israel controls all West Bank entry and exit points and, for the most part, only allows Palestinians to use the border crossing at the Allenby Bridge. But Israel prohibits many West Bank residents from using Allenby at all. Border soldiers refuse some travelers for ambiguous "security reasons" and often give no explanations. Many Palestinians don't learn they are on a travel ban until they arrive at the border. Furthermore, PA-issued travel documents are poorly received by foreign governments. Few countries allow Palestinians to visit without a visa and, as Ghassan Zaqtan learned, obtaining visas can be difficult. As a result, most West Bank Palestinians apply for temporary Jordanian passports from Amman. Poor Bedouins like Salha and her family can scarcely afford international travel anyway, even with all the proper documents. For them, leaving Palestine is as fantastical a notion as a sheep that can fly.

Salha was studying to finish her last year of high school. Each day she walks three kilometers to the highway where she catches a service taxi to her school. She spends most of her days on her schoolwork, but she still writes stories in her free time. "I don't like to share them," she said. "I keep them to myself." She plans on attending university in either Abu Dis or Ramallah and is considering studying creative writing. "It depends on my final high school scores," she said. "If I get good grades, I will study law. If not, I will become a writer."

I laughed and told her this was a wise plan. "Why do you want to be a lawyer?"

"Because the occupation makes the situation here so unstable. Because I want to make a change. And because my father is in jail."

Just like the father in *Hantoush*, Salha's own father is serving time in an Israeli prison. The court originally gave him a twenty-five-year sentence but recently increased the punishment to life. "The Israelis were unhappy with the original sentence," Salha explained.

"What was his crime?"

"They think he organized resistance groups and things like that," she said, not willing to give me any more details.

"Can you visit him?"

"Yes. We must leave here at four in the morning and don't return until eight or nine at night. He is in Ramla."

Our conversation quickly stalled. Salha started replying to my questions with disinterested one-word answers, and her brother occasionally stepped in to elaborate. At first I judged her sideways glances and fid-dling with her bracelets as evidence of Salha's shyness and modesty, but quickly realized I was wasting her time. Salha felt proud of winning the Hans Christian Andersen prize—"It showed that Palestinians can be achievers," she said—but four years' worth of attention from people like me earned her nothing. "The story became popular around the world. I expected something to change. I expected things to get better. But noth-ing really changed here." To Salha, I was just another foreigner taking advantage of her story with nothing to offer in return.

Salha didn't want much. She didn't expect me or her other inter-national visitors to challenge Israel's control over the wadi or free her father. All she wanted was a youth center where Bedouin children could play, and a better football field. The pitch next to the school, marked by a dented pair of drunkenly leaning goal posts, is too small and full of rocks. "If we had a place to practice and play we could get a Messi out of here," she said.

3

To Breathe Life into a Name

The prophet Mohammad began his night ascent to heaven from the stone that now lies beneath the shimmering golden dome of Jerusalem's Haram al-Sharif. Believers say his footprint remains visible in the rock, along with the handprint of the angel Gabriel, who held the rock down as it tried to follow Mohammad into heaven. Nearby, in the Church of the Holy Sepulchre, believers can put their own hand in the posthole of Christ's cross; a splinter of the cross itself lies locked away in a Greek Orthodox treasury. A church in Lod houses ambiguous fragments of the body of Saint George along with the chains that bound him in prison. This disputed land is holy land, after all, and full of the holy debris of holy men for Palestinian believers—be they Christian or Muslim—to meditate upon.

But not all revered objects in this place draw their sanctity from God. Not all relics are for the religious. The white coffee cup in Darwish's museum is rendered sacred not for the coffee it once held but for the poet who held it. So, too, the scattered pens and notebooks in his office at Sakakini Cultural Center that I dared not defile by touching them. During my time in Palestine I sought out books hallowed for their very existence, where the words written within were less important than the ink and paper they were written upon. The stories of the books themselves proved as compelling as the stories they contain.

I rode a service taxi from Ramallah to Jerusalem through the Qalandia checkpoint, where I watched a trio of boys in black leather jackets, like characters from an S. E. Hinton novel, sell car air fresheners to the waiting drivers. I walked from the bus station to the Old City, itself a walled reliquary of holy books, bones, and stones. When I entered through Damascus Gate, I was startled to see an old friend, Ali Jiddah, sitting at a café adjacent to the entrance. I first met and befriended Ali in Jerusalem in the waning days of 1999. Drinking coffee and listening to Ali pontificate about politics at his home in Jerusalem's African Quarter sparked my interest in the Israeli-Palestinian conflict. His was the first Palestinian story I ever heard.

Ali is an Afro-Palestinian, born in Jerusalem to a father from Chad and a Nigerian-Palestinian mother. Like Ghassan Kanafani, Ali joined the PFLP as a young man. In 1968, he planted a bomb in a trash bin near Bikur Cholim Hospital in a Jewish neighborhood in Jerusalem. "I was eating a banana," Ali told me, "and I had the bomb in a paper bag. When I finished the banana, I placed the peel in the bag with the bomb, put it in the bin, then walked away." I remember being struck by how matter-of-factly Ali told this story. How he seemed to savor the details without a smudge of regret. The bombing injured nine Israelis, and Ali served seventeen years in prison before Israel released him in a 1985 prisoner exchange.

Ali could be blunt and vicious in his discourse, yet he always expressed an optimism for peace that seemed less naive in 1999 than it does today. He was healthier then, too. He was thin and frail now. Ali told me he'd been ill—"My blood is too sweet," he said—and he walks with a cane. I don't know if Ali remembered me, but he pretended to, and we spoke briefly over coffee as we used to do. Before I stood to leave, he said that if I ever needed him, I could find him at the café. "I am here every day," he said.

Ali was one of many constants for me in the Old City. The scene had changed little since my first visit in 1999. The streets were still populated with helmeted IDF soldiers and robed monks. Christian tour groups still clogged the narrow streets carrying wooden crucifixes. The smell of freshly ground coffee still wafted from the shop at the top of Khan El Zeit Street. I recognized some of the same cooks sweating above the same kebab grills in the same restaurants. Palestinian teens still blocked the heavy doors to the Austrian Hospice of the Holy Family, whose garden remained one of my favorite places in which to write.

My affection for the city itself, though, has waned. I used to describe Jerusalem as my favorite city in the world: a place that always fascinated me and always seemed vital and exciting. But after many visits, I'd started to sense the darkness beneath the aesthetics of faith and history. Each sect and subsect lays claim to every stone and alleyway. Everything is disputed. Nothing is tolerated. Jerusalem is a city holy to everybody but welcoming to no one.

Then again, Jerusalem could never mean as much to me as it means to the Palestinians. My heart lays no claims on this place. I defer to writers like Mourid Barghouti, who wrote of the city:

> All that the world knows of Jerusalem is the power of the symbol. The Dome of the Rock is what the eye sees, and so it sees Jerusalem and is satisfied. The Jerusalem of the religions, the Jerusalem of politics, the Jerusalem of conflict is the Jerusalem of the world. But the world does not care for our Jerusalem, the Jerusalem of the people. . . . The Jerusalem of white cheese, of oil and olives and thyme, of baskets of figs and necklaces and leather and Salah al-Din Street. . . . The palm fronds in all the streets on Palm Sunday, the Jerusalem of houseplants, cobbled alleys, and narrow covered lanes. The Jerusalem of clotheslines. This is the city of our senses, our bodies and our childhood. The Jerusalem that we walk in without much noticing its "sacredness," because we are in it, because it is us.

After leaving Ali, I walked until I found Chain Gate Street and asked around until someone pointed me to the green door of the Khalidi Library. Haifa and Asem Khalidi, cousins and current caretakers of the library, were waiting for me. They scolded me for my lateness and escorted me inside.

The Khalidis are another constant presence in the city. "Our family knew Salah Eddin," Haifa said, referring to the Muslim sultan and warrior who wrested Jerusalem from the Crusader king in 1187. "We followed him into Jerusalem." Salah Eddin eventually departed for Damascus, but the Khalidis never left. They have long ranked among the city's most enduring and accomplished families. For the first thirty years of the nineteenth century, Sheikh Musa al-Khalidi held the post of judge of Anatolia, the second-highest religious post in the Ottoman Empire. In the latter part of the century, Yusuf Diya-uddin Pasha al-Khalidi served as the mayor of Jerusalem, as a member of the Ottoman Turkish parliament, and as the governor of a Kurdish province of the Ottoman Empire. In his scant spare time, he wrote the first Kurdish-Arabic dictionary. His nephew, Ruhi Bey al-Khalidi, was appointed the consul general of the Ottoman Empire in Bordeaux, France. He lectured at the Sorbonne, translated Victor Hugo into Arabic, and wrote a book about Arabic literature and Victor Hugo that is considered the world's first work of comparative literature. Dr. Hussein Fakhri al-Khalidi served terms as the mayor of Jerusalem, as Jordan's minister of foreign affairs, and, briefly, as Jordan's prime minister. The current senior member of the family, Walid Khalidi, taught at Oxford and the American University of Beirut, and founded the Institute of Palestine Studies at Harvard.

The Khalidi family amassed vast collections of books and manuscripts in their roles as scholars, jurists, writers, and intellectuals. At the end of the nineteenth century, Hajj Raghib al-Khalidi, a Palestinian judge working in Jaffa, decided to organize the family's books into a single collection. His idea was that any time a member of the family passed away, his books would be transferred to a core library. In 1900, Hajj Raghib established the al-Khalidiyah Library as a family trust, or waqf, with income generated from a public bathhouse the family owned elsewhere in Jerusalem.

I followed Haifa and Asem past the courtyard into the library's reading room. The chamber used to be a thirteenth-century mosque, and the polished stone mihrab, the niche that orients the congregation toward Mecca, was still visible. Haifa pointed me to a row of black-and-white portraits of her ancestors sitting on a shelf along the wall. The men all shared the same dark eyes. "In those days, the Khalidis all intermarried,"

Haifa said, explaining the remarkable resemblance. "You should look at me. My grandmothers are sisters and my grandfathers are first cousins. I am pure Khalidi." The twisting and intertwining branches on the Khalidi family tree resemble the ancient olive trees of Palestine.

After Israel captured East Jerusalem from Jordan during the Six-Day War in 1967, Haifa's father, Heydar Khalidi, was put in charge of all Khalidi properties in the Old City, including the library. One day, an Israeli official posted a notice on the library door that declared the building "Absentee Property 65." In 1950, the new government of Israel created the Custodian of Absentee Property to take possession of Arab property abandoned during the Nakba. The government administered the same policies following the Six-Day War. "Anything that was closed was considered absentee," Asem said. The absentee-property notice rendered the library officially under Israeli control and out of bounds to the Khalidi family.

Haifa remembers her father tearing the notice to shreds in front of an Israeli officer, who threatened to arrest him. Heydar pointed to the sign above the door that read AL-KHALIDI LIBRARY, then showed the officer his identity card. "As you can see," he said, "my name is Heydar al-Khalidi. This library belongs to me, and I am clearly here and not absent."

Heydar's boldness earned him a brief reprieve and the officer walked away, but the notice on the library door began a twenty-year legal struggle between the Khalidis and the Israeli establishment. "Uncle Heydar had so many confrontations," Asem said. "So many harassments. Even Haifa faced harassment." He turned to his cousin. "You got late-night visits from soldiers. They banged your door with the butt of their guns. Remember?"

Haifa nodded, and her eyes reddened. "Yes," she said. "I remember."

The Israelis confiscated the building next door to the library, which also belonged to the Khalidis, in 1968. A series of explosions rocked a nearby street and IDF soldiers decided to occupy the building in order to monitor the area. They stayed for over a decade. Afterward, the Israelis turned the building over to Shlomo Goren, an Orthodox rabbi, author, and Israeli war hero who was part of the military force that captured Jerusalem in 1967. Rabbi Goren would prove to be the Khalidis' greatest adversary. He established a rabbinical seminary next to the library, then demolished a connecting wall between the two buildings and installed windows that overlooked the library courtyard. The Khalidis fought in court for five years against the renovations, and eventually a court order required Goren to replace the wall and fill in the windows.

In November 1987, after waiting another five years for permits from the Jerusalem municipality to start their own renovations, the Khalidis began construction on a second floor. Rabbi Goren's lawyer presented his own court order stopping the construction a month later. The rabbi also claimed that one of the rooms of the library belonged to his seminary. The case lasted an additional five years. In the end, two Israeli scholars— an archaeologist and a historian—testified on the Khalidis' behalf, marking the end of more than two decades of legal struggle for the building.

I followed Haifa up a tight spiral staircase into the sealed main library holding room, where the Khalidis store nearly thirteen hundred books in plain gray boxes to protect them against acidity. Haifa had removed a few special manuscripts to show me. She held out an Ottoman-era Koran, handwritten nearly four centuries earlier. Blue and gold designs swirled around the verses, and much of the calligraphy was written in gold ink. Haifa pointed out the ornate *hezeb*, circular markings like golden medallions that act as dividers between the chapters and sections. These, too, were drawn with gold. I asked Haifa if I could hold the Koran. "Are you a Muslim?" she joked before she handed it to me. The weight surprised me. The Koran was laid with so much gold leaf it must have weighed twenty pounds.

Next, Haifa showed me a six-hundred-year-old medical book titled *Chanakya's Book on Poisons and Antidotes*. The book was a gift for a twelfth-century Indian ruler as a guide to prevent assassination. Among the deadly recipes in the book is a cautionary tale about a beautiful young girl transformed into a weapon by a team of assassins. They fed her small but increasing doses of poison so that her body would accumulate the toxin while resisting its effects. Eventually, the maiden was saturated with so much poison she was fatal to the touch. The assassins then presented her as a "gift" to an unknowing king.

The pages of *Chanakya's Book* were peppered with tiny dots I first mistook for overzealous punctuation. They were, in fact, holes made by worms. Haifa told me that the library was closed between 1950 and 1967, and the only protection the family could afford for the books was mothballs, which failed to keep away the maggots. Now the library's caretakers "smoke" the room twice a year to ward off silverfish and moth larvae.

The last book Haifa showed me was an eyewitness account of the 1187 Battle of Hattin, Salah Eddin's final battle with the Crusaders, a victory that marked the beginning of the Muslim reconquest of Jerusalem. The book, full of hand-drawn diagrams of Salah Eddin's military units and formations, is more than eight hundred years old and describes the city as the first Jerusalem Khalidis would have seen it. The entire collection bears witness to centuries of Khalidi scholarship, but this book in particular stands as a symbol of the family's—and, by extension, the Palestinians'—enduring presence in the city.

As we left the library, Haifa told me that someone suggested they move the collection to Birzeit University in the West Bank, safely out of reach of the Israeli authorities. The family refused. "If we remove the books from here, it means the building itself is going to be taken," Haifa said. Without the books, the library will be just another vacant building in the Old City, and this will put it at risk of confiscation.

The threat possesses its own sort of poetry. The Khalidis first established the library to protect the family's books. Now, a century later, the books protect the library.

Before 1948, the father of Palestinian philosopher Edward Said owned the Palestine Educational Bookshop on East Jerusalem's Salah Eddin Street where he sold books, stationery, and typewriters. Said's father sold the shop after the war, and the new owners divided the space into three tiny storefronts. In 1985, Ahmed Muna rented, and eventually purchased, the middle shop. He stocked the shelves with stationery, pens, pencils, and other school supplies and reopened the following year. He called the store the Educational Bookshop, dropping *Palestine* from the name. At the time, Israeli authorities associated the word *Palestine* with the PLO, which they considered a terrorist organization, and forbade the use of the word in areas under Israeli control.

Ahmed taught at the United Nations schools that operated in Jerusalem and didn't open the store until two in the afternoon, after he finished teaching. "It was not a serious business," his son Mahmoud Muna told me as we drank espresso at a sidewalk table on Salah Eddin. "It was an extra thing. His friends would come and hang out there."

Not long after the shop opened, Mahmoud's brother, Imad, returned from his studies in Jordan and took over the business. He was a more ambitious businessman than Ahmed. "He put new energy into the store," Mahmoud said, explaining how Imad added Arabic novels and poetry collections to the store's inventory. A greater opportunity arose when the First Intifada erupted at the end of 1987. Foreign journalists and NGO workers, most of them proficient in English, wanted to read about Palestine and the conflict, so the store started bringing in relevant English titles. "We started with books by Edward Said," Mahmoud said. Demand quickly soared. By 1992, Imad was picking up packages of books from the post office every couple of days. The bookstore made only small orders, usually less than five copies at a time, to avoid paying extra Israeli import taxes.

In 1995, Edward Said published *Peace and Its Discontents: Essays on Palestine in the Middle East Peace Process*, a book that railed against the recently signed Oslo Accords. The new Palestinian Authority, headquartered in Ramallah, banned both the English and Arabic editions of the book. The PA had no authority in Jerusalem, though, so the Educational Bookshop was free to stock it. "The book became one of our first bestsellers," Mahmoud said. Everyone wanted the book—in both languages. Even officials from the very PA ministry that banned *Peace and Its Discontents* ordered copies and sent their underlings from Ramallah to pick them up.

Sales of English books about the conflict continued to rise. In 1996, Imad made his first visit to the London Book Fair, one of the largest book industry trade fairs in the world. The trip marked the Educational Bookshop's entry into the proper book trade. But just as the store expanded its English-language selection, demand for Arabic books declined. In 1999 and 2000, Mahmoud watched the rows of Arabic books shrink month by month. Half a shelf of Arabic books would disappear at a time, replaced by English titles or more school supplies. Mahmoud made the painful decision to stock colored pencils in the place where Arabic books used to sit. "You are a businessman, yes, but you also love the books."

Mahmoud blamed the drop in interest in Arabic books on Oslo's disappointing legacy. "During the First Intifada, there were a lot of books about the cause. About the struggle. About liberation," he said. "Then Oslo came and didn't really deliver anything. People were reading and waiting for something to happen. And something completely opposite happened." Before Oslo, the store sold hundreds of copies of books by Palestinian negotiators and figures like Yasser Arafat. They sold books about Fatah and the philosophies of the struggle. "Suddenly no one wanted to read them," Mahmoud said. Palestinian readers felt betrayed by their own writers. "They felt like they were reading bullshit. They were reading lies." Mahmoud's customers opted, instead, for Arabic poetry and fiction. These were genres they felt they could trust.

In 2000, looking to expand the bookstore into a larger space, the Munas purchased a second storefront across Salah Eddin Street. Their timing was terrible. The Second Intifada erupted just before they planned to open, and the violence kept customers away from Jerusalem altogether. The building remained vacant until the Intifada eased in 2009. Only then did the Munas move their English books into the new space and add a café. They also expanded their selection to include books on topics beyond local politics. They added titles about Palestinian and Arab culture, tour guides to the region, popular magazines, and translations of Arabic novels and poetry. Educational Bookshop is now a destination for visitors to the city—especially those who lean left politically. Even liberal-minded Israelis occasionally drop by.

Mahmoud continues to sell Arabic titles in the original shop across the street, and sales are rising. Palestinians still avoid political books— the post-Oslo hangover continues—but they read poetry, short stories, and the occasional novel, particularly those by well-known North African authors. More young people are buying books, "especially if they are cheap," Mahmoud said. No title, though, ever competes with the year-end horoscopes. "They are the bestsellers every year."

Mahmoud knows his bookstore represents a rare success story in occupied Palestine. "The occupation did not stop me from starting a business, running a business, and opening every day," he said. The store sells books that are highly contentious and critical of the Israeli government, but the authorities have not interfered. At worst, and only rarely, airport officials will search his book shipments, and a particular cover might draw attention. He remembers how a book about Hamas that featured an AK-47 on the cover furrowed the brows of airport security personnel. "They are worried that this is *Chicken Soup for the Terrorist Soul*," Mahmoud said. But even books deemed suspicious are merely delayed. "The books are referred to a superior officer who may have already gone home, so they hold the whole shipment for a couple more days, during which time I must pay for their storage at the airport." Eventually, someone in charge signs off on the shipment.

The biggest threat to the book business in Palestine comes from copyright infringement by Palestinian printers. Arabic books are regularly pirated in Palestine. As soon as a book becomes popular, cheap forgeries appear. Mahmoud would rather not stock pirated books in his shop, but due to Israeli import rules, he often has no other choice. Lebanon remains one of the top producers of Arabic books, but the country—along with Syria and Iran—is a declared enemy of Israel, so the authorities forbid their import. The Israelis automatically classify books from these nations as propaganda. Pirates, though, will surreptitiously bring in a single copy of a Lebanese book, block out the words "printed in Lebanon," and make copies that can be "legally" sold.

Mahmoud sighed when I asked him if there was such thing as a Palestinian literature. "It is a puzzling question. There are definitely more Palestinians writing from outside Palestine than from inside Palestine, both in English and Arabic." This diaspora creates most of the writing about Palestine that Mahmoud deems "important"—whether politics, history, or literature. Only those living away from Palestine, like Darwish and Said, possess both the luxury and the time to articulate the struggle. "The rest of us are just busy struggling."

Mahmoud wonders what Palestinian literature would look like were it not for this struggle. "Most Palestinian literature has to do with Palestine, to do with the conflict, to do with refugees," he said. "What would it be if Palestine was not occupied? Would writers have the motivation? Would we have Darwish? Would he have gone as far as he's gone? What would we have talked about?" But Mahmoud believes this attachment to the same old narratives does not serve Palestinians or their literature well. "Why are we so stuck in the corner?" he asked. "Why are we not leaving?

We are just rewriting, reconsuming, recomposing the occupation. Truly, we deserve more."

Sometime during the first few days of May 1948, a carload of young Jewish men drove into the Talbieh neighborhood in West Jerusalem. They had guns and loudspeakers, and Anahid Melikian remembers them warning the residents of the mainly Christian neighborhood to "Get out. Get out or else." Anahid's family was living in the house her grandfather built after escaping the Armenian genocide more than thirty years earlier. For familiar reasons, the men with guns worried them. The British Mandate for Palestine wasn't due to give way to the newly established state of Israel until midnight of May 14, but most of the British troops had already left, and Anahid's family feared no one would protect them from the shouting armed men. The family fled their house in Talbieh and moved into the Lutheran Church of the Redeemer in the Old City.

Anahid was in her early twenties and working in Haifa at the time, but when she heard of her parents' evacuation she traveled to Jerusalem and stayed with them for a few weeks. She and her mother returned to the Talbieh house a couple of times to gather personal items they had left behind. "We took the stuff that had been in the family for a long time," Anahid said. "The things we could carry." They gathered up their carpets and good china. A cherished tea set. "And we took most of the books."

But Anahid's favorite books, twenty volumes of a German encyclopedia called *Meyers Konversations-Lexikon*, were too heavy to carry away. The encyclopedia was already an antique in 1948, but Anahid remembers how she used to thumb through the pages when she was a girl. "I used to look things up," she said. "It had some beautiful illustrations. And they were the old kind, a two-page fold-out picture always between a piece of thin paper." The books belonged to her father, Hagop Melikian, who was orphaned by the Armenian genocide and moved to Jerusalem in the care of German missionaries. The missionaries educated Hagop in German schools, and many of the books in the family library were written in German. He intended to pass them on to Anahid, who studied the language as a child. "The books were what my father bequeathed to me," she said.

Anahid's parents didn't think much of leaving the books behind.

Like Darwish and Abu Ahmed in al-Birwa, they believed their exile would be temporary. "We thought that this was going to last a few days," Anahid said. Weeks later, though, the soldiers stopped letting anyone leave the Old City at all. Then they briefly shelled the city itself. Anahid and her family hid in a basement near the church until the bombing stopped. "I don't think they meant to kill anyone," Anahid said. "They meant to say to us: 'Just so you understand, it is all over for you.' And it *was* all over. That was it."

Her father refused to dwell on all the family had lost. Each time Anahid's mother lamented some missing possessions—her linens or silverware, for example—Hagop interrupted her. "We are not talking anymore about anything we left behind," he said. "We are starting a new life now." That new life would eventually lead the family to Winnipeg, where I met Anahid in 2013 at the home of her niece and namesake, Anahid Melikian Helewa, who joined us in her sunroom.

Sometime in the early 1970s, after studying in the United States and finding a teaching job in Beirut, Anahid returned to Talbieh. Just like Kanafani's characters in *Returning to Haifa*, she wanted to see her former home, but the Israelis living in the house would not allow her to enter. "My grandmother had planted a jasmine in front of the house," she told me, "and the jasmine was in bloom. I walked up the steps on the outside, and I picked a few of the jasmine blossoms. Then we walked back."

Anahid would never see her father's library again. The loss of these books was "a sort of heartbreak," she said. She had long heard rumors that Israelis confiscated books from abandoned homes in West Jerusalem's Arab neighborhoods in the days following the Nakba. This was different than the indiscriminate looting of Palestinian homes and villages that occurred elsewhere at the time. The book collection was systematic. "I was told that trucks would go with librarians," Anahid said. "Soldiers would go and open the house, and the librarians would pick and choose the valuable books."

In 2010, an Israeli scholar named Gish Amit researched the collection of Palestinian books as part of his doctoral thesis and confirmed the stories Anahid had heard. A few weeks after the majority of West Jerusalem's non-Jewish population fled their communities, an official at the Hebrew University sent a memorandum to the provisional Jewish government under the laborious heading "Regarding the Urgent Need for a Central Authority Which Would Have Custodianship Over Abandoned Public and Private Libraries and Books." The university wanted the government to grant the National Library the responsibility of collecting and caring for books the Palestinians left behind. "The National Library has the means to keep the books in the proper conditions," the memorandum stated, "as well as to return them to their lawful owners, should such owners appear." The new government agreed, and it charged the military to assist in the collection. The operation gave rise to what Amit called "a sort of spontaneous intelligence service" in which bookish soldiers and civilians reported the libraries and the book collections, small or large, they knew about. In the end, nearly thirty thousand books were collected from abandoned homes in Jerusalem. Just like the Khalidi library nearly two decades later, the books fell under the authority of the Custodian of Absentee Property.

The custodian office indexed the books and stored them in a special section of the National Library of Israel. Documents from the time suggested the books would eventually be returned to their owners; their storage at the National Library was considered an act of preservation and safekeeping. Subsequent documents, however, showed the Israeli library hoped to keep the "lion's share" of the books—certainly all the most valuable titles. Nearly six thousand of these books, all marked AP, still occupy the shelves in a special room at the National Library and remain under the authority of the Custodian of Absentee Properties. None have been returned.

The National Library published a report in 1949 that listed sixty Palestinians whose books had been collected up until that point and the neighborhoods they'd lived in. The men on the list were scholars, writers, successful businessmen, and community leaders from influential Palestinian families. "The list constitutes a group portrait of a Palestinian elite already destroyed," Amit wrote. "When the war ended it became evident that in addition to their homeland, homes, and property, the Palestinian people had also lost their aristocracy." The list included author and translator Khalil Baydas, the cousin of Edward Said's father and a former deputy mayor of Jerusalem. A lawyer who represented the Arab League in talks with the United Nations was also on the list. So, too, was Khalil al-Sakakini, the educator and writer who opened the cultural center in Ramallah that bears his name. Al-Sakakini wrote about his lost books in his journals:

> Goodbye, my books! Farewell to the house of wisdom, the temple of philosophy, the scientific institute, the literary academy!
>
> How much midnight oil did I burn with you, reading and writing, in the silence of the night while the people slept—farewell, my books!
>
> I do not know what became of you after we left: were you looted? Burned? Were you transferred, with due respect, to a public or private library? Did you find your way to the grocer, your pages wrapping onions?

Anahid's father was also on the list, but she had no idea until 2012, when an Israeli filmmaker named Benny Brunner produced a documentary called *The Great Book Robbery*, based in part on Amit's research. Anahid's niece saw the film online and was startled to see "Hagop Melikian from Talbieh" mentioned in the documentary. "I was happy and surprised to see my grandfather's name," the younger Anahid said. Hagop had passed away in 1967, and seeing his name in the film sparked memories of him. "He is alive now," she told me. "His books are being talked about. I felt proud that his books are of value." She called the Israeli embassy in Ottawa to inquire about her grandfather's books. They said they didn't deal with such matters and suggested she contact the National Library of Israel. She tried, but they didn't respond to her requests. "So I left it at that," she said.

For the senior Anahid, her father's lost volumes stand as witnesses to a sophisticated culture that was lost after 1948. "You hear Israelis talk about Palestinians in a derogatory way," she said. "They want you to think that the Palestinians are poor wretches living in refugee camps. I say, 'Look at what was left behind in these houses. Look at the books.' Maybe they will say that those Palestinians were not illiterate after all." Anahid does not want the books back. Too much time has passed. "I just hope the books found a good home," she said. "I hope somebody appreciates them."

I traveled to Jerusalem's Hebrew University, where the National Library of Israel is located, to learn more about the AP books and search for Anahid's father's encyclopedia. I wanted to hold those books in my hand, perhaps photograph them, just to let Anahid know they still exist and are being cared for.

I first sat with Raquel Ukeles, the curator of the library's Islam and Middle East collection. Ukeles remains conflicted by the story of the AP books. "It was morally complicated," she said, "because, really, the authorities saved that material." Many books were destroyed during the violence and looting in the spring of 1948. The collection of books in Jerusalem can be seen as both a theft and a rescue. "There are stories I've heard from professors and academics in places like Haifa, where they saw rare Islamic manuscripts thrown on the sidewalks," she said. "At the end of the day, I think about what I would have done had I been there. I would have probably taken those books and saved them also. As I understand it, there was crazy looting going on all over the place, and anything that wasn't taken up disappeared."

What Ukeles finds unforgivable, however, is that library personnel eventually removed the family names of the original Palestinian owners and branded the books with the general AP label. After learning this from Amit's work, Ukeles "walked around for a few years thinking that of all the things the library did really wrong, that was the worst. How terrible to erase the names."

Unless, of course, this never happened. Recently, a senior librarian who worked at the library for more than fifty years claimed the accusation is nonsense. "And he is radical left," Ukeles said, "so not an apologist at all." The man showed Ukeles examples of academic articles written in 1950 mentioning Palestinian manuscripts already labeled AP, years before Amit claims the original family names were removed.

"So you're saying the library didn't erase the names but never recorded them in the first place," I said.

She nodded. "I am sorry they didn't do that, but at least they didn't consciously destroy the records."

I wasn't sure what to believe. In Gish Amit's research, library personnel from the 1950s and 1960s describe in detail sorting and cataloguing large flour sacks full of books according to their original owners. "Every book had a sequential number," one man said, "and beneath it we wrote an abbreviation of the owner's name in English. For example, the letters *SAK* stood for Sakakini, *NIMR* meant Nimer, and so on. Those letters appeared both on the inside cover and on the index card." As for the removal of these records, however, Amit is less precise. He states only that the owners' names were erased before the 1960s and admits he does not know how the decision to remove the owners' names was made. In his paper "Salvage or Plunder? Israel's 'Collection' of Private Palestinian Libraries in West Jerusalem," Amit writes:

> The fact that the books in the 1950s were catalogued to the extent possible by their Palestinian owners' names could indicate Israeli willingness in the early years to pay compensation for the abandoned property. Whatever the case, from the 1960s onward the direct personal connection was severed, eliminating not only any possibility of the books' return but also the unique and nonduplicable memory of human beings, preserved in the library for over a decade and now lost in a general archive.

Amit suggests that, by the 1960s, the Israeli government had changed its mind about what to do with absentee property. The fate of the Palestinian books mirrors that of deserted Palestinian villages at the same time, he notes. The Israel Land Administration bulldozed over a hundred such villages in 1965 "to 'clean up' the country and permanently prevent Palestinians from returning to their homes," Amit writes. "The purpose of both erasures, deliberate and premeditated, was to render the outcome of the war a final, irreversible reality."

Whether records of the original owners were erased or never compiled at all, both Ukeles and Amit acknowledge that, at the very least, the books were kept separate and distinct. The library could have easily swallowed the material into the general collection. Instead, they labeled the books "Palestinian" and dedicated a special room for them. "Thus these books constitute a strange monument that binds together destruction and conservation, demolition and salvage," Amit writes.

I wondered if the fact that the library stored the AP titles apart from the general collection signaled an enduring intention on the part of the government to one day return the books. Ukeles didn't know. "I've never talked to a government official about this," she said. Such a decision would be problematic, since returning the books might set a difficult precedent for the Israeli government regarding absentee property in general. If the Israelis give books back to their original owners, pressure would certainly mount to also return, say, Anahid's home in Talbieh or Abu Ahmed's family land in al-Birwa.

Ukeles told me that, aside from a couple of attempts by individual families, there has never been a collective request by Palestinians—not by the writers' union nor by any Palestinian university—to return the books. "Now I assume that hasn't happened because they assume it won't work," Ukeles said. "And it won't." But even if the Custodian of Absentee Property instructed the library to give the books back, the issue of original ownership remains. To whom would the library return the books?

Ukeles envisions ways this might work. Perhaps a team of graduate students from a Palestinian university could examine each of the nearly six thousand volumes, page by page, in search of dedications, ex libris labels, annotations, or other marginalia that might suggest the books' original owners. This would be a massive and time-consuming project and would undoubtedly leave most books unidentified, but it would be a start. Or perhaps the entire collection could be donated to a Palestinian institution as part of a future diplomatic settlement between the Israelis and Palestinians. This is magical thinking, and Ukeles knows it. "Still, I dream that there will be a Palestinian national library, and we will be able to give the books to them, and they would be the core of the collection," Ukeles said. "Wouldn't that be beautiful?"

Ukeles wants to see the issue of the Palestinian books solved one way or another. "Almost every conversation I have with any Palestinian cultural figure starts with the AP collection," Ukeles said. "It colors everything I do." Ukeles considers the library a public and nonpolitical space for all citizens: Jews and Arabs both. "Because I am American, I will cling to these naive ideas of a national institution that is supposed to serve as a stable place in civil society," she said. Ukeles would like to see more Palestinians living in Israel participate in the programming she designs, but she struggles to convince Palestinians to support an Israeli institution that holds their books hostage.

Ukeles and I looked for Anahid's *Meyers Konversations-Lexikon* in the AP collection. We couldn't find it. According to Amit's research, our failure shouldn't have been a surprise. Unlike the Arabic books collected in 1948, most foreign-language books like the German encyclopedia ended up absorbed into the general library collection instead of branded with AP. No doubt Hagop's encyclopedia once resided among the other collected volumes, but not anymore. Ukeles found a set of the encyclopedia on the library's regular shelves, but the first volume bore an ex libris from the library of Gertrude Brann, a Jewish woman who died in 1951. This was not the book that Anahid thumbed through as a child. Perhaps those pages ended up wrapping onions at the grocer.

I sent Anahid Melikian Helewa an email from Jerusalem. I told her I'd failed to find her grandfather's books and asked her to pass on my apologies to her aunt. She responded a few hours later:

Dear Marcello

We thank you wholeheartedly for all your efforts in trying to locate these books, which I believe ended with a fruitful result. This loss is nothing compared to the other losses Palestinians encountered because of the political situation in Palestine during both war and peaceful times. We never wanted these books back. None of the other heirs of Hagop Melikian read or write German and my aunt is almost ninety-two, but we wanted to know where they ended up. Now we know and we can put it to rest.

As for my aunt, she thanks you for your effort. She says that you are the last link and she hopes that these books found a good home with a book lover. She says that her father Hagop would say "forget about it."

Back in Ramallah, at the Ziryab Café where Mahmoud Abu Hashhash and his friends used to gather to discuss poetry, I met with Wisam Rafeedi. Wisam was born "two days before Jesus" in 1959 and, according to his mother, used to spend all of his pennies on comic books. When he grew bored of comics, he started to collect coins—an obsession that, oddly, gave way to a fascination with socialism. Wisam joined the Communist Party when he was fifteen years old and took part in political demonstrations he didn't tell his mother about. The sharp-eyed woman was no fool. "I knew something was wrong because his birth certificate was in the worst shape of all of my children," she once said. She guessed, correctly, that the document had grown ragged from Wisam pulling it from his pocket over and over to prove to the soldiers he was too young to have a proper Palestinian ID.

The police arrested and beat Wisam a few times for minor offenses when he was a teenager. His short jail terms grieved his mother but were hardly unusual for politically minded young Palestinians in the 1970s. Wisam served his first major prison sentence when he was sixteen. He spent a full year in jail after being convicted—wrongly, he claims—of torching a car. The judge originally gave him two years, but Wisam's sentence was reduced by half when he agreed to sign a "paper in Hebrew," a confession he couldn't read to a crime he insists he did not commit.

Wisam spent much of his yearlong sentence sitting in his cell transcribing from memory over one hundred poems and songs by Ahmed Fouad Negm, an Egyptian poet who rose to fame in the 1960s. Negm penned revolutionary verses that praised Egypt's working class and infuriated the political establishment of the time. Marxists like Wisam adored him. After writing out the poems, Wisam shared them with his fellow inmates. "My voice is not very good, but I would usually sing the poems," he said.

After his release, Wisam finished his high school education and started a degree program in Arabic literature at Birzeit University. He also became involved with the PFLP. Wisam didn't tell me his role in the group or what actions he involved himself with, only that one night in 1982, a little after midnight, Israeli authorities pounded on the Rafeedi family's door, looking to arrest him. Wisam was drinking tea with his mother and brother at the time. Wisam stood up, calmly told his mother to put his teacup in the sink so the soldiers wouldn't know how many people were at the table, and slipped out the back door.

He was gone for nine years. Occasionally soldiers came to the house asking for Wisam. Sometimes they came to tell his mother that Wisam was dead. Neither she nor the Israelis knew that he had gone underground. The PFLP arranged a safe house for Wisam and gave him a printing press so he could produce the front's communiqués. Wisam rarely left the apartment and never met with anyone outside the organization.

The Israelis intensified their actions against the PFLP in 1985. Wisam's superiors feared his safe house had been compromised and moved him into a different Ramallah apartment. His neighbors thought the place was abandoned, so in order to maintain his cover Wisam could not receive visitors or even turn on the lights. He lived alone in the dark for five months. "It was not a good house," Wisam said. "Every two weeks someone came and put food outside the room, knocked a secret signal, and went away." The PFLP moved him again during the First Intifada, and Wisam spent twenty-two straight months indoors.

The most challenging aspect of living in hiding, Wisam said, was the uncertainty. A political prisoner in an Israeli jail always knows his release date. Even those serving life sentences have faith they will eventually be swapped for Israeli hostages. But a man in hiding doesn't know his future. He could be arrested at any time. He could be shot. "Or maybe you will grow tired and decide you can't continue, and you will be smuggled to Lebanon or Syria. You don't know anything."

Wisam's superiors eventually moved him to a house in an upscale Ramallah neighborhood. "Bourgeois neighborhoods are best for safe houses. The neighbors don't put their nose on you. They don't care about anything," Wisam said, his Marxist colors showing. But Wisam was unlucky. In 1991, IDF soldiers knocked again on Wisam's door. They had been going house to house looking for local boys who had been throwing stones. They were not searching for Wisam at all, but when they realized who he was, they arrested him and took him away. The military interrogated Wisam over the course of five months, during which time he underwent surgery for intestinal problems brought on, he claims, by beatings he endured at the hands of his captors. Then the Israelis put him in prison.

In his first letters from jail, Wisam describes four months of being transferred "from interrogation rooms in Ramallah to torture cells in Moscobiyya and to solitary confinement rooms in Petah Tikva." And he assures his family that he is in relatively good health, despite a continuing intestinal illness and an injured foot that "is unpredictable and has a mind of its own." Wisam thanks his family for their support, expresses sadness

for being away from his mother for so many years, and admits his em-
barrassment for forgetting the names of his nieces and nephews. "Please
understand that my memory has worsened during the months of interrogation. Not being able to remember everyone's name bothers me." His
letters to his mother are remarkable for their florid sentimentality. "My
gift to you today from behind these prison walls is tens of kisses on your
rosy cheeks," he writes to her on Mother's Day. "After the kisses are some
hugs and ruffling of your hair as I used to do when I was a youngster." I
didn't expect such sappiness from a militant Marxist.

Wisam also writes: "Let me be very clear and up-front with you from
the beginning that the road I have chosen is a road of deep conviction.
The routines of life, such as having a wife, kids and getting a degree, do
not mean much to me. If I am able to fulfill these, all the better, as long
as it is not at the cost of my convictions. If I am not able to achieve these,
I will *never* regret one day of my life or look behind into my past! Long
live the life which has as its titles: change, adventure, and struggle." Still,
he admits he would like to marry. "If possible, I would like to meet a
woman that has a strong, independent personality, and who is organized.
I despise those women that only nod in agreement to everything their
husbands say."

As if in answer, Wisam soon received a smuggled message from
Rula Abu Dhou, herself a PFLP inmate in Neve Tirza women's prison.
Wisam knew Rula from his childhood—their families were friends in
Ramallah—but he hadn't seen or heard from her since she was nine years
old. "Abu Rafeedi, how are you?" she wrote in that first note. "Are you
still tall and skinny? Is your mind still working?"

Wisam sent a message back. "Yes," he wrote. "The only thing working well is my mind."

The messages marked the beginning of a long, smuggled correspon-
dence between Rula and Wisam. They wrote to each other about their
families and of time spent in Ramallah. Rula reminded Wisam that she
was part of a singing group that he had led, and he'd taught her the songs
of Negm. "I can't say they were love notes," Wisam said, embarrassed
when I asked him. "Sometimes we talked about politics, but mostly about
personal memories." Rula also sent Wisam her ration of cigarettes from
the Neve Tirza commissary. "She didn't smoke," Wisam said.

Rula was serving a twenty-five-year sentence for her role in the killing of Yigal Shahaf in 1987. According to news reports, Shahaf was walking toward Jerusalem's Old City with his wife when an agent with the PFLP shot him in the head at close range. The assailant passed the gun to an accomplice who, in turn, handed it off to nineteen-year-old Rula, who then disposed of it.

The different ways Shahaf's story is told speaks to the frustrating ambiguity that blurs nearly every narrative of the conflict. Wisam told me that Shahaf was an Israeli soldier and therefore a justifiable target. But while Shahaf had worked as a technician for the Israeli Air Force, he was no longer active and was not wearing a uniform when he was killed. Israeli news reports, instead, more often referred to Shahaf as an Israeli "civilian," a "student," or an "amateur basketball player" without mentioning his military service at all.

Rula's role also differs according to who tells the story. Israelis usually consider her a violent terrorist. Palestinians rarely do. One pro-Palestinian media source described her, simply, as "allegedly being a member of an armed cell and an illegal organization." Journalist Leila Diab, writing in the *Washington Report on Middle East Affairs*, obscures Rula's role in Shahaf's killing even further when she writes that the Israelis accused Rula of "transporting arms"—an obscenely misleading way to describe the disposal of a still-smoking murder weapon. Diab goes on to claim that Rula denied all charges and, like sixteen-year-old Wisam years earlier, was forced to sign a confession in Hebrew that she could not understand. Even if this is true, Rula openly admitted her guilt on her release. "I am not sorry for it," she told the *Los Angeles Times*. "On the contrary, I'm proud. And I wish I could do more for my country."

Such competing narratives meant I never knew which story to trust, if any at all. Even individual words were burdened with bias. Ghassan Zaqtan once told an interviewer, "There is here a struggle over the language. There are two narratives in this land, and each one has its own terms, and it has its ground rules." In much of Palestinian journalism, a Palestinian is "kidnapped" not "arrested" and "martyred" rather than "killed." Supporters of Israel's security barrier never call it a "wall," while its opponents never call it anything else. Israeli settlers often black out the Arab names of villages on road signs in the West Bank, leaving only

Hebrew and English behind. Right-leaning Israelis will only refer to the West Bank by the ancient Hebrew names of Judea and Samaria, while many Palestinian writers will not use the word *Israel* at all. There is no neutral lexicon. The conflict is fought word to word, phrase to phrase. Vocabulary is its own intifada.

In 1993, prison authorities transferred Wisam from Hebron Prison to the al-Naqab Prison near the Egyptian border. There he met a PFLP comrade who urged Wisam to write a memoir about his time living underground. Wisam hesitated at first. He didn't want to reveal any secrets to his captors. "Under interrogation, I gave them nothing," he said. Instead, Wisam decided to write a novel based on his experience, something that wasn't purely fiction but would not betray any secrets. He called the book *Al-Akanim Al Thalatha*, roughly translated as *The Trinity*.

Because Wisam wrote *The Trinity* on notebooks his colleagues smuggled into prison, and which were therefore contraband, he needed to keep the pages out of sight of his guards. Wisam and his fellow inmates devised a system for hiding such illegal documents they cheekily called "a fax." Prisoners would pull the soft white inside out of a loaf of bread, mix it with water, then form the wet dough into a ball. Once the ball dried and hardened, it became easy to throw. Prisoners tied messages to these faxes and hurled them back and forth between sections of the prison camp. "There were prisoners who specialize in faxes," Wisam said. "They are from villages and have good muscles from throwing stones." Some of the best fax throwers could launch the hardened bread balls more than two hundred meters.

During inspections, Wisam's colleagues would fasten his manuscript to a fax and throw it to sections of the camp that weren't being searched, thus saving it from being discovered. "But one time, they made a mistake," Wisam said. The thrower aimed poorly, and the fax landed within sight of prison guards who then confiscated the manuscript. Wisam had spent five months working on the novel and did not have the heart to rewrite it. "When we have the feeling to write something and we do it, and then we lose it, we can't have the same feeling to write the same something," he said. "So, *khalas*, I lost it."

The Israelis moved Wisam to another prison soon afterward. Years later, after several more transfers, Wisam ended up at the prison in Asqalan. He received a message from one of his comrades in Nafha Prison. The man wanted Wisam's advice on setting up a "cultural program" for PFLP inmates there. The man sent along a copy of their proposed reading list for Wisam to critique. Wisam was shocked: the list of books included *The Trinity*. Wisam sent a message back to Nafha asking where they had found his lost novel. All the man knew was that a prisoner at Ktzi'ot Prison, where Wisam was never interned, had somehow read Wisam's book and handwrote a copy for himself. When this prisoner was transferred to Nafha, he brought the copy with him and shared it with his PFLP colleagues. The discovery that his book had somehow survived felt like a miracle to Wisam. "Something like when Jesus was born," he said.

The Nafha prisoners sent the novel back to Wisam, who copied the whole thing out again. This time, Wisam didn't risk writing in a notebook that might be easily found. Instead, he rewrote the novel on thin squares of paper peeled from the back of cigarette package foil. "I wrote it very, very small," he said. Then he encased the tiny pages into fifty-four waterproof capsules he fashioned by melting cellophane from cigarette packages around the papers. This method was commonly used to pass messages from prison to prison. When an inmate was about to be transferred, he would either swallow the capsules or, as Wisam said, "put in from under." He pointed to his backside to indicate that they pushed the capsules into their rectums. Suppositories of words.

The prisoners sometimes smuggled entire books this way—hand copied, encapsulated, and either swallowed or inserted—especially titles by Marxist thinkers and PFLP founder George Habash, whose books were banned. Wisam once spent fifteen hours copying a 270-page book by Karl Marx onto cigarette foil papers and forming them into individual capsules. The following day, twenty PFLP prisoners each smuggled about a dozen capsules in their rectums during a prison transfer. "We have a method," Wisam said. "We tie each of the capsules together so we can pull them out one by one. It is very, very dirty." Wisam said that the papers smell so horrible after "delivery" that they cannot be read right away. "You must put them in the window for two days. And you will put aftershave or something on them."

Wisam eventually had to sneak his own book out of prison. A prison transfer order came without warning, and Wisam didn't have the time to distribute the encapsulated novel to his fellow transferees. So Wisam stuffed the fifty-four little pods into his underwear. The prison guard assigned to search Wisam noticed the resulting bulge and put his hand on Wisam's crotch. "I yelled, 'You are a gay! You put your hand on me, and you are a gay!'" The other prisoners started hollering, and guards rushed in to quell the noise. Wisam threatened to file an official complaint of sexual assault, and the guard eventually apologized. Wisam's novel was never discovered.

Unlike Hamas and some of the other Islamist resistance groups, the PFLP had always valued critical thought over religious faith. For them, the establishment of a Palestinian state was an ideological and intellectual goal, not a spiritual imperative. Going to prison during the First Intifada was "like being enrolled in a master's degree program," Wisam said. PFLP members within the prison held classes where they discussed strategy and introduced socialist philosophy to novices. New prisoners were given reading lists by their comrades and attended lectures by their senior members. "You studied everything: history, economics, novels, poetry." After two years in prison, any member of the PFLP becomes an intellectual, Wisam said. A member of Hamas leaves having only learned the Koran.

After the establishment of the Palestinian Authority in the 1990s, the Israelis closed the prisons at Nablus and Jnaid and transferred the inmates to detention centers inside Israel. Wisam was interned in Jnaid at the time, and his fellow inmates worried about what would happen to the library they'd amassed. Wisam suggested they donate all the books and handwritten manuscripts to the municipal library in Nablus. As he and his fellow inmates packed the books to be shipped out, Wisam found the original book of Negm's poems he'd transcribed when he was a teenage prisoner in Nablus Prison. Sometime in the preceding seventeen years, the notebook had been transferred to Jnaid's library. The discovery was another literary miracle for Wisam. "It was a very good morning," he said. "The book was my history. Thousands of prisoners read those poems." He flipped through the book for a while, seeing the poems written by his teenage hand, then placed it in a box with the rest of the books. Once all the books were packed, Wisam's mother picked up the boxes and brought them to the Nablus Library.

Wisam was released from prison in 1998. Rula Abu Dhou was waiting for him. They were engaged within three weeks and married the following summer. Soon afterward, Wisam traveled to Nablus to find his notebook again in the municipal library. "I held it in my hand," he said. "When I see it, I feel happy."

After speaking to Wisam, I went to see the "Prisoner's Library" in Nablus. Two Palestinian sisters, Beesan and Zeina Ramadan, took me to the third-floor room in the municipal library which houses about eight thousand printed books and eight hundred notebooks from Nablus and Jnaid prisons. Most of the inmates in these prisons would have been jailed for their role in the First Intifada, and a large number of titles discussed Marxism and socialist economics. These are the same books Wisam and his PFLP colleagues would have read, studied, and copied during their incarcerations.

Other books described the struggles of subjugated people elsewhere in the world. "The Palestinian movement has always felt connected to other independence movements, especially during the 1960s and 1970s," Beesan said. I found an account of America's destruction of its native peoples, and a workbook dedicated to Namibian independence. I also found a tattered book of songs about Nelson Mandela, himself a prisoner at the time, with both English and Arabic translations. Someone had written diacritical marks in pencil over the Arabic lyrics to indicate proper pronunciation, evidence that prisoners did not simply read the words but sang them aloud. I imagined a group of Palestinians, standing in their prison clothes, singing songs for a fellow political prisoner in a distant African jail cell.

Many inmates of the time were students who wanted to keep up with their studies while in prison, Beesan said, hence the large section of textbooks and dictionaries. Prisoners who had been educated abroad gave foreign language lessons to their fellow inmates. A shelf of English fiction held the sort of classics high school teachers assign to their students. Titles by Dickens, Hardy, and Hemingway stood alongside the occasional spy thriller or English translation of Dostoyevsky and Mahfouz. There were unexpected selections, too, such as a biography of Picasso and *The Burl Ives Songbook*. Elsewhere in the library I browsed a selection of English nonfiction, most dedicated to the Israel-Palestinian conflict, with titles like *The West Bank and the Rule of Law* and *Israeli Nuclear De-terrence*. Others, like *Silent Spring* and *Crime in America*, cast a dark light on the United States government.

The fact that the prisoners were allowed a library at all is itself a triumph. In the 1960s, decades before Wisam's long incarcerations, the Israelis did not allow prisoners to have books. Inmates staged hunger strikes to demand them. The authorities eventually relented and began to cooperate with the Red Cross to allow selected books into the prison. Many remained banned, especially political titles, and everything had to be approved by prison offi-cials. Nonetheless, inmates' families smuggled in forbidden books by adding false covers and changing the first few pages so that the volumes would pass a casual inspection by guards. "This library stands as an accomplishment of the prisoners' movement," Beesan said. "Each book means someone had to suffer inside the prison. This is real struggle."

The end of the Cold War in the years preceding Oslo also left an ideological hole in the Palestinian project, as the socialist independence movements suddenly found themselves aimless and without a core phi-losophy. In Palestine, as elsewhere, the Left left. Even Wisam, who maintains that socialism could be a solution to the Palestinian struggle, admits that the Soviet model is dead. Political Islam stepped up and filled the ideological space that socialism had left behind.

Compared to what came next—the violent excesses of the Second Intifada, the rise of religious extremism, infighting among Palestinian factions—the First Intifada seems a golden age of Palestinian resistance. The fighters have been cast as heroes, as better men fighting a more dig-nified and honorable fight. This is why their books are so important. "The prisoners who had these books in the seventies and eighties represent for me the prime of our civil struggle," Zeina said. "It was our revolution." For visitors to the library, like Beesan and Zeina, the books provide a tactile link to the prisoners and the time in which they lived. Nobody visits the library to read these books. They come to connect with the men who once held them, to put their fingers in the same place on those same pages—and, perhaps, to mourn what has been lost.

Beesan and Zeina's father, Mahmoud, was himself imprisoned in Jnaid for his political beliefs. He read many of these books, and he told his daughters that if they searched the volumes carefully, they might find his handwriting in the margins. "This is what I am looking for," Zeina told me. "This is part of who I am." As she flipped through books she guessed her father might have read, Zeina showed me some of the writing other prisoners had added. She found a couple lines of a Darwish poem scribbled in one book. Simple drawings of flowers and trees in another. The Palestinian flag rendered in blue ink. Passages underlined in red or notes made in margins. Following Zeina's lead, I did the same, searching the spaces between the printed text for the ink of men I can know no other way than by the hieroglyphs they left behind.

The librarian on staff waved me over. She lifted a thick hardcover book out of her desk and opened it to reveal a secret compartment hollowed out of the center. The librarian told us prisoners had used the book to smuggle messages back and forth. Slots cut adjacent to the compartment allowed the pages to be tied together just enough so a guard could thumb through the pages without discovering the inner cavity. The hollow still contained a stash of messages written on paper peeled from the backs of cigarette foil, just as Wisam had described. The delicate paper retained a scent of tobacco. The handwriting was exceptionally precise, almost puritan in its neatness, and nearly too tiny to read. These were hardly the writings of ham-fisted and uneducated thugs.

Holding the hollowed-out book in my hands and gently unfolding the messages gave me a sort of forbidden thrill. I imagined Wisam in his cell, peeling the diaphanous paper—slowly, slowly—from the cigarette foil. I imagined him with a cheap ballpoint in his hand, resting his cheek on the table to bring his eyes as close to the paper as he can. Only his cramping fingers can discern the movement of the ballpoint. He writes tiny words about his life underground. Reproduced ideas about Marx and independence and revolution, entire manifestos on paper as thin as gossamer. I pictured him wiping his aching eyes when he is done. Then he folds the paper twice, glances up from the table, and places the message inside the secret book.

The First Intifada prisoners, the men Beesan and Zeina so admired, starved themselves so they could read and then swallowed and smuggled the words they'd written. In a place where ideas are forbidden, words themselves become a valuable contraband.

I met Sharif Kanaana again to talk about the book *All That Remains*. Instead of sitting inside the shuttered and smoke-filled Café Ramallah, which made Sharif uncomfortable, we met in the brighter environs of his house. Sharif's home stood along the road to Qalandiya and near a park filled with pomegranate trees, cypresses, Italian pines, and pink blooming oleander. Sharif's wife, a woman from South Dakota named Pat, served coffee in a salon decorated with Southwest Americana. Framed cross-stitches of wild birds hung on walls next to glass cases filled with porcelain figurines of American Indian dancers from Arizona and New Mexico. Sharif sat next to me and pointed his good ear in my direction.

In the 1980s, Sharif worked as the head of the research center at Birzeit University. He launched a project to document the history and geography of each Palestinian village abandoned or destroyed in the wake of the Nakba. He and a staff of nine research assistants randomly selected villages from regions throughout what is now Israel. They administered a questionnaire to about a dozen former residents of each village who were old enough to remember what the village was like. "We collected information only from people who were at least fifteen years old when they lived there. People who were aware of things," Sharif said. His team also gathered old photographs and made family trees for all the various clans and families. Then they accompanied the residents to the village sites to search for and photograph whatever original structures remained, and Sharif collated the information for each village into a small booklet.

Sharif hoped to create a booklet for each of the nearly four hundred villages lost in the Nakba. "After I made fifteen of them, I realized I wasn't going to get very far. It was going too slow." The research also proved expensive, and Birzeit University lacked the resources to continue funding such an ambitious project. Sharif wrote a letter to Walid Khalidi of the Khalidi Library family, who was living in the United States. Sharif described the work his team had already accomplished. Then he suggested that instead of producing four hundred individual books, perhaps a better strategy would be to create a single volume with two or three pages devoted to each village. Sharif asked Khalidi if he'd be willing to support such a project.

Khalidi never answered Sharif directly. Instead, he contacted the administration at Birzeit University and offered to provide between four hundred and five hundred dollars for each village included in the project. With Khalidi's money in hand, Sharif devised an efficient system for working on the book. He reassembled his team into three groups, each with a geographer, a photographer, and a research assistant. He sent each team into a different area in Israel to seek out original residents from the villages who would accompany the team to each site. Back in Birzeit, Sharif tasked another group of researchers to collect statistics for each village from old British Mandate records that stretched back to the mid-1920s. Sharif also recruited a historian to write a short history of each village they investigated. "And when the material about a village was ready, we put it together in a package and sent it to Walid Khalidi," Sharif said.

Visiting the ruined villages with their former residents transformed the project from an academic pursuit into something heartbreaking. Finding one's home reduced to a few stones or, in most cases, vanished entirely shattered the villagers Sharif worked with. "I would take people from the village. When they got there, they'd break down," Sharif said. He started to recount for me the time a man found the sparse traces of the cemetery where his father was buried, but Sharif couldn't finish the story. He, too, broke down. His voice cracked, and he started to cry. Afraid he might spill his coffee, I took his cup from his quaking hand. Pat sat quietly with her head bowed, and I figured she'd seen this happen before. "I am sorry," Sharif said once he composed himself. "I cannot control this. I can still see the scenes when the people saw the remains of their homes. Or the graves of their relatives."

Sometimes anger usurped sadness on these journeys. Sharif once took an eighty-year-old man to visit the site of his former village, al-Shaykh Muwannis. The Israelis built Tel Aviv University on village land after 1948, and the man's former home was incorporated into the Eretz Israel Museum. "We wanted to go through the museum gate to get to the house," Sharif said, "but they tried to charge us admission." The man caused a scene, refusing to pay for a ticket to see his own house. Eventually, the woman at the ticket booth called for her supervisor, who allowed the man and Sharif's team to enter the museum for free. The man has since died, Sharif said, and the house itself was bulldozed in 2003.

The Institute for Palestine Studies published the book in 1992, in English, under the title *All That Remains: The Palestinian Villages Occupied and Depopulated by Israel in 1948.* An Arabic edition followed a few years later. Even though Sharif and his team compiled the entries for all but fifty of the 418 villages included in the book, the English edition names Walid Khalidi as the editor and Sharif as associate editor. In the Arabic edition, Walid is listed as "author" while Sharif and his team are only thanked six or seven pages into the introduction. The book also fails to credit Sharif el-Musa, the Palestinian-American writer who did the bulk of the editing. Both Sharifs felt Khalidi took undue credit for the work, and they met in Ramallah to discuss whether or not to confront him. "We sat and talked and in the end agreed that the book is good and that we shouldn't ruin its reputation. And to hell with Walid Khalidi."

I felt grateful that Sharif and el-Musa did not allow bitterness to darken the book's accomplishment. *All That Remains* succeeds in evoking both the pastoral splendor of a lost Palestine and the tragedy of that loss. As Khalidi writes in the preface:

> *All That Remains* is a manual, a dictionary of destroyed villages presented individually, yet in the context of their region and the events that swept them away. It is an attempt to breathe life into a name, to give body to a statistic, to render to these vanished villages a sense of their distinctiveness. It is, in sum, meant to be a kind of "in memoriam."

Amid the book's enumeration of fields overgrown with weeds, cacti, and Christ's thorn are entries that read like sad and accidentally beautiful poems. "There are two large, open graves on the northeast side," begins a description of Bayt Nattif. "The bones in the grave are visible." Of a village called Zayta, the book tells us, "there are no traces of houses; only a well, still in use, is left." The description of Darwish's al-Birwa mentions the schoolhouse I visited with Abu Ahmed and reads: "All of these landmarks stand deserted amid cactuses, weeds, and fig, olive and mulberry trees." Other times, the descriptions are so stark and clinical they leave the reader to fill in the sadness. In al-Haram, the "dilapidated cemetery overlooks the sea and is used as a parking lot for Israeli tourists." In Qastina, "there was also a thick undergrowth of *khubbayza*, or mallow, a wild plant cooked as a vegetable in Palestinian peasant cuisine. Later when a photographer returned to the site, he discovered that this undergrowth had recently been burned off." The banality of the language contributes to the feeling of absence.

But the book does more than this. When I first held *All That Remains* in my hands and felt the heft of its six hundred and fifty pages, something else struck me. The book renders the emotional heaviness of the Nakba into actual weight. Each time I lifted the book from my desk, I could feel in my hands a physical representation of all that was lost. In 2014, a left-wing Israeli nonprofit group called Zochrot designed a smartphone app called iNakba that used GPS technology to make an interactive map of all the villages lost in 1948. The app incorporated much of the material from *All That Remains*, along with updated information and photographs. For all its technological wizardry, though, the app lacks the book's striking physicality. Tapping a screen is not the same as turning page after page after page. Hundreds of pins on a virtual map cannot evoke the same sense of loss as two kilograms of paper and ink.

4

I Do Not Have an Account
in the Bank of Wars

Mourid Barghouti wrote about crossing through the Qalandiya checkpoint between Ramallah and Jerusalem in his 2009 book *I Was Born There, I Was Born Here*. Or rather, he refused to. "There's no need to describe the exceptional tragedies that take place here," he wrote. "It's enough to picture in one's mind the density and solidity of the fortifications, their iron-ness and cement-ness, and then to picture the fragility of the human body, any human body." Much as I admire Barghouti, I disagree with him on this point. It is not enough to simply imagine Qalandiya.

I once crossed on a Thursday morning during Ramadan when hundreds of people were trying to get into Jerusalem in advance of prayers the following day. The service taxi from Ramallah dropped me off in front of a large shed built of corrugated steel and lit by anemic fluorescent tubes. From here, the crowd pressed forward into a series of caged chutes, flanked by vertical steel bars and topped with a metal grate, that divided the crowd into tight single-file lines. The cages were so narrow that anyone carrying heavy bags had to enter sideways. Barbed wire coiled above us while the floor collected discarded cellophane from cigarette packages and other trash. The light through the bars cast striped shadows on patient but unsmiling faces. The steel and concrete surrounding us imposed a chill on the scene as Barghouti's "iron-ness and cement-ness" came in contact with the warmth of human flesh.

I inched forward through my cage then grabbed the bars of a revolving steel gate and pushed through. Elsewhere, full-height turnstiles are nicknamed iron maidens after the supposed medieval torture devices they resemble. According to Barghouti, Palestinians call them milking stalls. "I have seen a better setup for managing herds of cows," he writes. I emerged into another security zone with three rooms separated from each other by a concrete half-wall topped with a pane of bulletproof glass. Each room had a remotely controlled turnstile at one end with a light that was supposed to turn from red to green when the turnstile unlocked.

The lights didn't work. The fifty or so Palestinians crowded in the room had to listen for the soft metallic clunk that indicated the turnstile had been opened. Then everyone pressed forward. Those at the front had only a few seconds to navigate through before the gate locked again. People at the back shouted for them to move faster. I ended up huddled and compressed alongside a family with three young boys. The surging crowd terrified the boys into tears each time the assembled mass of bodies started to push and shout. Crossing Qalandiya means offering up your flesh—your body's fragility, as Barghouti would say. Bodily humiliation is the price of passage.

Almost an hour had passed by the time I managed to squeeze my way to the front of the crowd and clank through the rotating steel. A soldier on the other side regarded my passport with bored disinterest, seemingly oblivious to the compacted pilgrims waiting to pass. Then she waved me through.

I crossed through Qalandiya because I wanted to meet Palestinian writers living in what most of the world calls Israel and what most Palestinians call 48—shorthand for the territory belonging to Palestine before the 1948 war. Palestinians make up more than a fifth of Israel's population, numbering about 1.8 million. I wondered what it meant to be an urban Palestinian living as a minority citizen of the State of Israel, far from both the architecture of the occupation—the checkpoints, the settlements, the roadblocks—and the hills and villages of the Palestinian imagination. I decided to travel north to Haifa, Nazareth, and Acre and meet the writers there. First, I paused in East Jerusalem to meet poet Mohammed El-Kurd.

Mohammed's mother used to write poems for a Jerusalem newspaper. She would read them aloud to her husband in their house in East Jerusalem's Sheikh Jarrah neighborhood, seeking his feedback before sending them to her editor. When Mohammed was a child, he woke each morning to the sound of these tentative verses filtering into his bedroom from the kitchen. "That is how I became familiar with the way rhythm and rhyme float in a poem," he said.

Mohammed was still a child when, in 2009, a group of radical Israeli settlers stormed his home and took over half the house. In 1956, the United Nations had designated the property for Palestinian refugees, and the el-Kurds had lived there legally for more than fifty years. This did not dissuade the settlers. They came armed with a 1970 Israeli law that allows Jews to reclaim any property in Jerusalem that belonged to Jewish families before 1948. According to the settlers, the front half of the el-Kurd house occupied land once owned by Jews and was built without an Israeli-issued building permit. Under the protection of Israeli police, the settlers entered the house and tossed the el-Kurds' furniture and possessions into the front garden. Mohammed watched as settlers then set his three-year-old sister's bed on fire and warmed themselves around the flames.

Eight members of Mohammed's extended family now live in the extension at the back of the house built after 1948 and therefore safe from reclamation. A rotating group of six settlers occupies the rest. The settlers have spat on the el-Kurds. They hurl trash into the family's side of the property and kept a dog in the yard so vicious Mohammed's little sister wet herself in fear every time she saw it.

The el-Kurds' eviction attracted international attention and became the subject of a documentary narrated by Mohammed, then eleven years old, called *My Neighbourhood*. In the film Mohammed's face bears a sort of bewildered grimace. He expresses astonishment both at the settlers' actions and at the Israeli and foreign activists who rallied in support of his family. Six years later, Mohammed recalled the chaos of the eviction, especially the role of the women of Sheikh Jarrah who "weaved the first battle cry":

[It] was my aunt Nadia, 70-something then, and the rest of the neighborhood's women who protested with chanting and drumming on pots and pans, who tried to heal the pain and suffocation caused by tear gas with onions and yogurt, and who hid young Palestinian men and American activists escaping persecution and arrest. I will never forget the sight of my nineteen-year-old neighbor, freshly homeless, as she spray-painted the words "TREES DIE STANDING" on the gate of her stolen home, and on what remains of her tainted childhood. I will never forget my grandmother pushing the Israeli settler out of her jasmine garden with whatever body strength a 90-year-old might possess.

Mohammed met me on the corner near where my bus from Ramallah stopped. He'd grown into a slender young man of seventeen since the documentary aired, with a face darkened by a struggling teenage beard. His wet cough made him seem frail, and I suggested moving our meeting to a day he was feeling better. He assured me he was fine. We walked up the street toward the posh American Colony Hotel before turning down a cracked side street to his family's home. Around the same time as Mohammed's family was evicted, settlers took over four other Sheikh Jarrah homes, including the house across the street from the el-Kurds. In 2010, journalists filmed these neighbors singing praises to Baruch Goldstein, the American-born settler terrorist who massacred twenty-nine praying Palestinians at Hebron's Ibrahimi Mosque in 1994:

He took aim at the terrorists' heads and squeezed the trigger tight.
And shot bullets and shot bullets, and shot and shot bullets.
Dr. Goldstein, Dr. Goldstein, there is none like you in the world.
Dr. Goldstein, Dr. Goldstein, everyone loves you.

When we reached Mohammed's house, we stepped past the front entrance where settlers had spray-painted a black Star of David over the door and passed his grandmother's jasmine tree on the way to the back of the house. Blankets hung on a line strung between the back door and one of the windows in the front of the house. Mohammed told me the blankets acted as a curtain to block their view of the settlers, who often stand naked in the windows and make obscene gestures at Mohammed's mother and sisters. Then he led me inside to the salon where a small monitor displayed the feed from a security camera mounted outside. A collection of books, in both English and Arabic, filled a small cane bookshelf in the corner. Soon after we sat, his mother delivered a tray of mint tea.

Before Mohammed was born, Israeli doctors told his mother that Mohammed—but not his twin sister, Muna—would be born with Down syndrome. They advised her to abort. Mohammed believes that Israeli doctors often tell pregnant Palestinian women their sons-to-be will have some sort of serious illness or disability and encourage them to end the pregnancy. "It is a demographic strategy," he said, to limit the population of male Palestinian children.

This conspiracy theory made me uncomfortable. I had trouble accepting the idea that Israeli doctors would be involved in a nefarious government plot to abort Palestinian babies. Still, the fact that this plot is believable to Mohammed and others was evidence of the dark chasm of mistrust that separates Palestinians from Israelis. Could peace ever blossom between people who believe such things of each other?

Mohammed and Muna were born in 1998 on the fiftieth anniversary of the Nakba. Mohammed didn't have Down syndrome, but he had a hole in his heart that healed itself over time. He was also born with a preordained Palestinian future. "What do you do when your destiny is already embroidered in the womb?" he wrote in one of his poems. I asked Mohammed about this. "According to Islam, this is true," he explained. "Everything is written for you already. You are just following God's plan. There are two kinds of life in Palestine. You're either the martyr or just the person who is insulated away from politics—as if politics is not in your living room."

Unlike the other writers I'd meet, Mohammed wasn't a great reader when he was a small child. When he turned eleven, around the time the documentary about his eviction was filmed, Mohammed started to wonder about topics considered taboo by Palestinian culture. He struggled with questions about spirituality, atheism, and sexuality that he felt uncomfortable asking his parents. Mohammed sought answers in the public library. He wrote his first poem around this time, too. "It was about an Israeli policeman, and I was basically cursing him in a poetic way." His proud parents made him recite the poem to their Arab neighbors. Mohammed remembers the poem less fondly. "It was trash," he said. "Seriously terrible. I would kill someone if it was published."

Mohammed's writing eventually drew the attention of the teachers at his all-boys school. He wrote such compelling and mature essays in his eighth-grade English and Arabic literature classes that his teachers accused him of plagiarism. When they realized that he had indeed written them, his teachers urged him to recite the essays in front of the other classes. The following year, a paper Mohammed wrote about respecting women caused a minor storm at the school. "All of the other kids wrote about their mothers and sisters, and how we should respect women because they give birth to men," Mohammed said. His essay, though, suggested women have human rights that should be honored whether or not they decide to become mothers. "I wrote that respecting women had nothing to do with charity or sympathy. It was a responsibility." The paper criticized traditional Palestinian society for disrespecting women who divorce, those who choose not to have children, and those who decide to work outside the home. Mohammed's teacher accused him of blasphemy and advised him to direct such thoughts somewhere other than on the page.

Mohammed never heeded this advice. Much of his writing dares to tackle the problems he sees as inherent in traditional Palestinian society. His poems celebrate feminism and women's rights. He describes his first poetry collection, which he named after his grandmother Rifqa, as an ode to "Palestinian women, women of color, and women in general who are often dismissed and underrepresented in the narrative of struggle and resistance." Mohammed's poems also challenge Palestinian masculine ideals. "There is a definition of a man in Palestine that no one can refuse," he told me. "People have internal ideas of what they expect when they see a man. For example, the way I am sitting is not the way men sit here." He gestured to his legs, which he had crossed above the knee. "All the boys at school played soccer. I didn't. They all dreamed of getting married. I don't dream of that."

Mohammed suggested that everything that came to Palestine from elsewhere—the British Mandate, say, or the occupation—turned into disaster for Palestinians. As a result, they distrust Western concepts like feminism and equality. "I understand that I come from a society that is backward in some ways," Mohammed said. "But I am also saying that this society is undeveloped for a reason. We have a defense mechanism against anything that is foreign to us." His society will applaud and respect him for standing on a stage and reciting verses about Palestinian resistance. "But I will be seen as a deviant, as a threat that comes from the West, if I recite a poem about the liberation of women," he said.

"We have lost our land. We have lost our children. We have lost our future. The only thing my society can hold on to are the cultural habits and heritage," Mohammed said. "And some of our cultural habits are great. Some of them are disgusting. But we hold on to them." He paused then quickly added, "And, yes, I am blaming our social backwardness on the Israeli occupation."

Mohammed wants his poetry to make people feel guilty about their role in society's ills. "Some poetry has this real positive vibe that makes you want to go out and do something in the world," Mohammed said. "Unfortunately, I don't have that way with words. It's really hard for me to cheer myself up. To me poetry is truth, and I cannot just sugarcoat things. You can ignore and neglect any kind of power that comes from the outside, and you can become oblivious to whatever force is talking to you. And you won't care if you don't want to care. But if the provocative force is coming from inside you, it itches your soul. It goes into your veins. It is in our skin. You cannot ignore it. You will submit to it." Comments like this made me forget that Mohammed was a teenager.

Despite his poetic efforts, Mohammed finds Palestinians difficult to inspire. The reality in which they live is the only reality they've ever known. Their world is small, and their lack of liberty has come to feel normal. Mohammed traveled to the United States with the filmmakers of *My Neighbourhood* in 2012. "I was astonished by the fact that the train from Washington, DC, to New York didn't stop every fifteen minutes for me to be searched by police," he said. "We grow up on songs of liberation. But do we really know how occupied we are? Do we really know how imprisoned we are? Do we really know that we've never tasted freedom?"

Mohammed takes his own inspiration from the writers he reads, like Ghassan Kanafani and Fadwa Tuqan, a fiery female poet from Nablus who died in 2003. "And I just started reading Mahmoud Darwish," he said. "I used to think he was overrated, but his stuff is really amazing." Mohammed also admires the Egyptian feminist writer Nawal El Saadawi, whose 1969 book *Women and Sex* was banned for criticizing female genital mutilation. She is now in her eighties, and her writings and lectures continue to challenge religious and political elites. "That to me was so amazing, how words can be so powerful, and women writers are so impressive to me. Especially Arab women."

But the woman who has influenced Mohammed most, his favorite aunt, Maysa, was not a writer at all. Mohammed had little in common with Aunt Maysa, but he admired her fierce self-confidence and individuality. After she died of cancer in 2014, Mohammed wrote:

> She was a goddess, hiding and covering every fragile piece of her soul beneath thundery laughs, red lipstick, pearls, and sassiness. No outer power was able to touch her; not divorce, not notoriety, and not whispers from covered women on the *Anata* bus. I used to think of her as a superwoman: the woman who taught me everything I know about confidence and self-love. Indestructible and astonishingly careless, she seemed. The closest to freedom one could get in an occupied country.... The way she loved was generous. The way I loved was ordinary.

In the days following our meeting, Mohammed would write his high school finals and exams from the education ministry. The Savannah College of Art and Design in the United States had already accepted Mohammed into its creative writing program, so he simply needed to pass those last high school tests. Still, he wanted to do well. Palestinian newspapers publish the results of the government exams, and students feel enormous pressure to make their families proud. "My family isn't that happy that I've been accepted into college, but they are going to be thrilled when I pass my exams," Mohammed said. "It is a cultural thing."

I asked him if he would miss Jerusalem. "I have this love-hate relationship with Jerusalem," he said. "But it is mostly hate." He will be sad to leave his friends and family, to be sure, but he yearns to escape the plural occupations he endures here: the Israeli occupation, and also the occupation of religion, of gender norms, and of the oppressive traditions his poetry rails against. "Everywhere you go there is an enemy. We pick our battles in Palestine. You can either advocate against the occupation, or advocate against the cultural norms that are repressive, but you can't really be against both of them." Mohammed is only seventeen years old, but of all the Palestinians I met, he seemed the most weary.

When Mohammed first visited the United States in 2012, he wept on the day he returned to Jerusalem. He didn't want to come back. And yet, after only a few months at college in Savannah, Mohammed posted an entry on his blog titled "On Missing Jerusalem." He describes the birds and bus stops. His grandmother's jasmine, his father's stubbornness, and his little sister's dance in front of the mirror. He misses every "picturesque tragedy" and "every combination of the bizarre and just-about-right." Then, in another poem, Mohammed wrote:

sing me a song of home:
throw a stone or two
because the screams make me nostalgic
and now I almost don't fear the sirens.

I boarded a bus north to Acre, the city Ghassan Kanafani fled during the Nakba, and met with author Ala Hlehel in a seaside café overlooking the Bay of Haifa. He told me the first thing he ever wrote was a love letter to a girl named Isoris who sat near him in his grade two class. Ala's mother found the letter before he had a chance to deliver it. "She was so excited. She let all the village read it," Ala said. Mortified, Ala destroyed the letter and never gave it to Isoris. "But she had already heard all about it." Aside from such maternal embarrassments, Ala enjoyed a happy and safe upbringing. "I always joke that I am not lucky. Each writer wants a very bad childhood for his first novel."

Ala was born in Jish, a village close to the border with Lebanon—had the British drawn the line one millimeter south in 1916, Ala would have been Lebanese. His parents were from Qadita, a village of stone houses, grain fields, and pomegranate orchards that was lost in the Nakba. His parents were not enthusiastic readers, Ala said, and he did not inherit his love of literature from them. "Writing and reading was a very personal passion for me." When he was a boy, Ala used to read and imitate the poems of a Syrian writer named Nizar Qabbani, who wrote of love, women, and eroticism. "There were dirty things to read. I used to hide the book in secret places."

Qabbani made Ala want to write poetry, but he discovered early in his career that he was a terrible poet. Ala decided, instead, to become a visual artist. He studied drawing, painting, and sculpture at the University of Haifa, where he earned a Bachelor of Arts in mass communications and fine arts. Three months after completing his degree, Ala sat on the floor of his rented apartment drinking beer and smoking hashish with his friends. He looked up at the paintings he'd done and announced, "Guys, this is bullshit. I'm not an artist. I don't know how to paint." This was the moment he decided to become a writer. When he was twenty-six years old, the Qattan Foundation awarded Ala a writing prize and gave him the opportunity to read his work onstage in front of a crowd in Ramallah. The prize and the applause convinced Ala that he could be a successful novelist.

In the mid-1990s, Ala began writing for a communist newspaper in Haifa called *Al-Ittihad* (*The Union*). He wrote about the experiences of daily life, and readers were happy to find such stories in a serious and formal newspaper. "I wrote about making falafel," Ala said. Like Darwish and Zaqtan, Ala considers writing about the banalities of ordinary Palestinian lives to be a political act. "I want so much to write about the small details that make us human beings, because even us Palestinians write about ourselves as one-dimensional people. Either we are *shahid*s or future *shahid*s."

Palestine's intellectual elite, those most equipped to write the Palestinian narrative, fled en masse after 1948. "We were left with two hundred thousand fellaheen—peasant farmers—with no voice," Ala said. "There was no one left to tell the story." The authors and poets who remained wrote overtly political texts that focused on the heroic struggle of the nation but were artistically and emotionally unsophisticated. "As a writer, you were basically a soldier. You gave people texts in order to shape their identity. You wanted to be the voice of the people." The collective mattered more than the individual.

Just as Mahmoud Abu Hashhash had suggested in Ramallah, Ala believes the focus shifted after Oslo. "We were under the illusion that the struggle was over," Ala said. "We thought, we can have a Palestinian state now, so let's stop writing about Palestine. Let's start writing about sex." Ala was part of the generation of authors that began to write about Palestinians as individual human beings—whether in or out of the bedroom. "We stopped writing about Palestinians as a placard or a political poster. Suddenly we had feelings. It was not so bad if you cry."

The world outside Palestine was also changing. The internet granted Palestinians access to foreign literature and authors elsewhere in the Arabic-speaking world. Palestinian writers connected with their diaspora colleagues in Cairo and Beirut. The availability of so many new texts changed the perception of what it meant to be an Arab, especially for writers like Ala who lived in 48. "The internet was crucial for us as Arabs in Israel. We are surrounded. We are Israeli citizens, but we are not complete citizens because we are Arabs and not Jews." At the same time, the rest of the Arab world was suspicious of Palestinian-Israelis, with their Israeli passports and citizenship. The internet allowed writers to connect with each other beyond the confines of political borders and fraught nationalities.

The appearance of satellite television channels launched another "revolution." Broadcasters like Al Jazeera started interviewing Arabs living in Haifa and Nazareth. Palestinians in 48 edged closer to the rest of the Arabic-speaking world, and to the world in general. "You had a wider perspective of what literature is and what life is about," Ala said. "Not just the struggle in Gaza, or Nablus, or the Galilee."

Ala recalls writing only two stories set in the West Bank. He felt both were fraudulent. "If I want to write a novel about Ramallah, I should go there for a year," he said. "And, for me, Gaza is a myth. It is a place that does not exist in my real life. Just in headlines. If I want to write about the immediate Palestinian that I am, I will write about Haifa and Akka," he said, using the Arabic word for Acre. "This is the material that I know." Ala's stories center on Palestinian characters living in 48 and are often colored with ironic humor and frequent dashes of the erotic. The protagonist in Ala's story "My Husband Is a Bus Driver" looks forward to the travel she will do with her new bus-driving husband, but all she does is clean the trash and vomit out of his bus when he returns from a trip. "The Tent" gives a strained and complex portrait of a family living in the close quarters of a leaky refugee tent. In "The Passport," a Palestinian author desperately tries to retrieve his passport in time for a publicity trip to London.

Ala has endured his own passport problems. In 2010, he was named one of thirty-nine rising Arab writers and invited to a literary festival in Beirut. But the Israeli government considers Lebanon an enemy state and forbids citizens, including Arabs like Ala, from traveling there. Israeli prime minister Benjamin Netanyahu himself released a statement declaring he would not allow Ala's trip. Adalah, a legal center for Arab minority rights in Israel, decided to petition the Israeli High Court of Justice on Ala's behalf. Adalah felt the law was worth challenging out of principle, but it didn't believe it harbored any chance of winning. Neither did Ala, so he decided to attend a different literary event in the United Kingdom while his lawyers argued the case.

The High Court was in session while Ala flew to London. "When I landed, I had four hundred messages on my phone. They said, 'Mabrouk! You are going to Beirut!'" Inconceivably, the court had rejected arguments by the government's lawyers and overturned the travel ban. Israel's interior minister himself signed the order. The decision was groundbreaking. Ala would be the first Israeli citizen since 1948 permitted by Israel to visit an enemy state.

Ala told the newspaper *Haaretz*, "It is almost impossible to describe the joy that I feel right now." But his happiness was short-lived. He had been so certain his court challenge would fail that he hadn't bothered to arrange his attendance with the Beirut festival organizers. Now Ala faced another problem: Lebanon enforces a parallel law that forbids anyone from entering the country on an Israeli passport. "It was a disaster because I hadn't planned anything with the guys in Beirut. I spent three days in London trying to convince them to have me. They said, 'You didn't apply. You have no Palestinian passport. We have a law.'" Ala finally convinced the Lebanese embassy in London to issue him a laissez-passer that would allow his trip. He booked a flight to Beirut for the following Friday.

Then, on Thursday, the Icelandic volcano Eyjafjallajökull erupted and thwarted Ala's plans. Volcanic ash filled the skies around northern Europe and grounded all commercial aircraft. Ala never made it to Beirut.

He joked that the eruption was an Israeli conspiracy. Iceland's first lady at the time was Dorrit Moussaieff, an Israeli Jew born in Jerusalem. "She caused the volcano," he said.

Kidding aside, the prohibition against traveling to Lebanon struck against Ala's Arab identity. Beirut has always been a center of an Arab culture that has long included Palestinians. For generations, Palestinians in Jerusalem and the Galilee pursued university degrees in Beirut. They listened to Lebanese music, watched Lebanese films, and read Lebanese books. Beirut stands as a capital of the Arab nation that Palestinians have belonged to for centuries. "So why does Israel want us to forget this history?" Ala asked. "I write in Arabic. I dream in Arabic. I make love in Arabic. It is my immediate culture. And you want me to think Beirut is not a part of my personality? Why? I don't recognize your security discourse. This is my nation. This is my people. This is my language, for god's sake."

Perhaps Ala's greatest contribution to the wider Arab nation is Qadita, an Arabic cultural website named for his family's lost village. The site includes short stories and poems as well as sections for politics, cinema, theater, and other arts. Ala founded Qadita in 2010, and the site quickly became popular with the Arab cultural elite and creative classes. The section dedicated to gay literature attracted the most attention. This was the first inclusion of queer lit in a general culture website anywhere in the Arab world. "It caused a shock," Ala said. Furious readers called to tell him there was no gay scene in Palestine or that queer culture was "an Israeli thing." The harsh reaction lasted for only two or three months, and people stopped complaining altogether after a year. Ala eventually liberated Qadita's queer section from "the ghetto," and now gay literature appears throughout the site.

Most gay Palestinian writers live in 48, where organizations exist that advocate for homosexual issues. Ala said he couldn't run a site with queer literature from the West Bank. "This is one of the benefits of being in Israel," he said. "We don't like to admit it. It's not nice to say, but in Israel there are positives. You are not supposed to say good things about your enemy." Ala wants all Palestinians to enjoy the same freedoms Israelis do.

Half of Qadita's content comes from Palestinian writers, the rest from elsewhere in the Arab world. "We have no real lines. No taboos. You can write about gay issues, about politics—Arafat or Abu Mazen.

Qatar or the Saudis. There are no limits." The site receives material that cannot be published in the Arab states it comes from. Qadita even welcomes stories about atheism, a provocative idea in the Arab world and an actual crime in some countries. "If someone wants to write his deep and honest thoughts about God, we will publish it, too." Quality is Ala's only concern.

There are only two basic rules for writing, Ala said. Honor your reader, and love your characters. The latter rule holds particular relevance for Palestinian authors writing from 48. "I can't be a professional writer if I write a one-dimensional Jew," Ala said. When he teaches creative writing, he tells his students that if they lack "the power and the willingness to write about Herzl as a human, then don't write about him." Jewish characters in Palestinian fiction should be complete and well-shaped and not included as poorly drawn targets of hate. "Otherwise it is political bullshit."

This is another advantage writers in 48 have over their colleagues on the other side of the Green Line. The only Jews West Bank Palestinians ever see are soldiers or settlers. Mourid Barghouti wrote: "our problem with the Jew . . . is that all three or four generations of Palestinians have seen of him is his helmet. They've seen the Jew only in khaki, with his finger on the rifle's trigger." Palestinians in 48, on the other hand, live among Jews. Half of the residents of Ala's building are Jewish, and everyone wishes each other good morning. Ala even writes the occasional article in Hebrew and once signed a contract with an Israeli publisher to write a Hebrew novel. (He quit after only a thousand words, though, and paid back his advance. "I was young and foolish and wanted to be popular and written about," he explained.) Just like his Jewish neighbors, Ala is an Israeli citizen. "I am paying taxes for this country," Ala said, though this fact riles him. He hates knowing that his tax dollars fund settlements and help equip the Israeli military. "I am buying the bullets they are shooting at Palestinians," he said.

Ala doesn't like to admit it, but he realizes there is a cultural divide between Palestinians in the West Bank and Palestinians living in the 48. "The Israelis succeeded in separating us. Through borders, checkpoints, and military actions. And walls." West Bank Palestinians call those living in Israel *shamenet*, or Cream Arabs. The term comes from an Israeli epithet for someone who is spoiled from birth. "We are the rudest Arabs in the Arab world," Ala said. Palestinians in the 48 also earn more than those in the West Bank. "We tend to go to Jenin and Nablus to shop," he said. "With our five hundred shekels we are rich. The Palestinians there tend to look at us in our pockets."

But holding the same blue ID card as his Jewish neighbors does not mean Ala lives the same life. In 2012, an Israeli housing development called Nes Ammim, or Banner of the Nations, decided to expand into a multicultural community for Jews, Muslims, and Christians. The community's website promised a "unique, high-quality community based on the principles of openness to all religions, tolerance and acceptance of the other." This philosophy appealed to Ala and his wife, human rights lawyer Abeer Baker, who support the ideal of a secular democratic state for both Israelis and Palestinians. Besides, the community itself was beautiful. "Surrounded by trees," Ala said. He and Abeer felt Nes Ammim would make a good home for their two young children.

They applied to purchase a home there in 2014. In addition to arranging the relevant financing, Ala and Abeer had to be approved by the committee overseeing the community. They completed a four-hour computerized exam with "hundreds of questions meant to analyze our personality," Ala said. Near the end of their application process, they sat for an interview with a selection panel. Ala and Abeer considered the interview a mere formality. After all, by then they had already signed a contract, chosen a plot, and paid their deposit. "But the interview did not go well," Ala said. Nes Ammim's managers asked Ala and Abeer about their work and political leanings. Then they asked whether or not Ala and Abeer would accept an invitation to attend a community barbecue to celebrate Israeli Independence Day. Ala told them no. "It's not our day," he said.

This was not the answer the committee wanted to hear. When they called Ala and Abeer in for a second interview, the atmosphere was tense. One of the committee members, a man from Holland, told Ala and Abeer he found their political positions problematic. He objected to a column Ala once wrote comparing the Israeli Knesset to a garbage dump. The committee felt that this was vulgar and rude. The man said, "Ala writes as if he is shouting." Ala replied that, as a minority, sometimes you have to shout to be heard. The man said that wasn't polite. Ala told him that was a typical white answer. Another manager said that while he could see that Ala and Abeer were "very clever" people, he worried they would cause clashes in the community. By then Ala knew the committee was going to reject his application, so he asked if it would rather accept a stupid Jewish person than a clever Arab. Nes Ammim returned Ala and Abeer's deposit. "They wanted good Arabs," Ala shrugged.

In spite of the frustrations of being a Palestinian in Israel—the travel restrictions, the conflict with Nes Ammim—life in the 48 grants Ala a wealth of material to write about. "For a writer, it is a fortune," he said. Years ago, he decided to move to London. He lasted only a week. A promised newspaper job never materialized, and he quickly ran out of money. "I was lonely and terrified," he said. "It was the shortest immigration ever." Ala's quick return infuriated and embarrassed his mother, who had boasted to everyone in Jish that Ala had moved to London. She demanded Ala hide out in Haifa for a little while before showing up in Jish, just so she could save face with her fellow villagers.

Ala told me he won't leave again. "I don't want to give up on this place," he said.

In Raji Bathish's ironic short story "Nakba Lite," five young men decide to mark the sixtieth anniversary of the Nakba by collecting their families' stories for inclusion on a "Nakba Blog." They become disappointed, though, when they realize their stories lack sufficient tragedy. One man tells of how Israeli soldiers considered using his family's home as a command center, but never did. Another explains how his family fled the fighting in Haifa and ended up settling comfortably near Nazareth—hardly a desperate fate. A third speaks of his aunt, a spinster "who is expected to die of cancer at any moment because of the trauma she has been suffering for more than sixty years." She suffered nightmares of being raped by soldiers even though she was never actually raped. Finally, the fourth blogger tells the story of his mother's uncle, who kept the key to the house he fled in 1948, only to have it stolen during his wife's funeral. "And so, five years later, my mother's uncle died from grief over his key." The blog coordinator loved this story, and asked the man how he knew for sure that the uncle died out of grief for his lost key. The man replied: "Is there anything more tragic to die for?"

Raji is not unlike the men in the story. His personal history also lacks a compelling Nakba tragedy. "All of us Palestinians are melancholic figures. All of us are looking for sadness to write about, because it is not interesting for a Palestinian to write happy things," Raji told me as we sat at a pricey café in Nazareth near the gaudy Basilica of the Annunciation. "But I am not a refugee," Raji continued. "My melancholy is related to something different." Each Palestinian author writes about the occupation somehow, Raji said, but his work challenges collective symbols like lost orange groves or the sanctity of keys for stolen homes. Raji has set stories in Tel Aviv, "the capital of the enemy," which rarely appears in Palestinian literature. His characters are more vulnerable than heroic. And instead of patriotic clichés, Raji—like Ala Hlehel—would rather write about sex.

When he was a boy, Raji used to steal books and magazines his uncle left behind in his mother's family home. "It was like a passion for me. I wanted to read all the time. I read everything." Many of the titles came from Lebanon and Syria, and Raji realized later on how rare these books were. The books were illegal under Israeli law and likely smuggled in. Young Raji most enjoyed reading a Lebanese health magazine called *Your Doctor*, which always included a sex advice column. "I read about sexual problems and penis size," Raji said. The magazine taught young Raji the blunt carnal vocabulary he would later use in his work.

The sacred attracted Raji just as much as the sexual. He used to accompany his Catholic mother to church on Sundays. Raji was not particularly religious: even at nine years old he questioned why Catholics knelt before statues of stone saints and found little inspiration in the lessons of the Bible. But Raji loved listening to the priest recite religious texts during the Mass. He heard a beautiful music in the words of faith. In 2016, he told an interviewer, "At age six, when you discover words like *batul* (virgin) or *shafi'a* (patron saint), or the rest of the vocabulary of sin and sinfulness and sacrifice without understanding its meaning, an extremely rich lexicon opens up to you." Just as *Your Doctor* introduced Raji to the language of sex, his Sunday morning ceremonies taught him the language of purity and transgression.

He remembers, too, learning of the Sabra and Shatila massacre in 1982. Raji was twelve years old when one hundred and fifty Lebanese

Christian militiamen, allied with Israel, entered the Shatila refugee camp and the adjacent neighborhood of Sabra in Beirut. For three days the militia raped, murdered, and dismembered the residents. Israeli soldiers positioned around the camp did not stop the rampage. Instead, the IDF sent flares into the sky to illuminate the darkness for the militiamen. Mahmoud Darwish wrote of the massacre in his memoir *In the Presence of Absence*: "The night of Sabra and Shatila was all lit up so that the killers could peer into the eyes of their victims and not miss a moment of ecstasy on the slaughtering table." The Israelis also allowed reinforcements to enter the camp and provided bulldozers to dispose of the bodies. Between eight hundred and 3,500 Palestinians died in the massacre—the numbers, as in all such grisly accounting, remain disputed. Many of the victims were children.

"It was the first time that I smelled the odor of something horrible that happened to kids," Raji said. "The invasion of Lebanon by Israel in 1982 was something very violent that showed people my age that the world is not as good and simple as we children thought." The massacre coincided with trauma within Raji's home. His eighteen-year-old sister suffered a psychological breakdown that same week. Raji didn't want to tell me the details, saying only that it was a "a traumatic thing" that made him lose the "feeling of safety in the house." The two episodes, opposite in scale and intimacy, deeply affected young Raji. "That week changed the world around me," Raji said.

Raji started writing his own stories as a teenager, about the same time he started to have sexual experiences with older men. "I loved the feeling of sin," he said. "I started to write about my feelings in prose and in poems." When he graduated from high school, Raji left Nazareth to study chemical engineering at a university in Tel Aviv. He took lovers from among the other Arabs in his dormitory, and he continued to attract the affections of older men. He dabbled briefly with politics, but activism and nationalism quickly bored him. Raji was far more interested in writing. One of his first published stories was about a victim of child sexual abuse. As he continued to write, his work became more and more explicitly homoerotic.

"Yesterday I thought about what makes me write about sexuality," Raji said. "I thought about what makes me want to be penetrated by another man. I think it gives me the feeling that I am alive. That I am made of real material." I found this fascinating in light of what I'd already learned. Like Ala Hlehel, Raji belongs to the new generation of Palestinian writers that has jettisoned nationalistic flag-waving for domestic narratives. The focus tightened from the nation to the home. But Raji's work represents an even further and more intimate shift. Raji's explicit sexuality narrows in on the body itself.

Raji also dispenses with the common trope of heroic masculinity. "I like to write about vulnerable manhood," he said. His characters all share the illusion that they control the world in which they live. For Raji, much of this sense of vulnerability stems from his experiences as a sexually active gay man during the height of the AIDS crisis. "I remember when I started having sex in public places. I always used protection, but every time I started to feel symptoms—if I was sweating or something—I believed that I was HIV positive. It was something that ruled my life." Then he told me, with startling nonchalance, about an encounter with a man in a Haifa park when he was in his twenties. Raji was giving oral sex to the man, and he ejaculated without warning. "I was crazy for months. I thought I was going to die. And not just die, but die with shame."

Raji paused then asked me, "Do I make you uncomfortable when I talk like this?"

"No. I am just surprised," I said. "I've never met anyone who speaks so explicitly about these things."

"My work is explicit," Raji said. "I wrote a story about intercourse between me and a colleague in my office. It was fiction, of course, but the story was very pornographic. When I published it on the internet, people were very angry. I asked myself, what is the problem with writing pornographic stories? Why should they have less value?"

"What do your readers think?" I asked him.

Raji shrugged. "I live in my own bubble here," he said. "Nazareth is a small town. People don't have anything to say." The crowd Raji draws when he travels to give readings and lectures always surprises him. "I realize I am a very well-known name in queer writing." Raji is not a typical gay rights activist. He doesn't encourage people to come out of the closet, and he doesn't march in the Tel Aviv Pride Parade. "I don't know what to be proud of," he said. But Raji often speaks out against what he considers Israeli pinkwashing. He rejects the idea that Israel's accommodation of the LGBTQ community stands as evidence of the country's humanitarian virtue. "You cannot be a fascistic state, with apartheid and occupation, and be proud of your gay integration."

Especially when Israel's domestic intelligence agency, Shin Bet, blackmails gay Palestinians into becoming informants. In 2014, the *Guardian* printed the testimony of a Shin Bet refusenik. "If you're homosexual and know someone who knows a wanted person—and we need to know about it—Israel will make your life miserable," the man said. "Any such case, in which you 'fish out' an innocent person from whom information might be squeezed or who could be recruited as a collaborator, was like striking gold for us and for Israel's entire intelligence community." He went on to suggest that this practice was Shin Bet policy. "During my training course in preparation for my service in this assigned role, we actually learned to memorize different words for 'gay' in Arabic."

For its part, the Palestinian Authority is hardly innocent of such crimes. Reports surfaced in 2013 about PA policemen threatening to out gay Palestinians in Ramallah unless they informed on political activists. In either case, outed Palestinians in the West Bank—where homosexuality is not illegal but often considered sinful—face humiliation, shame, and violence.

I asked Raji if he could write such explicit homoerotic stories if he lived in the West Bank or Gaza instead of in 48. His long pause before answering surprised me; I'd thought my question was rhetorical. Raji said he never thought about it. "I know people in the West Bank who write openly queer stories. Some of the villages are very conservative, but I could live in Ramallah and write." He feels queer writing occupies such a small niche in Palestinian culture that few would even notice his work. "I think that I can write everything I want everywhere," he said. "But I told you I live in a bubble. I don't know what people say about me."

"Are you happy in your bubble?"

"I am protecting myself," he said.

He's protecting not just himself. Raji has a son. A few years earlier, one of Raji's female friends told him she wanted to have a baby and planned on going to what Raji called "the bank of sperm." Raji stepped up. "I wanted to fulfill my biological potential," he said. "My thinking was very scientific. I produce millions of sperm every day. If one of them meets an egg, the right egg, it would be a human being. And I wanted that."

I laughed. "That is the least emotional reason for having a child I've ever heard."

He shrugged again. "It is a fact."

Raji was living in Tel Aviv at the time, and his friend lived in Haifa. When she gave birth to their son, Raji moved to Nazareth—a short drive from Haifa—so he could be close to his child while also caring for his dementia-stricken mother. She passed away in 2016. Raji sees his son, Habib, four times a week, and the boy spends every second weekend with Raji in Nazareth. Unlike a lot of Palestinian fathers, who "don't get involved in the Pampers things and want the child very clean and clothed," Raji embraced the muck of parenthood. "I got involved in the liquids," he said. Raji dealt with the long illnesses and deaths of his parents, both of whom needed his constant care in their final years. Then he tended to his infant son's vulnerabilities. "It is the real life," he said. "This is very tough. You have another human being. You should protect him. And you can't always protect yourself."

In 2014, playwright Bashar Murkus decided to develop a play about Palestinian political prisoners in Israeli jails. "The issue of prisoners is important," Bashar told me as he chased an espresso with a ginger ale at a restaurant called Fattoush in Haifa. "Palestinians see them as heroes. Israelis see them as terrorists. But neither a hero nor a terrorist is a human being." Bashar began by conducting general research about political prisoners around the world before training his focus on prisoners in Israel. He learned about Walid Daka, a PFLP operative serving a thirty-seven-year sentence for his involvement in the 1984 kidnapping and murder of an Israeli soldier named Moshe Tamam. Bashar was drawn to Daka after reading a letter he wrote to his unborn son. "I loved the letter," Bashar said. "I loved how well he wrote it."

Daka is undeniably an evocative author. In 2005, *Haaretz* published another of his letters. He wrote:

Here we are not allowed to use a paper and pen during the visits. Memory is our only means. I forget to look at the lines that began years ago to be etched in the face of my mother, forget to look at her hair, which she started to dye with henna to conceal the white, so I won't ask her real age. And what is her real age? I don't know how old my mother is. My mother has two ages: her chronological age, which I know, and the age of my imprisonment, the parallel age, which is 19 years.

I am writing to you from the parallel time. We don't use your ordinary units of time, like minutes or hours, except during the moments when our time meets your time next to the visitors' window. Then we are forced to pay attention to those same units of time.

The letters motivated Bashar to learn more about Daka. He met with Daka's wife, lawyer and human rights activist Sana Salameh-Daka. The two married in prison in 1999 but had never consummated their marriage. Bashar also met with Daka's lawyer, his mother, and his brothers. And he began to exchange letters with Daka in prison.

Bashar wrote a play inspired by Daka's life in prison. He titled it *A Parallel Time*, based on Daka's letter, but the play is not a biography. Daka is not named and does not appear as a character. The killing of the Israeli soldier is not mentioned. Instead, the story centers on the life of five fictional political prisoners. As the play opens, one of the inmates is planning on marrying his girlfriend. Another prisoner arrives, an oud player, and his fellow inmates try to find a way to secretly build an oud so he can perform at the groom-to-be's prison wedding. "The play is about how the prisoners fight time inside the jail," Bashar said.

Al-Midan Theater, a Palestinian company based in Haifa, staged the play in Arabic several times over the course of two years without incident. In 2014, though, Midan included Hebrew supertitles for Jewish audiences. "Then the storm started," Bashar said. Protesters accused Bashar's play of showing sympathy for a convicted terrorist. Tamam's family was outraged. Israel's education minister, Naftali Bennett, removed the play from a list of performances available to Israel's schools. The Ministry of Culture and Sport, led by minister Limor Livnat, abruptly suspended funding for al-Midan. So did the Haifa Municipality. Bashar said he wasn't surprised by the response. "But the strange thing is that not one of these people actually saw the show or read the play."

Walid Daka read it. According to a story in *Haaretz*, Sana brought a copy of the play to Daka at Hadarim Prison during one of her biweekly forty-minute visits. "Doesn't Israel have any other problems? Such as the Palestinian problem, or Iran? Only the play about Walid Daka?" Daka asked her. "Did anyone among all those who are now on the attack actually see the play?"

Later that same year, Bennett and Livnat railed against another Palestinian artist living in Haifa, filmmaker Suha Arraf. Arraf's film *Villa Touma* was set in Ramallah, filmed almost entirely in Arabic, and included no Jewish-Israeli characters. The Israeli ministers, though, were outraged that Arraf listed the film as Palestinian at the Venice Film Festival. The film had received a $353,000 grant from the Israel Film Fund, the Ministry of Economy, and the Mifal Hapais lottery commission—all Israeli public entities. Arraf defended herself in a newspaper op-ed, saying, "Films belong to those who create them. They never belong to the foundations that helped fund them, and they certainly never belong to countries. I define my film as a Palestinian film because I am first of all a Palestinian." Arraf also reminded her detractors that while Palestinians make up a fifth of Israel's population, Arab-Palestinian cultural institutions receive less than 2 percent of Israel's budget for culture, and less than 1 percent of cinema funding. "If anyone should be complaining," Arraf wrote, "we are the ones who should be doing so."

Arraf failed to convince the ministers. They wanted the grant money back. Livnat demanded that the Israel Film Fund return Arraf's grant to the Ministry of Culture and Sport, which provided the money, and the Ministry of Economy wanted Arraf to pay the money back herself. In the end, the Israel Film Fund returned the funding. Since the controversy, both the Israel Film Fund and the Yehoshua Rabinovich Foundation for the Arts, the only cultural organizations in Israel to fund feature-length films with government money, require their grant recipients to declare their films Israeli. Now Arraf describes *Villa Touma* as stateless. Her movie has become another sort of Palestinian refugee.

The *Villa Touma* and *A Parallel Time* controversies revealed to Bashar that the only way for a Palestinian artist living in Israel to ensure auton-

omy over his or her own work is to be untethered from government funding bodies. "It is really important for all artists here to remember that we
are living inside an occupation," Bashar said. "I am making art to save my
identity. It is why I am working. It is crazy to believe that the occupation
will give me money to make this."

Bashar's own theater company, Khashabi Theatre, remains independent. Bashar and four of his theater school colleagues formed the
Khashabi ensemble in 2011. They spent three years producing shows at
various theaters in Israel and the West Bank before building themselves
a permanent home in an Ottoman-era building in Haifa's Wadi Salib
neighborhood. The building was a Palestinian family home before 1948.
For a while it housed a carpenter's workshop, then a nightclub, but it had
been shuttered for a decade like most of the buildings in Wadi Salib.
Bashar and his friends took possession of the building in 2015 and ren-
ovated the space into a theater. "We didn't take money from Israel to
make the renovations," Bashar said. "Not from the municipality or the
Ministry of Culture. We chose to make the theater truly independent."

Khashabi Theatre's inaugural season focused around the theme of
Haifa. They opened with *Sitt bil Ouffeh*, a play named after a Palestinian
dish of bulgur and rice. The play centered on the idea of inherited memory. Bashar told me that Palestinians have vivid memories of events they
did not experience firsthand, especially of the Nakba and the tumultuous
years that followed. "We took these stories from our fathers or grandfathers. And we believe that they are our memories. But they are not our
memories at all, because we didn't live it." The first generation of post-
Nakba Palestinians, those whose parents endured the traumas of 1948,
often suffer a sort of inherited PTSD.

But for Palestinians of Bashar's generation, the second after the
Nakba, this inherited trauma has faded—especially for those living in
Israel and away from the daily pressures of occupation. "My grandfather
lived through the Nakba, and he lived in fear until he died. My father
took this fear from his father, and he lives with it, too. But our generation
did not take it." Bashar told me a story about one of the ensemble members who lives in her grandmother's house in Nazareth. Each time she
travels to Haifa for rehearsals, her grandmother calls to make sure she
arrives safely. "Her grandmother still believes that it is really dangerous

to go from Nazareth to Haifa. She still has this fear, even though now it is just a half-hour bus ride." This enduring anxiety and the despair for all they'd lost paralyzed his father's and grandfather's generations. They didn't create anything new while looking fearfully backward.

The absence of inherited fear gives Palestinian artists like Bashar the psychological space to build something for themselves. Palestinians in the West Bank continue to struggle with the daily pressures of a military occupation. "But in Haifa, our war is not about geography," Bashar said. "We are working to save our identity and determine how we want to live." Bashar understands his experience as a Palestinian in Haifa differs from those living elsewhere. "It is different from what is happening in Jerusalem, for example, where the war is still about whether you exist or not." Instead of facing death, Palestinians in Haifa and elsewhere in Israel face questions about the life they want to live. "Here it is about *how* to exist." The Palestinian struggle in Haifa, then, is to create a life for themselves. "The Palestinian people are building their own Haifa," Bashar said.

The center of this new blossoming of Palestinian culture in Haifa is Masada Street. I walked to Masada after my time with Bashar. Dreadlocked Palestinians walked their dogs past afternoon beer drinkers. I eavesdropped as a man in a backward-facing yellow baseball cap rolled up his sleeve to show off his new tattoo to a pair of women at a café, and I wondered if he'd gotten inked at the tattoo parlor named Oops a little up the street. I browsed the antique shops and vinyl record stores, passed the tiny bars that can scarcely hold a dozen drinkers at a time, and took a coffee at Elika café. If Masada Street existed in my hometown, I would spend all my time there.

It would be easy to dismiss what is happening on and around Masada Street as simple gentrification. The phenomenon of creative young people transforming a low-rent neighborhood into a popular bar-and-café scene is hardly unique. But there is a political edge to what is happening on Masada. The Palestinians in Haifa are building themselves a cultural life in a city where they are a minority. Jewish Israelis are welcome here, and I heard almost as much Hebrew as Arabic coming from the café tables, but this is undeniably Palestinian space. The scene is also undeniably hip. None of these places resemble the dusty old-fashioned coffee shops in the West Bank where I smoked away my hours with gray-haired men in tweed blazers. Masada is where the young writers and artists gather. Here the hairstyles are modern and the music on the stereo current. Contemporary artworks rather than photos of Jerusalem hang on the walls. I found it ironic that one of the places where I found modern Palestinian culture manifested so clearly was in an Israeli city.

That night I met poet Asmaa Azaizeh in a café one street up from Masada. She is almost supernaturally beautiful, with the sort of eyes Arab poets wrote ghazals about. Asmaa started to load the bowl of a briar pipe with tobacco as soon as she sat down. She laughed when I told her I'd never seen a woman smoke such a pipe. "It is my boyfriend's," she said. "I've been smoking it lately instead of cigarettes because I feel I smoke less this way. Maybe it is a fantasy." She declined my offer to buy her a beer. "I have been drinking since ten this morning," she admitted. A planned hiking trip with her friends devolved into a daylong bout of outdoor drinking. "And we didn't hike anywhere," she said.

Asmaa comes from a village called Dabouriya in the countryside near Nazareth. She moved to Haifa when she was eighteen years old to study at the University of Haifa. Now she lives with her twin sister in an apartment across the street from the café. Asmaa's father was a farmer who used to recite classical Arabic poetry from memory at the dinner table. "He learned the poems from school," she said. "He loved them. And he was a good reader, too." By the time Asmaa was seven years old she, too, was reciting poetry from memory and writing jabberwocky verses full of gibberish and made-up words.

When she reached her teen years, Asmaa exchanged her poetry for the regular pursuits of kids her age. She hung out with her friends, listened to music, and played basketball. This sounded familiar. "You have a lot in common with Ghassan Zaqtan," I said. "You are both poets who used to play basketball. Do you know Ghassan?"

Asmaa smiled. "He used to be my father-in-law."

Ghassan and Asmaa met in 2007 when he published some of her poetry in the culture pages of *Al-Ayyam*. The two had coffee together whenever Asmaa was in Ramallah. Ghassan brought along his son Shadi, a fine guitarist and songwriter, to one of those café meetings in 2010. "Ghassan thought he would bring Shadi to meet me and maybe something would happen. He set it up. And it happened." Asmaa moved to Ramallah, where she and Shadi lived together for a couple of years before getting married. They broke up three years later. Shadi stayed in Ramallah, and Asmaa returned to Haifa. "On paper we are still married," she said, but the legal logistics of divorcing across the Green Line have proven to be complicated. For the time being, Asmaa and Shadi remain territorially divided but legally bound.

Asmaa studied journalism and English language at the University of Haifa. She admits she was not a good student, but she considers her time at university as her cultural awakening. "I started to write. I started to see culture. To see theater. To read." She also embraced politics. Asmaa joined the Abnaa el-Balad, or Sons of the Homeland, a movement of Palestinian citizens of Israel and like-minded Israeli Jews who advocate for a single democratic state in all of historic Palestine. Asmaa edited the movement's monthly magazine but eventually left the organization when older members of the movement started to shut the younger members out of decision-making. Asmaa also found the strict ideology of her Abnaa el-Balad activism crippled the freedom of thought she required to write her poetry. A poet can write about politics, but "you cannot be ideological in real life and be free in your poetry. You cannot be schizophrenic." Asmaa opted for poetry.

Like Bashar, Asmaa possesses a collective Palestinian memory of suffering she did not personally endure. Asmaa told an interviewer in 2017, "I was born in a peaceful village. I have never seen shooting in my life. I've never seen a dead body or a killing, but my memory and my collective consciousness has seen all this." She addresses her lack of firsthand trauma in her poem "Do Not Believe Me If I Talked to You of War":

Do not believe me if I talked to you of war, because when I spoke of blood, I was drinking coffee, when I spoke of graves, I was picking yellow daisies in Marj ibn Amer, when I described the murderers, I was listening to my friend's giggles, and when I wrote about a burnt theatre in Aleppo, I was standing before you in an air-conditioned one . . .

Do not believe me when I talk to you of war
Because I've never heard a bullet shot besides the one my father threw from his double-barreled gun into Marj ibn Amer's doves. And I've

never scented blood from a wound except for that which I smelled with
my mother the first time I menstruated.

I do not have an account in the bank of wars, but a Hourani woman
reassured me that my cheques are valid.

Asmaa won the A. M. Qattan Foundation's Young Writer Award
in 2010, and a Jordanian press published her first book of poetry, *Liwa*,
in 2011. I wondered when she found the time to write it. I've never met
anyone more engaged in the Palestinian cultural scene, in Haifa or anywhere else, than Asmaa. She began editing the arts and culture sections
of local magazines and newspapers midway during her university studies.
After graduating in 2006, she started working in radio and television.
She hosted talk shows, worked for a Ramallah television station, acted
as a cultural correspondent for an Arabic television channel in London,
wrote for magazines in Haifa and Lebanon, and edited the poetry section
of Ala Hlehel's Qadita website. She curates events at Haifa's Fattoush
Art Space and Bookshop and manages a poetry initiative called Poetry
Lab. She also handles media for various arts organizations, such as the
Khashabi Theatre, and coordinates a booking agency for musicians.

In 2011, the Mahmoud Darwish Foundation in Ramallah surprised
Asmaa by offering her another gig: the directorship of the new Mahmoud Darwish Museum. "You don't see young people in charge of these
things in Ramallah," Asmaa said. "The people who built the museum
and established the Mahmoud Darwish Foundation are all old guys. Dinosaurs. So when they offered me the job, I couldn't believe it." Asmaa
spent two months writing a formal seventy-seven-page proposal for the
museum, including everything from strategic planning ideas to long-
and short-term project proposals to outlines for running the museum gift
shop. She consulted with her contacts in the arts and culture scene, in
Palestine and abroad, and researched similar museums in Europe. She
wanted to partner with Birzeit University to establish a creative writing
college at the museum which would offer bachelor's or master's degree
programs in creative writing, the first such programs in the Arab world.
Asmaa envisioned the museum evolving into the one of the leading cultural institutions in the Middle East.

The dinosaurs, though, didn't bite. "They threw my idea in the trash, man!" Asmaa said, growing agitated at the memory. "They are fucked up in the head!" Instead, two months after the museum opened in 2012, the dinosaurs considered renting out the museum's theater to one of the nearby embassies for a cocktail party. Asmaa, mortified, refused. "This is not a wedding hall," she said.

The museum canceled the cocktail party, but it became clear that the founders would not implement any of Asmaa's ambitious ideas. "I was begging for them to let me work, but they didn't want to do anything." She quit after seven months. "I really got bored," she said. Now the museum screens films and hosts occasional poetry readings. "Big deal," Asmaa scoffed. "I can do that here in this coffee shop."

Asmaa prefers living in Haifa to Ramallah anyway. "The Palestinian places and spaces are known to us, and everybody knows everybody," she said. "I think Haifa is a calm city. I like the sea. I like the mountain. I really feel connected. My friends are here. My work is here." For Asmaa, the cultural initiatives she and other young Palestinian artists in Haifa engage in, on Masada and elsewhere, are "nothing short of a political revolt." To open a music venue or start a theater in an Israeli city stands as an act of cultural resistance, a dynamic movement that battles what Asmaa terms the "linguistic and cultural occupation of Haifa." The expression of a Palestinian identity here is a political act.

"Do you have challenges, though, being a Palestinian artist living in an Israeli city?" I asked. "Or do you have your own scene and your own people?"

Asmaa frowned. "You are describing it as if we live in a cultural ghetto. It is not a ghetto. It is more of a cultural bubble. In my daily life, I don't feel I am the Other. I don't feel as if I live in an Israeli city. I really feel it is my place. I feel connected to the streets, to the people, to the bars, to the theater, to the nature. I don't feel something is wrong."

"But is the whole city yours?"

"No. I don't go to Carmel Center to drink beer," she said, referring to a part of Haifa that is almost entirely Jewish. Still, over the years, she stopped seeing herself as part of a simple us-and-them binary. "We started to see ourselves as our own thing. We've gone beyond the realization that we are a minority, that we are oppressed and depressed. I felt this more when I was younger. I came from a village and wasn't used to living among Israelis. I wasn't used to the two systems. Now I feel different. I am still touched when I see what is happening in Gaza and Ramallah, and also here. But in Haifa, this odd place, in this small bubble where we live, we are a little bit isolated from it all."

If the Masada Street scene houses Haifa's Palestinian culture in the present tense, Wadi Nisnas represents its past. The neighborhood was founded in the nineteenth century for Arab workers. Most left after 1948, but the three thousand residents who remained preserved the neighborhood's rural atmosphere and Arab closeness. Narrow alleys still divide the low stone houses where laundry hangs from wrought iron balconies. Pomegranate trees still rise over garden walls, and church bells still ring on Sundays.

Khulud khamis's father was born in this neighborhood and grew up in these alleyways. Khulud, though, was born in what was Czechoslovakia to a Slovakian mother. The family moved to Wadi Nisnas when khulud—who spells her name with lowercase k's—was eight years old. They stayed in her grandmother's house until her mother, valuing privacy and space more than her new Palestinian in-laws and neighbors, insisted khulud's father find them another place to live.

Khulud knew only two words in Arabic when she arrived in Wadi Nisnas: *habibi*, the common term of endearment her father and grandmother no doubt called her, and *kanun alththani*, which means January. "My father tried to teach me all the months, but I got stuck on January. *Kanun alththani* has a kind of melody," khulud said, betraying her writer's sensibility.

"It is a beautiful word," I agreed. We were sitting in her living room in Vardia, a neighborhood far from Wadi Nisnas on Haifa's Mount Carmel. "How do you say *February*?"

"*Shbat*." Khulud laughed. "You see? You can't go from *kanun alththani* to *shbat*."

When she moved from Czechoslovakia to Haifa as a child, khulud endured the uniquely Palestinian anxiety of immigrating to a place she didn't know but was compelled to call home. The move was hard for her. Haifa's culture did not resemble what she knew in Slovakia, and she didn't speak the language. "I remember the experience of trying to fit in, and always failing somehow." Khulud sat quietly on the fringes of life in Haifa—not bullied, but left out. "I was always an outsider. Always, always, always."

Like many of the Palestinians I spoke to in Israel, khulud's family was not displaced by the Nakba. She has no refugee story. Khulud's grandfather even served as a member of the Israeli Knesset. ("We are not going to talk about him," khulud said.) But while khulud's youth did not bear the typically Palestinian scars of post-Nakba dislocation, khulud endured her own personal brand of self-imposed exile. When she was eighteen years old, an American ship bound for Russia broke down in the Mediterranean and docked in Haifa for repairs. Khulud met and promptly fell in love with the ship's chef, an American man twice her age. When he returned to the United States, khulud followed. They married in Las Vegas and lived for a while in an RV, driving through Mississippi and New Mexico before settling in a dingy basement apartment near Atlanta. Her husband had a fondness for Jack Daniel's that he didn't have for work, and khulud's parents sent money every few months to help support her. Khulud and her husband eventually had a daughter, Michelle.

Khulud's parents flew to America three times—each separately once, then together—to try to coax their daughter back home. Khulud was stubborn. Finally, in the middle of the night and at the end of a long conversation, khulud's mother made her realize the sadness of her basement-dwelling American life. A few months later, after khulud organized Michelle's travel documents, the two packed up their few possessions and returned to Haifa. The husband stayed behind. They never divorced, but she and Michelle rarely hear from him.

After earning a master's degree in English literature at the University of Haifa, khulud wanted to be a writer, but her own fragmented identity intimidated her. She wasn't sure whom she represented in her work and wondered what a writer with her unique heritage was permitted to express. Would she be seen as speaking for all Palestinians or the Palestinian minority living in Israel? Or was she an immigrant writer from Slovakia? The fact that she writes in English rather than Arabic or Hebrew raised further questions about for whom she was writing.

Khulud finally found her voice as a writer in 2008 when she started to work for Isha L'Isha, a radical feminist organization in Israel. Feminism connected the various strands of khulud's splintered self and gave her the "legitimization" to write about individual lives without worrying about representing the collective Palestinian experience. On the page, khulud was a woman first, before all else.

She remains a perennial outsider, though, and has spent her life trying to figure out where she fits in. "The feeling of wanting to belong is a primal instinct," she said. "We need to belong to something. Whatever it is. I think this is something that always drove me: to find the group or the place I belong to. And I could never find that. The Palestinians, the people I want to belong to, don't really accept me fully. Not in the total sense. Because, at the end of the day, I am a foreigner." Khulud spent years of "moving between the spaces of belonging and not belonging" in search of an emotional home before realizing that such a place did not exist—at least not for her.

But khulud discovered that her fluid identity possesses its own sort of power. "Its strength lies in its movement: sometimes being positioned at the very center, at other times on the margins." Khulud feels this mutability offers her a broad view. She views the complicated social-political structures of her world from various perspectives and can "make intricate connections between phenomena that otherwise would seem unrelated." Khulud may not belong anywhere, but from where she stands she can see everything.

Her outsider identity also offers khulud certain permissions not granted to other women she knows. The regular cultural taboos—against living with a partner outside of marriage, say, or marrying someone from a different religion—do not apply to her. A few years ago, khulud co-founded a Facebook page where Palestinian victims of sexual harassment and assault could share their experiences. "This is something that is not talked about even in intimate circles," she said. "Even between sisters." Many women posted their stories on the page, but only khulud used her full name. Her colleagues praised khulud for her bravery and for being a "revolutionary," but khulud knows she only got away with doing this because she was a foreigner and not "wholly Palestinian."

Khulud wrote her first novel, *Haifa Fragments*, while working two jobs, raising a daughter, caring for two dogs, and tending to her mother, who'd suffered a stroke. The novel follows Mayysoon, a Palestinian jewelry designer living in Haifa, and her relationships with her Muslim boyfriend, Ziyad, her secretive Christian father, and a young woman, Shahd, who lives in a village on the other side of the wall. All of these characters are Palestinian, but their individual histories, experiences, and values are diverse. Each character's life represents a fragment of what it means to be a contemporary Palestinian and challenges the Western perception of Palestinians as either stock victims or militants.

Comparing Mayysoon's urban existence in Haifa to Shahd's rural village in the West Bank raises the question of which woman enjoys the better life, and reminded me of Ala, Raji, and the other Palestinians I met living in Israel. Is there an advantage to living as an admittedly second-class Palestinian citizen of Israel compared to being the subject of Israeli occupation in the West Bank? Khulud used to think so. "And this kept me silent for many years. Who am I to write about Palestine when I am living in a luxury of sorts? During active military operations, they are suffering. Being killed. Murdered. Who am I to say that I am being discriminated against here in Haifa?" But khulud started to accept the fact that Palestinians on her side of the wall also feel pain. "We don't need to compare whose suffering is worse."

This real-life anguish inspires many of khulud's short stories. Or "fictionalized realities," as she calls them. Her story "Conflict Zone Date" draws on the attempted lynching of a Palestinian man in 2012. Ibrahim Abu-Taah was escorting a female Jewish colleague home from a staff party in Jerusalem when a group of Jewish teenagers heard the woman refer to Ibrahim by name, thus outing him as an Arab. They pummeled him with an iron rod. Ibrahim ended up in hospital with a broken leg. In the days following the incident, Jerusalem police officials said that their investigators were still trying to find the motive behind the attack.

The police didn't have to look far. Three weeks earlier, dozens of Jewish youth ambushed a group of Palestinians in Jerusalem's Zion Square and beat one seventeen-year-old nearly to death. A week after that attack, Lehava, an extremist group that opposes relationships between Jews and non-Jews, and whose leader advocates the burning of churches and mosques, circulated an online poster reading:

Dear Arab guy:
We don't want you to get hurt!
Our daughters are valuable to us,
and just as you would not want a Jew to date your sister
we are also unwilling for an Arab to date a girl from among our people.
Just as you would do anything to stop a Jew from dating your sister—
so would we!
If you are thinking of visiting Jerusalem malls or the pedestrian street
with the intention of dating Jewish girls—this isn't the place for you.
You may walk around in your own village freely and find girlfriends
there, not here!
Last week an Arab who thought he might find Jewish girls got hurt.
We don't wish for you to get hurt,
So respect our daughters' honor
As we mind it dearly.

In the eyes of his assailants, Ibrahim had not heeded this warning, and so they broke his leg. Police promptly arrested five of Ibrahim's attackers, three of whom admitted to the beating. Ibrahim recovered from his injuries. Still, khulud couldn't get him out of her mind. "He just kept coming back somehow. He kept bugging me at breakfast." Eventually she wrote a fictional account of the incident, moving it from Jerusalem to Haifa and focusing on the days before the attack. "The story is ten pages long, but the lynch is only a paragraph. I went back two weeks before the lynch and imagined the daily life of this person. He is a regular person. Why would you want to beat him up?"

Another real-life attack, this one a 2003 suicide bombing, inspires a scene in *Haifa Fragments*. Ziyad boards Haifa's number 37 bus with two schoolgirls, a teenage boy eating a McDonald's ice cream cone, and a young man he pegs as a university student by "the bulging backpack on his shoulder, the bloodshot eyes and the haggard body." The student is Mahmoud Kawasme, and his backpack does not contain textbooks. Khulud wrote:

> There was one thing [Ziyad] would strain to forget but which kept creeping back into his mind. Those numbered seconds Mahmoud had his eyes locked on his. The small dark eyes spelt death. But they were also telling him to get the hell off the bus—immediately. That is, if he wanted to live. Ziyad's brain stopped working. The only thing it did was send rapid instructions down his legs to get off the bus. And he did. Seconds later, the earth shook.

Khulud often uses the real names of both the attackers and their victims in her stories and poems. In *Haifa Fragments*, she names both Kawasme and thirteen-year-old Qamar Abu Hamad, the only Palestinian killed in the bus attack whose death haunts Ziyad. In a story based on the 2003 attack on Haifa's Maxim restaurant, khulud names both the bomber and Arab restaurant staff killed in the explosion. Khulud's poem "Set My Body on Fire" describes the 2016 murder of a nineteen-year-old Palestinian, Raneen Rahal, at the hands of her brother.

Khulud's decision to render incidents like these in her work, and to use the victims' real names, made me uneasy. I wondered if mining other people's tragedies for art was a kind of exploitation, an appropriation of personal trauma. "This is part of my reality here in Haifa," she said. "The bus I wrote about, the number 37, is the bus that my daughter used to take to school back then. Michelle could have been Qamar. I am writing from my perspective as a citizen of Israel."

Palestinian victims of violence—whether at the hands of bombers, mobs, or their own family members—are too often rendered invisible. "The media would always focus on the Israeli victims, running the stories of their lives, interviewing family members and friends, while the Palestinian victims like Qamar are all but ignored," khulud said. "Same with murdered women. Palestinian murdered women rarely make it to the news, and when they do, the coverage is lacking and portrays the Palestinian society as a violent society." By putting their names in her writing and telling their stories within her own stories, khulud grants these victims an identity they've been denied.

Even though her Slovakian passport allows her to live anywhere in the EU, khulud remains here. "I'm in love with Haifa. Totally," she said. "As much as I feel that I don't belong here, I don't feel that I can belong anywhere else in the world." She loves Haifa's topography. Using the mountain and the sea as markers, "you can always orient yourself," she said. And she's fascinated by the geographies of identity, the invisible borders of language and culture, that a mixed city like Haifa creates—especially in regard to her own fragmented self. "The way I am perceived in different parts of Haifa is different," she said. "If I walk in Carmel Center, a Jewish area, and I talk on the phone in Arabic, I might get looks." I thought of Maya Abu-Alhayyat's *Bloodtype* character answering her phone in English on the Jerusalem train.

As we talked, Michelle walked into the living room from her bedroom. She snuggled up to khulud on the couch and placed her head on khulud's shoulder. Khulud sensed a con. "You want money, don't you?" she asked. Michelle giggled and nodded. "I was wondering why you were cuddling with me." Khulud pointed to my voice recorder on the coffee table. "You are being recorded. Say 'Mommy, I love you.'"

"Mommy, I love you," she obliged. "Now give me money." Khulud sighed and pulled a few banknotes from her wallet and handed them to Michelle, who said goodbye and bounded out the door.

Khulud and Michelle live an exclusively urban life. They don't have a village in the hills or a centuries-old olive grove that they consider their ancestral home. I wondered if khulud felt any attachment to the archetypical Palestinian landscape I hiked through in the West Bank. "I don't have a personal relationship to that land," khulud said. "For Palestinians in the West Bank, their land is under constant threat. Mine isn't. My future is not shrunk and obscured. I know where I am going to be tomorrow." The absence of this particular anxiety means she doesn't address issues of land and territory in her work—the same reason Maya avoids writing about Israelis and why Ala doesn't set his stories in Ramallah. "I have solid ground under my feet, you know? That's the thing. When you have certainty, then it becomes less urgent for you to talk about it that much. I don't worry that I need a permit to pick my olives."

Khulud experiences a different brand of anxiety, though: that of a minority Arab living in Israel. She worries about wearing a shirt with

Arabic writing on it, or using her laptop on the train when it is covered with Arabic stickers that say "Free Gaza." This anxiety intensifies during times of conflict. "When my daughter was younger—I can't remember which war we were going through—I called her on the phone and told her not to speak Arabic on the bus."

These concerns peaked during the 2014 summer war in Gaza. Khulud and a group of fellow feminist activists, Jews and Arabs both, wrote the word *Enough* in Arabic, Hebrew, and English on their hands and traveled to Carmel Center to join a peaceful protest against the war. In the days leading up to the demonstration, social networks had lit up with incitement against the planned demonstration. "Even the mayor of Haifa wrote on his Facebook page that radical elements were coming to Haifa to disturb the city's peaceful coexistence," khulud said. When she and about two hundred of her fellow demonstrators arrived at the start of the march, at least two thousand extreme right-wing activists were waiting for them. "They had huge flags of Israel. They were chanting 'Death to Arabs' and 'Death to Leftists.' I knew it was going to get violent."

Khulud had planned to take a few photos of the demonstration then quietly return home before the march was over. "I don't like to be on the front lines. I don't need to be arrested," she said. "All these kids, these twenty-two-year-old protesters, they don't care. They don't have any children. They want to show that they are big heroes. I don't need to be on the front page."

When the demonstration ended, most of the marchers boarded buses and the police started to disperse. Khulud found herself among about forty or fifty remaining protesters, most from Haifa, who just wanted to walk home. But counterprotesters blocked all the streets leading away from the demonstration. "They were spread in groups in all the alleys surrounding us, behind bushes at the entrances to buildings, everywhere. They were ambushing protestors trying to leave," khulud said. She and about a half dozen of her friends tried to escape through a backyard, but a group of angry protesters chased them back to the main group. Later, khulud learned that five of her friends managed to sneak away. Two of them were attacked and one ended up in the hospital with a concussion.

Khulud and the rest of the protesters decided they were safer if they stayed together, so they moved away from the march venue as a group. The counterprotesters tailed and harassed them. The dozen or so police officers remaining at the scene did little to deter the extremists, who continued their chants. Then they began to hurl stones. The demonstrators crouched on the street, held their hands over their heads, and shouted at the police to do something. "I actually feared for my life," khulud said. "These people had death in their eyes. I saw it."

Eventually, officers in riot gear arrived and escorted the protesters along a road to a nearby junction. The mob behind them continued to throw stones. "The police told us to sit down. They started talking to each other, trying to decide what to do." When a city bus came up the road, one of the officers signaled the driver to stop. The officer then ordered all the passengers to get off the bus and all the protesters to get on. Once aboard, the protesters updated their Facebook pages to let their friends know what was going on. Khulud's friends asked where the bus was taking them. "I don't know. Maybe to Gaza," she joked.

The commandeered city bus stopped at Maxim restaurant, of all places, where a battalion of armed riot police, a water cannon, and a private bus were waiting. The demonstrators switched buses. "We still had no idea what was happening or where we were going," khulud said, but as soon as the second bus started moving, they all began to relax. "Then suddenly, all the windows shattered." Broken glass littered the floor of the bus as the protesters cowered and shouted at the driver to keep going. The extremists had been tailing the demonstrators in their cars, and waited for them to pass before launching a coordinated assault. "I guess they had military tactics," khulud said. She was shaken, but after this final attack, the extremists left them alone.

The bus dropped everyone off in Wadi Nisnas. "That is the first moment I felt safe," khulud said. But comfort quickly morphed into anger. "I felt like I was home. And why? Because I am in my own ghetto. I am angry that this is the only place in Haifa where I can feel completely safe." Khulud believes that if the protesters had demonstrated in Wadi Nisnas, or in another Arab neighborhood, there would have been no such violence. Israeli riot police occasionally disperse demonstrations in Wadi Nisnas and in the Arab villages of the Galilee, but marches there rarely fuel such hatred and violence. "We demonstrated in Carmel Center. It is not a Palestinian area. We invaded the Jewish public space. This is why they came after us."

Khulud leaned back on the sofa, weary from retelling this particular story. Then she glanced at my coffee cup. "Do you want more coffee?" I told her I didn't. "Can you please eat something, then? I don't want you writing that you went to khulud's house and she is such a terrible host. I'm really bad at these kinds of things." She pointed at a bowl of fruit on the table. "Have an apple." I grabbed one, and khulud said, "I need a cigarette."

I followed her outside into her garden, where she lit a Pall Mall. From her garden we had a clear view into the green valley below. "You can hear coyotes at night. And we have wild boars," she said. Khulud lives in a conservative Jewish neighborhood that is the territorial and cultural opposite of Wadi Nisnas. "I have right-wing neighbors," she said. "My friends laugh at me. They ask how I can live here. I'm playing it dumb. I am not getting into any political arguments or discussions with anybody. I don't need that in my life, because I know that these are not people I can convince."

When we went back inside, khulud mixed me a cup of Nescafé—"I never developed a taste for Arabic coffee," she said—then led me back to the living room. I told her about the photograph of the girl in the green dress. "These are the sorts of pictures we need to reach the West," she said. "Not pictures of bloody bodies. We are good at showing the world pictures of bloody bodies. But they shut it out. They don't see it. It's too difficult to see. In my writing, I have to talk about everyday things. This is what I do. I talk about the daily realities. A bus being bombed is one of them, but it is not the only one."

5

If You Can Hear the Rockets,
Then You Are Alive

I wanted to go to Gaza because of something Mahmoud Abu Hash-hash in Ramallah told me about the writers there. The honesty of their work—what he called "the poetry of destruction"—astonishes him. "When you go through a frightful experience of war, and you see death with your eyes, and you lose some people close to you, it is a real experience," he said. "And you want to reveal that experience in those texts." Nowhere in Palestine did literature, and art in general, seem so vital. "Art is the only way to keep their balance and humanity."

More than this, I wanted to visit because all I knew of Gaza came from reports of cruelty, death, and destruction. Gaza is one of the world's most overcrowded places. The 2016 birth of a boy named Waleed Shaath bumped the population of this tiny finger of land—forty kilometers long and only six kilometers wide at its narrowest point—to two million souls. But Gaza is more often defined by tragedy than the statistics of geography. The territory stands as a physical embodiment of despair. Gaza is where rockets fly and buildings fall and children die. There is no word imbued with less beauty than *Gaza*. No word less poetic. Gaza is the buzz of fighter jets tearing the sky. Gaza is the drone of a drone.

Plutarch, though, named Gaza *aromatophora*—the dispenser of perfumes. Darwish wrote that Gaza "is the most beautiful among us, the purest, the richest, and most worthy of love." Gaza lies along the Mediterranean Sea, after all. There must be more to this ancient sliver of coastline than rubble and ruin. Surely I could find something beautiful.

"I don't usually pick up hitchhikers," the Israeli driver said as she reached back and moved some boxes aside to clear a place for me in her backseat. "Especially with all that is going on. But I heard your voice and could tell you are not an Arab."

What was going on was a wave of violence that some observers called the Third Intifada or, luridly, the Intifada of the Knives. It was autumn 2015, and the attacks had been going on for a few weeks. Already Palestinians had killed seventeen Israelis and injured many more. One man stabbed four civilians and a soldier with a screwdriver in Tel Aviv. Another killed a rabbi by running over him with his car. Most chilling was how young some of the attackers were. A boy pretending to sell candy tried to knife a security guard. A thirteen-year-old Palestinian stabbed and nearly killed a thirteen-year-old Israeli riding past on his bicycle. None of the attackers appeared to be affiliated with any particular militant group. Israeli security forces killed many of the terrorists at the scene, sometimes well after the assailants posed any danger. The practice angered observers in Israel, Palestine, and elsewhere, who accused police and soldiers of summarily executing attackers on the street instead of arresting them.

The randomness and gruesome intimacy of the attacks left me shaken. Blood had puddled in the streets near my hotel in East Jerusalem the day I arrived. Police stood behind barricades everywhere, and a white surveillance blimp hovered lazily over Jerusalem's Old City. One night, after indulging in my triptych ritual of Palestinian vice—Arabic coffee, nargileh pipe, and Taybeh Beer—I realized I'd forgotten my wallet at my hotel two streets away. The fifteen-minute walk to fetch my wallet, bring it to the restaurant, and then return to my hotel terrified me. What if one of these young stabbers chooses me? What if I accidentally stumble into a fracas of blades and bullets? The fear was illogical, no doubt. Most fear is. But in all my travels to Jerusalem over the years my chest had never felt so tight.

I'd planned on entering Gaza a few days earlier, but an Israeli jet had bombed an apartment building there, killing a pregnant woman and her three-year-old daughter. I feared this attack would mark the beginning of another war, so I opted to stay in Jerusalem to see if the situation escalated. My decision frustrated Nedal, my fixer in Gaza, who considered my hesitation unwarranted. "There are no problems here," he wrote to me in an email. I hung back anyway, passing a couple of nervous days in Jerusalem reading the news, listening to the sirens outside my window, and wondering if I was in over my head.

The Israeli airstrike turned out to be an isolated incident rather than the opening salvo in a larger conflict. So I took a bus to Asqalan, the closest city of any size to Gaza, where I figured I could find a bus to Gaza's Erez Crossing. This was foolish. Israel's public bus company does not offer service to Gaza, a territory Israelis are forbidden to enter. I decided to walk the four kilometers to Erez and had made it about halfway when the Israeli woman picked me up. She dropped me at the checkpoint, where a crowd of about a dozen people waited for the Israeli border guards to open the gate. Most of those waiting were elderly and infirm Palestinians returning from hospital appointments in Israel. They sat in wheelchairs or hobbled along on crutches. I waited on a metal bench for two hours before the gate clanged open, but only Palestinians were allowed to enter. "There are too many boys at the border fence throwing stones," a young soldier said from her glassed-in booth. "It is not safe for you." She suspected the demonstrations along the fence would not end until sundown and suggested I return the next day. "Come early. Before the stone-throwers wake up."

I hired a taxi to return to Asqalan and arranged for the driver to bring me back to Erez at eight thirty the next morning. I'd beaten the protesters to the border, but the soldier at the gate said I still couldn't cross. She gave me no reason. "Maybe it will open at ten o'clock," she said. It didn't. The gate finally slid open at noon, and I entered the Israeli border post, a bright and clean building laid with polished tile. The feeling of welcome startled me. The place resembled the arrivals lounge at Ben Gurion Airport.

The checkpoint's aesthetics of hospitality faded once I showed my documents to a soldier in a glass booth and navigated the gauntlet of security architecture behind her. I followed a yellow arrow and a sign reading, simply, GAZA in Hebrew, English, and Arabic and went through a door. More yellow arrows led me into a tight passageway flanked with high steel walls. I wrestled my backpack through the metal turnstile at the end of the hall, then walked across a fenced outdoor courtyard to another turnstile built into a gate of vertical bars. The entire labyrinth reminded me of the checkpoints at Qalandiya and elsewhere in the West Bank. Only here at Erez, no press of bodies struggled to get through. I was completely alone. According to the Israeli agency COGAT (Coordination of Government Activities in the Territories), hundreds of Palestinians pass through Erez each day. But for all I could tell, I was the only person entering Gaza that afternoon.

Once I clanked through the turnstile, I faced the wall of the gray concrete slabs forming Israel's security barrier around Gaza. A thick steel panel at the base of the wall rumbled eerily to the side, remotely triggered by someone watching me through a security camera, revealing a small opening in the wall. Sunlight poured through.

I stepped through the portal into a wide cement pad. A long paved corridor, hemmed in by wire fence and topped with a wavy roof of corrugated steel, stretched across the buffer zone between the wall and Gaza proper. There was still nobody else around. I walked along the corridor until I heard the whir of an approaching golf cart. I stepped aside to let the cart pass, but the Palestinian driver stopped next to me and, without saying a word, gestured for me to take the seat behind him. He turned the cart around, and we sped down the kilometer-long cage until we reached the other side of Gaza's buffer zone. Through the fence, I could see the Israeli guard towers on the border wall looming over a weedy swathe of no-man's-land.

Next, I navigated Gazan security. First, I presented my documents to a Fatah official sitting in a white security trailer at the Hamsa-Hamsa checkpoint. Israel and the Palestinian Authority both regard Hamsa-Hamsa, or 5-5, as the official border post for Gaza. Still, as the man in the trailer flipped through my passport, a poster of Yasser Arafat hanging on the wall behind him, the inspection felt perfunctory. The PA has exercised little authority here since June 2007, when long-simmering tensions between Hamas and Fatah factions erupted into open war on the streets of Gaza. The weeklong battle left more than one hundred people dead and Gaza under Hamas's control.

Darwish railed against the Hamas-Fatah fratricide in one of his last poems, "From Now On You Are Somebody Else." Darwish asks the sparring factions: "Did we have to fall from a great height, and see our own blood on our hands, to realize that we are not angels, as we used to believe?" And he calls Hamas leader Khaled Mashal "the prisoner whose ambition is to inherit the prison." Darwish considered the sort of Islamic fundamentalism espoused by Hamas a disaster for democracy, and he declared that dialogue between the two main Palestinian factions could occur only "if Hamas apologizes for what they did in Gaza." Hamas was unmoved. After Darwish died in 2008, Mashal passive-aggressively sniped that while the poet's death was, indeed, a great loss, "Palestine can give birth to ten Mahmoud Darwishes."

Hamas refused to recognize any sign of Fatah's authority in Gaza. They operated their own border checkpoint, Arba-Arba or 4-4, about a kilometer down the road from Hamsa-Hamsa. Nedal waited for me there. He shook my hand, kissed both my cheeks, and handed me my Hamas-issued entry visa. Hamas officials checked my passport again and searched my bag for alcohol and other contraband. I had nothing illegal with me, but I was less worried about Hamas's rules than Canada's. My government considers Hamas a terrorist organization, and by paying them for my entry visa and temporary residency permit, I'd broken Canada's terrorist financing law. I tried not to think about this.

Nedal and I boarded a taxi to drive us into Gaza City. Our driver, Munir, traveled along Saladin Street, the major thoroughfare connecting Gaza's north and south. Once we passed through the fetid stench of open-air sewage ponds near the Jabaliya refugee camp, we left the smooth highway and turned west toward the seafront through a forest of broken streets. Ramallah's creamy white stones are not found in Gaza. Nor is the pink limestone of Jerusalem. Instead, the same gray of Erez's turnstiles and steel doors extends over the cinder block buildings that rose unsteadily around us. A week later I would meet a young woman who told me about seeing Gaza from a rooftop. The grayness was too ugly to bear, she said, and she never went to the roof again.

We shared the road with packed buses and strange motorcycle-cart hybrids that resembled mechanical centaurs. Women were in hijab or niqab. Children crowded the sides of the streets, boys and girls both, kicking around soccer balls or walking in school-uniformed groups. They added some color to the surrounding drab. So, too, did the graffiti, the soda bottles heaped on donkey carts, and the laundry hung to dry on cracked balconies. Once on the coastal road, we passed a row of fishermen's shacks and chicken coops built of scrap wood and rusted panels of corrugated steel standing on the trash-strewn beach. The sea and sky above were as gray as gunmetal.

I rented an apartment in a building near the port. The building custodian was a young man named Ahmed with slicked-back hair and no English. He lived in a tiny office in the lobby, equipped with a cot and a gas burner on which he brewed coffee. I arrived during one of the city's rolling electricity blackouts, so Ahmed had to switch on the generator to power the elevator. I stood inside the darkened cabin for a few seconds until the fluorescent lights flickered on. Then Ahmed gave me a thumbs-up and pushed the button for the eighth floor.

My two-bedroom flat was far larger than I needed, and full of the sort of polished wooden furniture my Italian relatives favored in the 1980s. A note on the table from my landlord explained how to manage the "eight hours on, eight hours off" electricity schedule, something I never did figure out in the nearly two months I lived there. The note also told me to drink from the plastic tank of water on the kitchen counter. When I ran out, I was to place the empty tank outside my door with a one-shekel coin on top, and Ahmed would refill it. The brackish tap water made for foul showers and left a crystal crust on the rim of my coffee cups each time I washed dishes. My first sip of coffee each morning always tasted of salt.

I could see Gaza City's main fishing docks and the hotels along the seafront road from my window. I felt a jolt when I spotted the Al Deira Hotel. This was the only building in Gaza I knew by sight. I recognized the hotel's red facade from news reports I'd seen during 2014's summer war, Operation Protective Edge. The stretch of beach beside the hotel was where the Bakr boys were killed.

Sometime in the late afternoon on July 16 that year, a group of boys played on the beach and atop a retaining wall near Al Deira's seaside terrace. They were kicking a soccer ball on the sand when an IDF shell struck and the retaining wall exploded into flames. The boys scattered. Then a second shell, fired forty seconds later, hit the boys as they fled. Those who could still walk carried those who couldn't to Al Deira, where international journalists in Gaza to cover the war tended to the bleeding bodies.

The boys were all between nine and twelve years old, which according to Gaza's cruel chronology means they'd already endured two previous wars: the first in 2008, the second in 2012. Ismail, Zakaria, Ahed, and Mohammed Bakr would not survive their third. They lay dead on the harbor wall. The cousins were members of a renowned fishing family that has plied the Gazan coastline for centuries. Family lore claims the Bakrs originated in Saudi Arabia, where they fished the Arabian Sea. Now, however, the Bakr family considers the Mediterranean a source of death and sorrow rather than sustenance. "We were devoted to the sea," Ismail's father told a reporter a year after the attacks, "but not anymore." The broken man still wanders the beach looking for parts of his son's body.

The IDF investigated the incident for a year then exonerated itself.

Military officials declared the killing of the boys a tragic accident, but no laws had been broken. A spokesman said the strike targeted a Hamas compound in an area used "exclusively by militants." The claim contradicted testimony from journalists who witnessed the attack from Al Deira's terrace and saw no militant activity anywhere near the boys.

I've seen a photo, taken the day after the attack, of the four boys laid out on blue stretchers. Their bodies, unnaturally gray in death, lay swaddled in bloodstained sheets and wrapped in the yellow flag of Fatah. Cuts and burns scar the boys' faces. The boy in the immediate foreground seems to be grimacing in pain or fear, as if even death failed to ease his trauma. But I am struck most by the smallness of their bodies. The children were scarcely bigger than my own six-year-old son, and I wondered who could mistake such boys for men.

On his blog, Ala Hlehel wrote a short essay, gnashing and sarcastic, from the perspective of one of the murdered boys:

We ran fast. Children run fast because their bodies are light, and excitement usually controls our movements. We used to run fast in the narrow alleys of Gaza. We are familiar with all of its curves and rough areas. We know by heart all the worn-out houses accumulated over each other, even when they are intermingled and look the same: their construction is not finished. Their colors are like dry cement. Believe me. We are familiar with aesthetics. In class, they taught us about Leonardo da Vinci. But Gaza lacks cement and paint. Even if they were available—poverty is much stronger. . . .

Allow me to apologize to anyone for whom we have ruined the delight of the "rational" and calculated attacks, and Israel's ability to be humane while killing us. We have ruined for you the delight of the "international solidarity" with Israel's pain. Here we are, once more as you see, insisting on dying at the wrong time. Even in death, we are illogical and impractical. Is there any enemy like us? Cruel and coarse as such?

A few days after I arrived in Gaza, a woman named Haneen, whose sister I know back in Canada, brought me to the same stretch of beach. Haneen's children were involved in a youth sailing program run by a Norwegian NGO, and we watched as a group of preteens practiced piloting tiny fiberglass boats. While they waited their turns, the others ran and splashed in the water, the girls in sodden T-shirts over their bathing suits and the boys bare chested. The setting sun gilded their bodies gold.

I couldn't help but think of the Bakr cousins, and I told Haneen I was surprised there was not some sort of memorial built here on the beach for them. She shrugged. "It was four boys," she said. "Five hundred children died in that war. What do we build for the rest of them?"

A Palestinian in the West Bank once told me that Gazans are lucky. In 2005, Israel dismantled its settlements in Gaza and marched its military out of the strip. Gaza is now the only place where one can fully live as a Palestinian among Palestinians. There are no Israelis in Gaza. No settlers and no soldiers. Gazans don't face humiliations at checkpoints or gaze upon the settlements that loom atop the hills. In Gaza, at least, the occupation is invisible.

Abeer Ayyoub draws little comfort from this unseen occupation. I met the young journalist for breakfast a couple of times during my stay in Gaza. On one of these mornings, she told me about a recent—and rare—visit to Jerusalem. It was the first time she'd seen Israeli soldiers in thirteen years. Abeer recounted how a friend in Jerusalem told her how hard it was to look the occupation in the eye on a daily basis. "I told him how much harder it was to feel the occupation every minute in Gaza," she said, "and never have the privilege to look it in the eye."

But Gaza is less under occupation than under siege. After the Hamas takeover in 2007, Israel declared Gaza a "hostile entity" and imposed a sweeping blockade on the territory. Israel controls who can travel in and out of Gaza. Usually only merchants with permits, medical patients, and a weekly quota of worshippers who want to pray in Jerusalem are allowed to pass through Erez. For most Gazans, leaving the territory via Erez is impossible. Israel vets all goods that enter Gaza, too, and decides which Gazan products can be exported and sold outside the territory. Israel even determines how long the lights stay on. Israel bombed Gaza's only power station in 2006 and then restricted the import of parts needed to rebuild it. This, combined with ongoing disputes between Hamas and the PA over who should pay for the station's fuel and another Israeli airstrike on the plant in 2014, means that for a decade most Gazans have not enjoyed more than eight consecutive hours of electricity.

Ziyad Fahed Bakr does not feel lucky to be in Gaza. The young fisherman—no doubt related somehow to the slain Bakr cousins—took me out in his boat one morning and told me about trying to make a living under the blockade. Israel decides how far from the coastline Gaza's fishermen can sail, expanding and shrinking the zone as they see fit. High-quality fish like sea bream and tuna prefer the distant reefs and rocks to the sandy sea bottom near the shoreline, but fishermen who dare cross the navy-enforced line risk being boarded, detained, or shot. Ziyad rolled up his pant leg to show me the smooth round scars from Israeli bullets. Few fish are left swimming in the nearby waters. "Sometimes I get lucky on windy days when the sea bream drift close to shore," Ziyad said. Usually, though, he only catches tiny sardines that fetch low prices at the market. "Some days I make no money at all," he said.

Farmer Abdusalam al-Manasrah did not feel lucky, either. His family has owned land in eastern Gaza since the days of the Ottomans. "Every speck of soil is mixed with my sweat and the sweat of my father, my grandfather, and my grandmother," he told me. But ancestral ownership means little in the shadow of the border. During the Second Intifada, the Israeli army bulldozed Abdusalam's ancient olive trees to create better sightlines from their positions along the border fence. Abdusalam planted wheat where his trees used to be, but the army burned the fields when the wheat grew too high. The IDF expanded the buffer zone in 2005 and again during the war in 2008. Abdusalam's family fields lie completely in no-man's-land now. He cannot access them at all. "Maybe you can reach the buffer zone line," he said when I asked what would happen if I tried to walk to his fields. "After the line, the soldiers will shoot warning shots. If you keep walking, they will shoot the ground in front of your feet. Within one hundred meters, I don't know. Maybe your legs. Maybe your heart."

The Karawan Café stands down an alleyway just off Omar al-Mukhtar Street, a boulevard of clothing stores, restaurants, and ice cream shops that forms Gaza's main commercial thoroughfare. Although the café was a twenty-minute walk from my apartment, Karawan immediately became my local haunt, my Gazan replacement for Café Ramallah. I'd go there most afternoons to sit on a plastic chair and write in my notebook on one of the café's wobbly tables. Young men in jeans and ball caps stared at their smart-phones while older men in open-collared shirts played cards. Occasionally, school-aged boys walked through the café selling cigarettes. Although posters of both Yasser Arafat and Hamas founder Sheikh Yassin hang on Karawan's tiled walls, fixed in place by black electrical tape, everyone in Gaza knows that Karawan is a café for Fatah supporters. Hamas sympathizers, known as *hamsawi*, take their coffee and nargileh elsewhere.

The head waiter patrolled the café taking orders. He was tall and thin and as constantly in motion as the flies that tormented the glasses of sweet tea he delivered. He carried tongs and a tin brazier of burning coals to replenish shrunken briquettes on his customers' nargilehs, and he shouted tea and coffee orders to his minions in the back. After only two visits, he already called me *habibi* and brought me an Arabic coffee and a lemon-mint nargileh as soon as I sat down.

I first learned of the Karawan Café from *The Drone Eats with Me*, Atef Abu Saif's diary of 2014's Operation Protective Edge. Atef writes of coming to the café from his home in the Jabaliya refugee camp every morning for seventeen years and the importance of keeping up his daily routine in the midst of war. "We have to recapture some normality, to reclaim some of the life we had before," Atef writes. "The Karawan Café is a very important ingredient of this normality." I was pleased, then, when Atef suggested we meet at Karawan. We sat outside the front door with our coffees while traffic noise from the nearby Saraya junction filled the spaces in between our conversation.

Atef never intended his journals from the war to become a book. On the fourth day, his London editor sent him an email to ask how he was doing. In reply, Atef translated what he'd written in his journal into English and sent it to his editor, who in turn posted the journal entry on the publisher's website. Atef liked the idea of people outside Gaza reading his account of the war, so he started writing his daily journals in English and sending them to London. Atef didn't know that his editor was also passing the entries along to newspapers, such as the *New York Times*, the *Guardian*, and the *Sunday Times*, which were reprinting them. "During the war, sometimes we only had electricity for two hours. I would use those two hours just to write my diaries, so I wouldn't check the internet," he said. Occasionally, Atef walked to the camp's internet café to write on its computers because it had a generator. The café owner knew Atef and chased out the kids playing video games. "He would say to them, 'Leave mister to work,' then he would lock the door until I finished my story."

Atef derived no pleasure from writing his war diaries, but he considered them necessary. During the two previous wars in Gaza—Operation Cast Lead in 2008 and Operation Pillar of Defense in 2012—Gazans knew places where they could feel safe from the Israeli bombing runs. They waited out the fighting in the homes of friends and family who lived in neighborhoods they figured would be spared. But nowhere felt safe in 2014. The destruction was widespread. Everyone I spoke to about Protective Edge told me the same thing: they never knew if they would see another day. "The action of writing is a testimony of my survival," Atef said. "When I am writing, I am proving that I am alive."

Atef also felt compelled to tell stories that the journalists sent to cover the war refused to tell. "I wanted to get out the humanity which war wants you to lose," he said. Atef describes how his family endured the fifty days of fighting and struggled to observe Gaza's Ramadan traditions during the bombings. He writes about how his son just wanted to go to the internet café to play soccer video games, and about a distraught man living in a UN-run shelter who begged for a few minutes of privacy to make love to his wife. In the media, Gazans appear as mere pieces of news. Atef wants to make them pieces of literature. That way they last forever.

In the footnotes of *Drone*, Atef gives the full names and ages of those killed in the fighting. The long list of victims, often members of the same family, challenges the sterile statistics of conventional war reporting. This was another of Atef's intentions: to honor those lives that, through their ending, have been reduced to numbers. Atef writes:

> When a human being is made into a number, his or her story disappears. Every number is a tale; every martyr is a tale, a life lost. . . . The Kawareh family—from Khan Younis, whom the drone decided to prevent from enjoying a meal on the roof of their small building under the moonlight—they were not just "SIX." They were six infinitely rich, infinitely unknowable stories that came to a stop when a dumb missile fell from a drone and tore their bodies apart. Six novels that Mahfouz, Dickens, or Márquez could not have written satisfactorily. Novels that would have needed a miracle, a genius, to find the structure and poetry they deserved. Instead, they are tales that have cascaded into the news as numbers: moments of lust; onslaughts of pain; days of happiness; dreams that were postponed; looks, glances, feelings, secrets. . . . Every number is a world in itself.

Atef does not write about Hamas in *Drone*, nor about the rockets they sent over the border into Israel, which many observers blamed for the Israeli airstrikes. I asked him if this was a deliberate omission. "I am not reporting on the war," Atef said. "I am writing from the perspective of a family. A family that is besieged and being attacked. Feeling that they might die suddenly. Feeling like they don't belong to the minute. Things happen out of their control, and they want to bring order to their little world. Their little living room. Their little kitchen. The rockets are always in the background, but it's not me who can write about them."

The Drone Eats with Me is something of a departure for Atef. He is best known as a writer of short stories, a genre particularly associated with Gaza's unique geopolitical history. Many of Gaza's writers fled after the 1967 war, and the literary scene collapsed under the weight of occupation. Israeli authorities shut down all the printing presses in Gaza to cripple communication between Palestinian resistance groups. Gazan novelists had no way to publish their work. Young writers, not to be defeated, started to write short stories and novellas, which were more easily hand copied and smuggled to Jerusalem, where they could be published. According to Atef, Palestinian literary circles once knew Gaza as "the exporter of oranges and short stories." Few oranges leave the territory these days, and Gaza now boasts a wealth of writers in all genres, but the short story remains a Gazan specialty.

Atef's parents and grandparents fled their home and orange orchards in Jaffa in 1948 and settled in Gaza City's Jabaliya refugee camp. Atef was born in the camp in 1973. By then the camp, like all Palestinian refugee camps, had grown from a collection of tents into a crowded ghetto of cinder block buildings. Atef always longed for Jaffa, even as a boy, and named his daughter after the city his family was forced to abandon. "For Palestinians, Jaffa is the lost dream," Atef said. "When Palestinians talk about the Nakba, they talk about Jaffa, because it was one of the biggest Arab cities at the time. It was the second most important cultural hub after Cairo." Before 1948, Jaffa's newspapers were published throughout the Arab world, and the city hosted the second-largest Arab radio channel. "If you were a big singer, you had to come to Jaffa to sing."

Atef learned about Jaffa from his blind grandmother, Aisha. "She lost her ability to see because she cried too much for her son, who died in the war," he said. When he was a boy, Atef used to sit with his grandmother and listen to her endless stories—many about her "beautiful youth" spent in Jaffa. Atef believed that she would have been a great novelist. "She could take your heart for five hours," Atef said. "Her way of telling stories was brilliant, and I hope by the end of my life I can manage to tell stories like she used to."

When he was ten years old, Atef started writing his grandmother's stories down. Once the First Intifada began in 1987, he began to write his own. "I was a very naughty boy at that time," Atef said. He and his friends used to hurl stones at Israeli soldiers at the military checkpoints. During one of these clashes, an IDF soldier shot Atef in the face with a rubber bullet. The wounds were severe. "I was supposed to die," he said. "My family even dug a grave for me." Atef continued his actions against the IDF at the checkpoints after he recovered. He was eventually arrested and jailed for three months in an Israeli prison in the Negev Desert.

Atef realizes that many of his readers, both in Palestine and abroad, expect his work to be overtly political. "People are not ready to listen to you if you are not talking about wars or Hamas," he said. But for Atef, who was born in Gaza and still lives in Jabaliya's narrow alleyways with his wife and children, Gaza is no metaphor. "Gaza is not only a place that produces news. It produces life as well." Gazans don't want to read shouted refrains of resistance or vows to survive in the face of the siege. They want to read stories.

In addition to *The Drone Eats with Me*, Atef has published five novels and two books of short stories along with several books of political writing. He also edited and contributed to an anthology of Gazan short stories called *The Book of Gaza: A City in Short Fiction*. Atef's last novel, *A Suspended Life*, was shortlisted for the 2015 International Prize for Arabic Fiction, a prestigious award dubbed the Arab Booker. Atef wanted to attend the award ceremony in Casablanca, but Hamas authorities stopped him at the Erez checkpoint and denied him an exit permit. In response, Atef penned a long screed against Hamas. He accused the authority of silencing artistic expression and contributing nothing to cultural life in Gaza since coming to power in 2007. "How many books has Hamas printed?" Atef wrote. "How many literary festivals has it sponsored and organized? . . . How much talent was nurtured? How many cinemas have been built? How many literary competitions were held to strengthen the contemporary literary scene?" Public support for Atef compelled Hamas to relent, but not in time. He never made it to Casablanca.

The award itself meant little to Atef. "I don't need anyone to clap for me," he said. The only audience Atef cares about is his storytelling grandmother Aisha. "One of my dreams is that I write a novel so good that my grandmother will come from out of her grave to enjoy it."

In his 2008 diaries, *A River Dies of Thirst*, Mahmoud Darwish wrote about destroyed houses, and the objects they contain, as victims of war. "The house as a casualty is also mass murder, even if it is empty of its inhabitants," Darwish wrote.

> In every object there is a being in pain—a memory of fingers, of a smell, an image. And houses are killed just like their inhabitants. And the memory of objects is killed: stone, wood, glass, iron, cement are scattered in broken fragments like living beings. And cotton, silk, linen, papers, books are torn to pieces like proscribed words. Plates, spoons, toys, records, taps, pipes, door handles, fridges, washing machines, flower vases, jars of olives and pickles, tinned food all break just like their owners. . . . Rent agreements, marriage documents, birth certificates, water and electricity bills, identity cards, passports, love letters are torn to shreds like their owners' hearts. . . . All these things are a memory of the people who no longer have them and of the objects that no longer have the people—destroyed in a minute. Our things die like us, but they aren't buried with us.

More than twenty thousand houses were casualties of Operation Protective Edge. The fighting destroyed nearly every home in Khuza'a, a town in southern Gaza near the Egyptian border. International donors provided Khuza'a's residents converted shipping containers to live in. More than a year had passed since the war ended, but most of these people were still living in the "caravans." Haneen needed to interview the caravan residents for the NGO she worked for, and she invited me to come along.

Aside from a few demolished buildings, I hadn't seen much evidence of the 2014 war in Gaza City. Much of the rubble had been cleared in the year since the bombing stopped. But the remnants of war littered the road to Khuza'a. We passed buildings with concrete roofs that sagged, almost comically, on the broken bodies of houses. Chunks of concrete hung suspended on dangling rebar like nightmarish necklaces. Salvage crews had sorted the wreckage into tidy heaps of pipe, smashed cinder block, and twisted metal the size of the atomized homes they'd originally come from. Enormous tangles of rebar resembled the nests of something giant and demonic. I saw a freakish pile of bicycle wheels. Bullet holes spread over walls like a pox.

The caravans seemed cheerful in the midst of this destruction. Dozens were assembled into little neighborhoods divided by dirt roads where women hung laundry and young boys kicked soccer balls. A woman shelling beans outside one of the caravans greeted Haneen and me, introduced herself as Fadda, and invited us inside. Fadda lived in the caravan with her sons and their families. Nine people in all shared the two bedrooms, single bathroom, and sitting room. After their homes were destroyed in the war's early days, the families waited out the bombings in one of the United Nations Relief and Works Agency (UNRWA) schools that had been repurposed into a shelter. When the war ended, the family lived in tents for three months while waiting for the caravans to be set up. They had been living in the caravan for over a year.

The family had expanded the caravan during that time, adding a larger kitchen space and a sitting area laid with rugs. A television stood in one corner of the room while posters of martyred men hung on the walls. A cluster of dates dangled from the ceiling in the middle of the kitchen next to a fridge and a pair of gas burners. A set of shelves strained under enough cookware and dishes to supply a small restaurant.

Food itself, though, was scarce. UNRWA hands out food coupons for staples such as rice, cooking oil, and powdered milk—though not nearly enough, Fadda said. Her husband cannot work, and her sons are all unemployed. The family earns a little money in the fall helping local farmers with the olive harvest, but only enough to buy vegetables, dry beans, and perhaps a weekly chicken. Sometimes they receive lamb when somebody performs *aqiqah*—a religious tradition in which a family who has been blessed with a new child pays their good fortune forward to the poor. If a woman gives birth to a boy, her family will slaughter two sheep and distribute the meat to the poor. A baby girl warrants only a single sheep.

Cooking no longer brings Fadda and her daughters any pleasure.

She told me she lost the emotional connection to food she had when she cooked in her home instead of a temporary shelter and slaughtered the goats and chickens she raised herself. "We don't have the same soul," Fadda said, "and we can't be as generous as we were before." Still, Fadda offered to heat up some of the pumpkin stew she'd made for lunch that day.

Haneen and I left Fadda and her daughters to visit another cluster of caravans next to the crater where Khuza'a's mosque once stood. In the precarious shadow of the leaning minaret—the only part of the mosque left standing—a team of salvage workers straightened tangles of twisted rebar from the rubble. En route to the caravans, we passed a makeshift kitchen assembled out of plastic tarps, broken cinder blocks, and sheets of corrugated steel. Inside, a woman baked bread in a clay oven. She waved us in.

The woman knelt in front of the squat oven between a basket of flattened dough and a pile of hot pita. An olive branch protruded out of the side of the oven, its one end burning red inside. Two eggplants softened atop the oven next to a bubbling pot of lentil stew. The eggplant would be for dinner, the woman said, the lentils for lunch. She would line a tray with torn pieces of fresh pita and top it with the stew. Her family would eat this with lemon, olives, and slices of raw onion—a healthy but meatless meal typical in Gaza's poorer households. The woman put down the wire rod she was using to turn the bread and, without looking up, scooped me a wooden spoonful of lentils. "Have some," she said. "Does it need salt?"

Gazans have long prepared meals in such a way. Clay ovens are as old as Gaza itself. But their resurgence has the blockade to thank. With cooking gas expensive and often inaccessible, many Gazans cook in the clay ovens their grandmothers used to use. The wood-fired ovens are a practical return to an ancient routine. I wondered, though, where Gazans found the firewood. Gaza boasts no forests, after all. The woman told me that firewood is plentiful these days. Gazans fuel their wood-burning ovens with the carcasses of fruit and olive trees the Israeli army bulldozed in the last war.

I traveled to Bayt Lahiya, a village just south from the Erez Crossing, to meet Nedal and his family for a Friday lunch. His mother roasted a chicken for us, which we ate with a mound of yellow rice in her cool kitchen. Afterward, Nedal flagged down a car, and we drove into the orchards outside the village where his family grows citrus near the border. They keep a small shack on the edge of the property, but Nedal couldn't find where his father had hidden the key. We dragged our fingers along the top of every window ledge and probed every space between the stones until we gave up. Instead, we sat outside and ate oranges off the trees. A heap of peels had formed at my feet by the time Nedal's father arrived to pluck the key from its hiding place—hanging on a tiny nail on a fence post we'd failed to examine.

Bayt Lahiya is better known for its strawberries than its oranges. Everyone agrees that Palestine's best strawberries grow in the rich and sandy soil here. At least they used to. Before the blockade, Bayt Lahiya's farmers exported their sweet berries as far afield as the Netherlands. Now few strawberries leave Gaza at all. Restrictions on the import of herbicides and irrigation equipment and the rising cost of fuel used to power the water pumps mean that many farmers have decided to grow less water-intensive crops.

Nedal fetched a kettle and burner from inside the shack and brewed tea. As the water boiled, I heard gunfire nearby and saw black smoke rising from near the border fence. Nedal pretended not to notice until I asked him if there were clashes. I'd read a story the previous day about Gazan youth burning tires at the border to provide cover for their attempts to breach the security fence. Nedal said no. He said the smoke and gunshots came from military exercises being held by Palestinian Islamic Jihad, an Iran-inspired militant organization devoted to the destruction of Israel. The PIJ operated a training facility and firing range nearby. Nedal pointed to its watchtower and black and yellow flag, brazenly within both the sight and range of the Israeli outposts on the other side of the border fence. I wasn't sure I believed Nedal about the exercises. I suspected my initial hesitation entering Gaza convinced Nedal I was easily spooked, and I wondered if he was downplaying the clashes so I wouldn't worry.

Another farmer came up the dirt path to greet us. Nedal introduced me to him, and the farmer insisted I see his trees. I followed him into his orchards and filled my pockets with lemons and kumquats he plucked for me—I would crush them into lemonade in my apartment the next day.

When we reached a grapefruit tree, its branches sagging with the weight of ripe fruit, the man invited me to choose a grapefruit for myself. He nodded at my selection, as if I'd picked a good one. We used the man's knife to tear away the peels and ate our grapefruits beneath the tree that bore them. When we were finished, fingers sticky with juice, the man gave me a pomelo nearly the size of my head as a final gift.

Nedal and I returned to the shack, and he prepared another pot of tea. As we lounged, Nedal told me that unlike most Gazans, he'd rather spend time in these orchards than on the beach. "I hate the sea," he said. "The sea is only for dark things." He told me how Israeli sailors shoot at fishing boats, and how their naval vessels shell Gaza during the war. And the sea brings nothing to Gaza. No escape. No life. Nedal harbors no affection for long blue Mediterranean views. "My color is green," he said. He gestured to the citrus trees that surrounded us. For Nedal, the trees represent the hard work of people trying to provide for their families under the pressure of the blockade. "This is what I love," he said. "I want to see rows of trees. One after the other." Especially, he said, in the winter when the oranges grow cold on their branches. "I sit beneath them and drink tea and smoke nargileh." Huddled in his family's orchards, Nedal cannot see the horizon, but there is nothing for him in the distance anyway. "Everything I need is here."

Lara, my soft-voiced translator, was one of the few people I knew in Gaza who was not descended from refugees. Her family were true *Ghazzawis* who lived in Gaza long before the Nakba. At twenty-three years old, she is already a professor of war. Lara can identify Israeli ordnance by the different ways the ground shakes after each explosion.

I joined Lara and her husband, Jehad, frequently at their apartment or at the garden café nearby, where we'd pull long drags on nargileh pipes. I met no Palestinian who smoked as much nargileh as Lara. I recall one of these nights in Lara and Jehad's flat. We were listening to music, drinking tea, and discussing our favorite movies when the power in the apartment suddenly went out. Jehad stopped talking in mid-sentence, looked up at the darkened lamp in the corner, and said to no one in particular, "They always have to remind us where we are."

The first interview Lara translated for me was with the author Gharib Asqalani. He welcomed Lara and me into his home on the edge of the Shati refugee camp. Like every Palestinian whose home I visited, Gharib offered us coffee. But instead of making some himself, he directed Lara to the kitchen. "There is the pot on the sink and the coffee on the shelf," he said to her. Lara shot me a look of bemused irritation but dutifully stood to make our coffee.

Gharib was still an infant in 1948 when Israeli soldiers swept through what was then known as the Gaza subdistrict. The occupation forces emptied forty-five out of fifty-six towns and villages in the area, including al-Majdal Asqalan, where Gharib had been born a few months earlier. He and his family escaped into the Gaza Strip along with the more than two hundred thousand terrified refugees who sought sanctuary among Gaza's eighty thousand residents. Gaza swelled. The territory represented only one-hundredth of the area of Mandate Palestine but housed a quarter of the Palestinian population after the war. One historian wrote that Gaza had become "an involuntary Noah's Ark."

Gharib's family settled in Gaza City, where his father found work as a tailor and cloth trader. They lived for a while in a rented house until Gharib's father realized that the family might lose its refugee status unless they lived in a camp. They moved their home and business into Shati refugee camp, where his father operated a textile factory. "Other high-quality cloth was imported and expensive," Gharib said. "My father sold his cloth to the other refugees for a good price."

Like many Palestinian adolescents in the 1950s, Gharib grew up reading the works of Marx and Engels, but this leftist philosophy made little sense to Gharib as a young Gazan refugee. "In the camps, I didn't see the rich living on the blood of the poor as Marx described," Gharib said. "Here the rich and poor were both expelled from their land. And there was no work for anyone."

Gharib's father, though, knew how to create work. He purchased a small plot of land near the Bureij refugee camp and planted strawberries and orange trees. He urged Gharib to study agriculture. "I have land," his father said. "So if you get an agriculture degree, you will have a job." Gharib agreed and traveled to Egypt in 1965 to study agricultural engineering at Alexandria University. Gharib had completed only his second year when Israel occupied Gaza in 1967. His family could no longer export their oranges, and the Israelis restricted the amount of water allocated to the farm. Gharib suggested to his father that they should either sell the farm or build homes or warehouses on the land. His father refused. "This is a farm, and it will remain a farm," he said. Gharib's father uprooted the orange groves and planted olive trees in their place. He knew olives could survive the drought the Israelis imposed on them. "My father taught me another form of resistance. Not to resist by weapons, but by staying," Gharib said. This was another example of *sumud*, the Palestinian concept of steadfastness.

The olive trees would take years to mature, so after graduation Gharib worked on agricultural projects in the Palestinian refugee camps in Jordan. When political friction between the refugees and the Jordanian government hit its peak in 1970, Gharib left for Damascus. He worked in Syria's al-Raqqah camp—"now full of ISIS," he said—then as an agricultural engineer on the Euphrates Dam. During this time, he married a woman he'd met while a student in Egypt. "She was from Gaza, we married in Jordan, and we lived in Syria," Gharib said. They returned to Gaza after the birth of their first son.

The sort of large-scale agricultural and irrigation projects Gharib had worked on in Jordan and Syria did not exist in Gaza. "The Israelis would not allow it," he said. "They wanted the Gazan economy to be controlled by Israelis, not Palestinians." His father's olive orchards were not yet bearing fruit, and Gharib did not want to labor on someone else's farm. He found a job teaching biology and physics. "I thought this would be a temporary job, but I ended up teaching for twenty years."

Gharib had been writing songs and love poems since he was a teenager, but he never had ambitions to become a professional writer. After his return to Gaza, though, he started gathering with the other authors he knew. "We thought we were the most important people in Gaza," he said. "We were the master intellectuals." Gharib and his colleagues wrote political poems and stories and considered themselves "resistance writers."

On Fridays, Gharib and his writing friends would find seats on the early morning buses that brought *Ghazzawi* day laborers to their jobs in Israel. The writers would alight in Tel Aviv and walk to Jaffa, where they'd buy Arabic-language newspapers from a communist shopkeeper they all knew. "We had to go early, otherwise the workers would buy them all," Gharib said. From Jaffa, they'd travel north along the coast to Haifa to visit Emile Habibi, a writer and communist member of the Israeli Knesset. They would sit in the offices of *Al-Ittihad*—the communist magazine Habibi edited—to drink coffee and listen to Habibi pontificate. "We used to call him colleague, but he always called us boys," Gharib said. Habibi published much of their early work in *Al-Ittihad*, and he encouraged them to enter writing contests. "He was like a prophet for us," Gharib said.

After their time with Habibi, Gharib's caravan traveled eastward to Nazareth to meet with "another prophet," Tawfiq Ziad. Like Habibi, Ziad was both a writer and a left-wing politician. He served as the mayor of Nazareth and the head of Rakah, a Palestinian communist political party.

During these visits, Ziad would chat with his Gazan comrades and sell them cheap translations of Russian books Rakah used to get for free. Gharib and his weary friends would then head back to Gaza. The entire journey took about fourteen hours.

I envied Gharib's Palestinian *On the Road* adventures. "I would love to do this trip," I told him.

He laughed. "Bring me permission from the Israelis, and we can do it together."

Gharib and his friends occasionally wrote romantic stories and poems, but they never published them. Their work was proudly political. Gharib's 1978 novel *The Collar* described an Israeli siege on Gaza when Palestinian fighters ambushed IDF soldiers in Shati refugee camp's narrow maze of streets. "The resistance used the alleyways as a trap," Gharib said. Ariel Sharon, the Israeli defense minister at the time, ordered the army to bulldoze a row of houses to widen the roads. Then they surrounded the camp with a fence—the collar of the book's title. Gharib wrote about the siege, the rubble left behind by Israeli bulldozers, and how women tossed oranges over the fence to feed the trapped fighters. Copies of *The Collar* were smuggled to political prisoners inside Israel. A sympathetic librarian in Gaza helped the wives of prisoners disguise the books by replacing *The Collar* covers with covers torn from benign-sounding romance novels. "We smuggled five hundred copies to political prisoners this way," Gharib said.

While his stories have always been overtly political and fueled by a sense of resistance, Gharib was no propagandist. He claims to be one of the first Palestinian writers to abandon overt sloganeering and turn his gaze toward issues of daily life. "After all, you cannot send your lover a kiss with a Kalashnikov," he said. Gharib wrote stories about the lives of regular people decades before the false promises of Oslo compelled Palestine's next generation of writers to do the same.

My favorite story of Gharib's is "A White Flower for David," which Atef Abu Saif included in his *Book of Gaza* anthology. The story examines the complicated relationship between two Palestinians, Mahmud and Haifa, and an Israeli couple, David and Esther. The two couples share a warm and nearly familial friendship. Early in the story, David and Esther visit Gaza to celebrate the birth of Mahmud and Haifa's son, Husam. "Esther was flying high that day as she cradled Husam in his cot. She was captivated by him, swooning over the blackness of his eyes. She caressed his neck and cried out: 'If only we could have a daughter with Arab eyes!'"

David and Esther are written with sympathy. Gharib never casts them as villains even when, years later, inevitable violence strains the bond between the families. During a confrontation in Shati refugee camp between Palestinians and the IDF, Husam joins the boys slinging stones at the soldiers. David, now a soldier himself and on duty in Gaza, points his rifle at Husam. In a panic to save his son from being shot, Mahmud hurls a rock at David and cracks open his friend's skull. In the story's final scene, the two families meet again, this time in David's home in Israel. Esther wears the Palestinian robe Mahmud's mother gave her years earlier, and Mahmud kisses the wound he inflicted on David's forehead. (The "scar was still moist.") The old friends forgive each other. Still, when Husam looks out of David's window and sees a group of soldiers waiting at a bus stop, he longs for his slingshot.

Gharib is hardly a humble man. He believes his life in Gaza was more complicated and nuanced than that of the new generation of Gazan writers. "I've experienced things they have only read about in books," he said, adding that they concern themselves with winning prizes and writing for foreigners. Despite his boasting, it is true that only a Gazan writer from Gharib's era could have written "A White Flower for David." Gharib represents the last generation of Gazans to have known Israelis personally. He grew up in a time when Palestinians could leave Gaza to work for and alongside Israeli Jews. The power dynamic between the occupier and the occupied hung over every friendship, surely, but the walls were not as high and strong then. Palestinians and Israelis did business together, attended each other's family celebrations, and exchanged gifts. Friendships like David and Mahmud's were not uncommon. Two Intifadas and the blockade put an end to this. I was reminded of Mourid Barghouti's claim that Palestinians have "seen the Jew only in khaki, with his finger on the rifle's trigger." Palestinians in Gaza rarely see Israelis at all, and all they exchange are rockets and stones for bullets and bombs.

Some of those bombs rained on the olive orchard Gharib's father left for him. During Operation Cast Lead in 2008, Israeli warplanes destroyed a third of the olive trees his father had planted back in the 1960s. "The grove was close to the border," Gharib said, "and the Israelis thought there were resistance fighters hiding among the trees." Gharib planted new trees after the war. These trees bore fruit for the first time in 2015, and Gharib pressed them into oil. He stood from his chair to fetch a bottle of oil from his kitchen. He held it out for me to see, gold and gleaming, as proud as a grandfather showing photos of his grandchildren. I thought he might give me the bottle, but this oil was too precious to give to a casual visitor. "My sons and grandsons will go to the land and see the trees I planted after the war," Gharib said. "I will pass away one day, but what will remain are my books and my olive trees."

Nearly every Palestinian writer I met in the West Bank and Gaza had some relationship to the Tamer Institute for Community Education. Each one of them referred to the organization as Tamer, with the same inflection and affection they would reserve for a beloved uncle.

Tamer began in 1989 during the height of the First Intifada, when the Israeli military shuttered Birzeit University near Ramallah. Their classes canceled, a group of lecturers from the university decided to teach children at the Shuafat refugee camp in Jerusalem, who were confined to their neighborhoods by regular police roadblocks. The Birzeit teachers gathered the young students together wherever they could find space—in someone's salon, in the shade of a neighborhood tree—and taught them the school lessons they were missing.

The children went back to their regular schools when the Intifada eased, but the teachers who organized the informal classes saw an enduring need for what they called community education, especially regarding child literacy. The volunteers opened an office in Jerusalem and implemented reading programs in both the West Bank and Gaza throughout the early 1990s. After Oslo, they moved their main office to Ramallah, where they organized themselves as the Tamer Institute of Community Education, registered as an official Palestinian NGO, and sought funding from foreign donors. Tamer now runs various literacy campaigns in Palestinian schools. It also organizes writing workshops for young writers, public art projects, and storytelling events with local authors. Tamer's publishing arm prints and distributes children's books by Palestinians like Maya Abu-Alhayyat as well as Arabic translations of books by international authors.

Tamer runs an annual reading campaign every April that it advertises with beautiful posters and billboards. The poster for the 2015 campaign featured a painting of a girl, her arms held aloft and her hair loose, bounding over rooftops beneath the slogan "Something awaits you in this world. Stand for it." The campaign includes storytelling events in schools, libraries, and public spaces throughout Palestine and as far afield as the refugee camps in Jordan and Lebanon.

Part of the programming always includes the Donate a Book campaign. Tamer invites youth to organize into groups and knock on doors in their communities to collect used books from their neighbors. The kids announce they are from Tamer and ask for any books the family may have already read. It is a sort of literary Halloween. Tamer sends the books to poor neighborhoods to supplement their library collections. If the children gather enough books, an entirely new library can be established.

The Donate a Book campaign added a new focus in 2010. Tamer organizers in Gaza realized that most of Gaza's children were born in the 1990s and 2000s and, because of the closed borders, had had no opportunity to see Jerusalem. As they went door to door collecting books, the children also asked their adult neighbors if they'd ever traveled to

Jerusalem. If they had, the volunteers would ask them to recount a story from their visit. The children wrote the stories down so they could have a record of the city they loved but might never reach.

Among all of Tamer's activities, though, I found the My First Book program the most compelling. Every year the foundation invites children between eight and fifteen years old living around Palestine to write a story and send it to Tamer. They ask for illustrations, too, and encourage the young writers to team up with a friend who likes to draw. Hundreds of Palestinian children submit stories each year. Tamer assembles a reading committee that chooses the best fifteen or so stories to be published, along with the illustrations, in the annual edition of *My First Book*. Copies of the collection are distributed to libraries all over Palestine.

Each annual edition of *My First Book* stands as a time capsule of Palestinian life in a given year as seen through the eyes of children. Taken together, the books offer a sort of child's history of Palestine. The *My First Book*s reveal that the time between the two Intifadas, from 1994 to 2000, was an age of optimism for young Palestinians. Children in all regions of Palestine wrote about camping with their families or visiting the sea. They wrote the sort of stories children anywhere might write. Beginning in 2000, however, the traumas of the Second Intifada—soldiers, shelling, checkpoints—started to feature in the texts. Before the Israeli army evicted the settlers from Gaza in 2005, Gazan stories often featured the checkpoint boys of Abo Holi, the Israeli roadblock that divided Gaza in half. Drivers knew they had a better chance of getting past the soldiers if they had children in the car, so enterprising boys charged drivers a few shekels to sit in their backseats. West Bank kids started to write about the "separation" wall as soon as the wall began to rise. Gazan kids started writing stories about wars when bombs started to fall.

For the most part, though, conflict darkened only a few of the stories I read. In the 2013 edition of *My First Book*, a ten-year-old named Saddin from Tulkarem writes about a "scary dinosaur" that becomes a lifelong friend. Shorouq writes of the day the sky over his village rained red mulberries. The young olive tree in Nora's story longs to travel but feels pride when her olives are pressed into oil and become part of the Palestinians who care for her. The girl in nine-year-old Umniya's book wants to be a doctor, and wear glasses and a stethoscope, so she can heal the sick turtle in her garden. Only one story in the collection, about a girl whose painting of Palestinian suffering was censored by the Israelis, was overtly political. The rest possessed an innocence I'd assumed the children of Palestine had long lost. These children wrote like children. I felt a strange relief reading about a world of friendly dinosaurs and magic mulberries rather than a world on fire.

Tamer endured an uneasy relationship with the Hamas government when it first took control of Gaza. Hamas disapproved of boys and girls mixing freely in Tamer's various programs, and the Ministry of Education banned a few of Tamer's published books from Gaza's school libraries. The most bizarre of these was *Election Day in the Savanna*, an illustrated children's book by French author Sandrine Dumas Roy that Tamer translated into Arabic in 2006. In *Election Day*, the animals of the savanna gather to elect a new king. Several animals announce their candidacy, including Jo the Lion, whose father was the previous king, and Jim the Crocodile, who bases his entire platform on security issues. "I will sink my teeth into anyone who should try to attack you," Crocodile says, and his unsophisticated message earns jeers from the other animals, who consider him a "brainless crawler."

But Jim the Crocodile wins the election anyway. He quickly appoints his brothers and cousins to all the important ministries and assigns young soldiers to secure the savanna's borders. This suits everyone fine until the dry season, when the local water holes dry up and the animals must travel to the North Lake. The crocodile border patrol stops them, telling them that the border is closed in both directions. The king, who has access to the Royal Pond and no need of the North Lake, ignores the animals' protests. When a gazelle tries to breach the border at night, the crocodile soldiers devour her whole.

The animals gather to plan a coup. They consider poisoning the Royal Pond or kidnapping some of Jim's children to ransom them for water. They decide, instead, to feed Jim and his royal family a banquet of magic mushrooms. The plan works. The stoned crocodiles become so convinced they've grown wings that they rush to the cliff and hurl themselves over the edge to their deaths. "We dodged a bullet—what a narrow escape," the other animals cry out. "We will vote much better next time." The end.

I've never read a stranger children's book than *Election Day*, but I didn't understand Hamas's objections until a volunteer at Tamer's Gaza office explained it to me. "Don't you see?" he said. "The lion is yellow. This is the color of the Fatah flag. And the crocodile is green, the color of Hamas." The plot of *Election Day* too closely resembled the 2007 election in Gaza, when a security-obsessed party of green unseated the long-reigning party of yellow. Critics accuse Hamas officials of crocodile-levels of corruption and nepotism. Even Jim's two-way border guards echo Hamas's frequent refusal to grant exit visas to its political opponents. Apparently, Hamas did not want Gaza's children to associate their party with the book's villains or, I suspect, to give them any revolutionary ideas.

I contacted the book's original French author. Roy hadn't heard about the ban. She told me she wrote *Election Day* as an allegory of another election, the 2002 French presidential contest that saw the troubling rise of the right-wing National Front party. Jim the crocodile was named after National Front leader Jean-Marie Le Pen. Hamas's censure of the book surprised Roy, but not the staff at Tamer. Nor did it stop them from reprinting the book in 2008 as a gift for the children of Gaza, who had just endured another war. Tamer also adapted the book into a play that they performed in eighteen different places around Gaza. In the end, the Hamas ban of *Election Day* had fewer teeth than Jim the Crocodile.

On a Saturday, I met with a Tamer employee named Hani to attend the final event of the Baba Read to Me Campaign, an annual Tamer program that encourages parents, especially fathers, to read to their children. Hani raced his rental car along the coastal road to the Deir al-Balah refugee camp in central Gaza. Like the other camps I'd seen, Deir al-Balah consists of mostly unadorned cinder block buildings. A field of tall date palms towers over the camp, and ramshackle fishermen's huts line the beach. "Everyone in Deir al-Balah is a fisherman now," Hani told me, but many of the families came from a farming village called Kawkaba where, before 1948, they lived off grain, grapes, and figs. Nearly eight hundred Palestinians from Kawkaba fled to Gaza during the Nakba.

The community had gathered in the bright, walled-in courtyard of Deir al-Balah's Women's Program Center. Women, all in hijab, occupied the rows of plastic chairs at one end while their children sat cross-legged in front of them. All the babas—fathers, grandfathers, or male relatives standing in for them—were the honored guests of the event and sat sprawled on thin foam mattresses laid around the perimeter of the court-yard. Some wore red keffiyehs held in place with black cords, but all had beards and cell phones in common. Everyone seemed excited. "The men are happy to see the changes in the children that the Tamer programs inspire," Hani said. "They enjoy school more. Their grades improve. They start to write stories. This makes their fathers proud."

Hami and I sat on the mats beside a group of local sheikhs. Their leader sat next to me. He wore an impeccable white beard and a white *taqiyah* on his head. His blazer and brown robe smelled of a spicy woodsy fragrance often worn by important men in Palestine. The sheikh wel-comed me and urged me to sit closer, but I opted to lean against a metal pole holding up the canopy. Even after all my time on the foam mats of the Middle East, I have never learned how to sit comfortably cross-legged unless I can prop my back against something.

A wide brazier stood in the center of the courtyard with a half-dozen brass coffee urns warming on the hot coals. Tall clay vessels supported trays of tiny ceramic cups and fresh dates. After Tamer volunteers served the guests, they unveiled a new mural painted on the courtyard wall de-picting scenes from the camp: a refugee house, clothing hanging on a line, the lifeguard tower that stands on the nearby beach. Afterward, another volunteer recited a well-known folktale the older people in the audience recognized. Then my sheikh, who usually gives the Friday ser-mon at the local mosque, stood to address the crowd with a speech about the important roles of fathers, mothers, schools, and mosques in the up-bringing of children. In particular, he urged the children to respect and honor their fathers "so that your own sons will help you in the future."

Then the volunteers handed out books to each of the babas and urged them to read it to their children. Two or three children crowded each baba to hear the story. The Western practice of parents reading bedtime stories to their children is not common in Palestine, and the children en-joyed the novelty of having their baba read to them and hold up the illus-trations for them to see. Afterward, another Tamer volunteer encouraged the children to read a story every day. "And not just your schoolbooks. Read stories you like to read."

A troupe of skilled dancers followed the storytelling session. They wore black pants and shirts, purple vests, and keffiyehs tied on their heads. They performed a traditional wedding *dabke*, then a modern dance to a song called "The Dove of al-Aqsa." The dance started with the performers pretending to hurl stones at an invisible enemy. One boy mimed being shot, and the other dancers surrounded him to mourn his death. The dance ended with fists in the air. In a final speech, an organizer insisted that "al-Quds will return to us if we know our culture."

These final words struck me. They suggest the pathway to justice, embodied best by Jerusalem's return to the Palestinians, is paved with culture. Art will bring change more than bullets, bombs, or politics. A people who continue to read their own stories and poems, who sing their songs and dance their dances, cannot be defeated. They sing, dance, and write themselves a continued existence. Just as the old books in the Khalidi Library testified to the historical presence of the Palestinians on this land, these new books, and their young readers, ensure this presence endures.

There are those who would interpret this longing for al-Aqsa as a call for Israel's destruction and a declaration of war. They forget the war was declared long ago and three generations of Palestinians have known nothing but. To reach for Jerusalem is to express Palestinian resolve—to remember all they've lost and what they continue to lose.

A spray-painted portrait of author Khaled Juma colors a wall near Karawan Café. His face, adorned with glasses and a mess of black hair, hovers over a depiction of the border wall and a tangle of blue graffiti that reads, "They are as beautiful as the cities they came from," the title of one of Khaled's poems. Though I met Juma in Ramallah, where he now lives, he reigns as one of Gaza's most beloved authors.

The Juma family fled to Gaza during the Nakba from a village called Hatta, and Khaled was born in the al-Shaboura refugee camp in 1965. He doesn't remember when he started writing, but his mother recalls how Khaled made up lyrics to his favorite songs when he forgot the original words. He wrote his first poem when he was seventeen years old: an ode to a sunrise Khaled now considers "very silly."

Khaled published his first poetry collection in 1992. His greatest challenge as a poet, he said, was to rid his own poems of Mahmoud Darwish's voice. "That is why I waited until I was twenty-seven years old to publish my first book of poetry, because I felt there was something that was not me in my poems," Khaled said. "The moment I could show that Darwish was out of my poems, I started to publish them. I love him, but I don't want to be a copy of him."

Khaled placed poems in newspapers and magazines while pursuing a degree in architectural drawing from Hebron University—back before the blockade, when Palestinians could easily travel to and from Gaza. Architectural drawing bored him, but he worked as a draftsman for the local municipality for over a decade before quitting in 1998 to write full-time and head the culture department of the Palestinian Authority's news agency.

In 1992, Khaled wrote a song for a Tamer Institute reading campaign that encouraged children to read books in order to find answers to all of their questions. Why is the moon a circle and not a square? Ask a book. Why does rain fall in the winter and not the summer? Ask a book. Tamer's campaign organizers loved the song. So did the children. "Once they put the song to music it was like a bomb going off. Every child in Gaza was singing it."

The song's success inspired Khaled to write his first children's book, a tale about the importance of hygiene called *Diaries of a Germ*. He wrote seventeen more books for children, many published by Tamer with whimsical titles like *The Rabbit Who Did Not Like His Name* and *Sheep Do Not Eat Cats*. "I've written articles, novels, and poems, and I am telling you the 100 percent truth that writing for children is the most difficult thing you can do in your life," Khaled said. "You have to turn yourself into a child, and that is difficult. You have to lose everything you've learned after you've turned six years old. You have to give it all away."

An abundance of self-confidence can poison a children's writer, Khaled said. "When you write for children, you have to be scared all the time. They either like your story or dislike it. They love or hate. They don't have something in between." Before Khaled sends new work to his publisher, he gathers a few children into an informal focus group and lets them read his manuscript. "Then I take their notes," he said. Adult readers can critique Khaled's language or comment on the messages his stories attempt to convey, but the children don't care. Khaled's young readers don't want to be lectured to. "They want the good guys to win. They want the bad guys to lose. They want to be happy. That is what they are looking for. They are not looking for signs and struggles."

Despite his success in the genre, Khaled doesn't consider himself a children's writer. "I am a poet doing other things," he said. In his poems, Khaled aims to "shine a light on the things that people can't see." Instead of depicting a bereft mother dancing for the cameras at her martyred son's funeral, Khaled imagines her alone at night, long after the public theatrics of mourning, staring at her son's photo. Instead of writing about the overt humiliations imposed by Israel's checkpoints, Khaled describes how a closed crossing once prevented his friend's fiancée from leaving Gaza. "He was happy," Khaled said. "The checkpoint made his lover return to him."

Khaled remembers fondly the time between the Intifadas. "Gaza was open," he said. PA salaries were being paid, and workers could cross the border to high-paying jobs in Israel. Gazan cinemas, restaurants, and hotels were busy. Licensed clubs and dance halls—where Gaza's Nawar, or "Gypsies," danced onstage—were full of men drinking and smoking. Stores sold alcohol and rented videos. Then, in 2000, the Second Intifada began and weakened the Palestinian Authority. Hamas operatives in Gaza saw an opportunity to flex. The Intifada was hardly two weeks old when vandals torched the liquor stores. Then the video stores, the cinemas, and the beachside nightclubs were burned down. "Hamas was ready," Khaled said. "They had been hiding. You think they stole Gaza just in one night? They were prepared. For thirty years they had been preparing."

In 2005, Hamas took erroneous credit for Israel's decision to force Jewish settlers out of Gaza. Khaled remembers carloads of hamsawi driving around Gaza City, waving their flags and declaring, "We did this." Gazans were happy to see the settlers go, but their absence put Gaza into immediate peril. With no Israelis left in Gaza, Khaled said, the Israeli government "started to see Gaza as another country that they could bomb and fight. Before, Israel was the occupation. Now the situation is much more dangerous."

Hamas also put a chill on Gaza's writing community, but the lack of attention Hamas paid to Khaled unnerved him. "I knew that a few of my articles were on Ismail Haniya's desk," Khaled said, referring to the Hamas leader in Gaza at the time. "Every other writer Hamas investigated was asked about 'the communist Khaled Juma.' But I was never called in myself. Why did they not send for me? I was scared."

"Did you have relationships with the communists in Gaza?" I asked.

"Do you know what Hamas means by *communists*? They mean anyone who is not Hamas."

A PA contact helped Khaled secure a permit to leave Gaza and enter the West Bank for a wedding in 2014. On his second day in Ramallah, Khaled asked a friend to bring him to Darwish's grave. They spent twenty minutes standing in front of the tombstone. "Nobody spoke," Khaled told me. "We just stood there." Darwish's gravestone is inscribed with lines from his poem "The Pigeons Fly."

Sleep, my love
With my hair over you, peace be on you.

Khaled didn't believe these were the verses Darwish would have chosen for his gravestone. So Khaled lifted a fistful of soil from the nearby garden and scattered it over the white stone. Then he wrote with his finger a few lines from one of Darwish's last poems:

Tell the absence: You missed me
And I am present . . . to complete you

"I think he wrote this to be put on his grave," Khaled said. "It is something very philosophical. Very deep. Very beautiful." Khaled held up his phone and showed me a photo of his gravestone edit. Darwish's words curled through a thin dusting of reddish soil.

Khaled decided to stay in Ramallah for a few months after the wedding to finish a project with his West Bank colleagues. That way, he'd have the chance to meet with the people he worked with face-to-face rather than having to rely on dropped phone calls, unreliable Skype connections, and Gaza's buggy internet service. When 2014's summer war began, Khaled could not go home. He was forced to watch the fighting from a distance. "I lost twelve kilograms during the war, just sitting and writing. Watching the TV and my mobile and the internet. Sleeping for only one hour a day."

The international media's coverage of the wars frustrated Khaled. Journalists act as accountants rather than storytellers, tallying corpses but ignoring the lives that remain. He reminded me of what Atef wrote about war reducing humanity to mere numbers. "The media shows only demolished houses and dead people. The sound of blood is louder than the sound of tears," Khaled said. "But the most dangerous thing that happens in war is what is not said, what is not photographed, and what is not talked about."

Instead of describing the dead, Khaled wrote about the injured, especially those who lost limbs and for whom the war never ends. "At first, people will say they are champions, but after a time, they are just handicapped." He wrote about the storehouse of memories lost each time a family home is destroyed, about the guilt and trauma endured by fathers who cannot keep their children safe, and the ironic cruelty of rockets. "Explosions travel faster than sound," Khaled said, "so if you can hear the rockets, then you are alive. You can't hear what kills you because it kills you before you hear it." Even when he writes about the children killed in the 2014 war, as he did in his heartbreaking poem "Oh Rascal Children of Gaza," Khaled writes about their lives rather than their deaths:

Oh rascal children of Gaza.
You who constantly disturbed me
with your screams under my window.
You who filled every morning
with rush and chaos.
You who broke my vase
and stole the lonely flower on my balcony.
Come back,
and scream as you want and break all the vases.
Steal all the flowers.
Come back.
Just come back . . .

Khaled planned on returning to Gaza until ISIS threatened to slit his throat. In December 2014, the Gaza affiliate of the Sunni extremist group fighting in Syria and Iraq published a statement on Facebook. The notice accused eighteen Gazan poets, authors, and journalists of apostasy and immoral writings and threatened to kill them within three days if they did not repent. Khaled's name was on the list. Few considered the threat serious. Some believed Hamas wrote the notice to garner support against suspected ISIS threats. For its part, Hamas denied writing the statement and claimed the Gaza ISIS affiliate did not exist at all. Three days later, instead of the promised executions, a second Facebook notice appeared, apologizing for the first. The whole episode was bizarre, and many dismissed it as a bad joke.

Khaled, though, wasn't laughing. The ISIS letter spooked him, and he hasn't returned to Gaza since.

"But that list turned out to be a hoax," I said.

"It doesn't matter. If someone stupid reads that, they will not think about whether it is fake or not. If he shoots me, it doesn't matter."

Actor and theater impresario Jamal Abu al-Qumsan wanted a place where Gaza's writers, artists, and intellectuals could meet and drink cheap coffee. "Many intellectuals don't have any money," he explained. He opened a café in a gallery inside Gaza's Ministry of Culture building in 2005 and named it, suitably, Gallery Café.

The place quickly evolved into an impromptu arts center and the informal heart of Gaza's cultural community. "I wanted to put a sign on the door that said, 'There is no need to shake hands at Gallery, because everyone already knows each other here.'" Established writers like Gharib Asqalani and Khaled Juma used to come and give readings, while young poets came to seek their advice or perform poems aloud in front of Gallery audiences. Stage and film actors met over tea and nargileh with directors and producers. Musicians rehearsed at the café's tables—though Jamal once exiled a young oud player to a table in the farthest corner of the café until his atonal playing improved. Jamal's customers floated from table to table, frustrating the waiters when the time came to pay their bills. "I had a big book of unpaid tabs," Jamal said.

When Hamas took over Gaza in 2007, officials told Jamal he could continue to operate his café at the ministry as long as he enforced separate sections for men and women. Hamas also insisted Jamal prohibit his female customers from smoking nargileh or playing music. Jamal feared the new rules would destroy the free and congenial atmosphere he'd fostered, so he decided to move Gallery elsewhere. Owners of a café called Laturna offered Jamal a partnership, but he turned them down. Jamal knew they were proper businessmen who wouldn't tolerate his ease with unpaid bills. So Jamal rented a large outdoor space that used to belong to the construction workers union. He called the place the Union Gallery Café, but didn't put up a sign. Jamal didn't want Hamas to know where it was. Three thousand customers came to the new café's opening day.

"Gallery went back the way it used to be," Jamal said. "In every corner you'd find someone playing music or doing something interesting." Jamal added a small reception hall on the property that could be used both as a stage for musicians and a studio for artists, and he filled it with paints and easels. Jamal rented out space for arts events at very low prices, sometimes for nothing at all. "I also had to put in a kitchen because my customers would sit all day long and get hungry," Jamal said. The café earned a reputation as a venue for Gazans to cheat on their Ramadan fasts.

Gallery became a refuge for Gazan women seeking respite from the strict morality rules imposed by the new Hamas government. "Women could feel free at Gallery. Laugh. Be loud. They could sing. They could do whatever they wanted." Aside from Jamal's own prohibition on gambling—"I didn't want Gallery to turn into a card place," Jamal said—Gallery had no rules. "And that is why Hamas thought we were bad."

Hamas started sending undercover security agents to harass Jamal and his customers, especially the young women. They scolded them for smoking nargileh and demanded to know the identities of the men they socialized with. "The agents always dressed the same," Jamal said. "We knew them by their beards, vests, and sandals. The sandals are key." Occasionally, agents forced Jamal's customers up from their tables and brought them to the police station for questioning. Hamas knew nothing illegal was going on at Gallery, but Jamal suspects the continuous harassment was intended to frighten customers away so the café would eventually go out of business. "The good thing about the Gallery visitors is that they were strong," Jamal said. "They argued. They were not afraid."

Not even a bomb could discourage Jamal's regulars. In October 2009, a phone call woke Jamal at around four in the morning. Someone had detonated a bomb at the front entrance of the café. The night watchman, Jamal's nephew, suffered minor injuries to his leg. The bomb turned out to be small and handmade, but it caused serious damage to the café entrance and to some of the tables and chairs near the door. The police told Jamal they would look into the attack, but no one was ever arrested. "Apparently, they still are investigating," Jamal joked. He is convinced Hamas planted the bomb to scare off customers. This tactic failed, too. Gallery was as busy as ever following the explosion.

Hamas wasn't finished with Gallery, though. The following May, security agents appeared at the café entrance during an exhibit of graffiti photography by Swedish artist Mia Gröndahl. The agents started to pester Gallery's visitors. One of the waiters called Jamal and told him to come to the café. When Jamal arrived, the agents told him they had been looking for him for the past two months. "Really?" Jamal said. "I've been here the whole time." The agents took Jamal to the police station where they accused him of holding the graffiti event without permission from the Ministry of Culture. Jamal told him that he did, in fact, have a permit. Then the police told Jamal there were Israeli collaborators among the patrons at the café. "Then you should go and arrest them," Jamal suggested.

His interrogators switched strategies again. "You meet many women at the café," one said.

"What is wrong with meeting women? This is none of your business."

The officer swore at Jamal and shouted: "You are having sex with these women!"

Jamal told them this was not true, that he had a wife and children and was an honorable man. The police, though, spent hours questioning him about imagined sexual improprieties. Then they demanded he return the next morning for further interrogation. When Jamal came back, the agents asked him the same questions again, from nine in the morning until four in the afternoon, and told him to return again the next day. On the third day, they confiscated Jamal's mobile phone and scrolled through his messages. They pointed to numbers and email addresses belonging to female names. "Which of these women do you have sex with?" one officer demanded.

"None of them," Jamal said. "And even if I did do it, I would not admit it."

An interrogator leaned forward and snarled, "I can make you admit it, even if you didn't do it."

The officer ordered Jamal to stand and place his hands on the wall. He tied a blindfold over Jamal's eyes. Then the man took a long stick and struck Jamal across his buttocks. Instead of crying out, Jamal laughed. He knew that by beating him, the interrogator had escalated the situation beyond his authority. The man hit Jamal twenty times. When he was finished, he told Jamal to return the next morning at ten.

"I will be here at nine," Jamal said.

He did not return home from the police station. Instead, Jamal called all the foreign journalists and human rights activists he knew in Gaza and told them to meet him at Gallery two hours later. He figured this was enough time for the bruises on his buttocks to start to color. Then he stood before his makeshift press conference and declared, "I invited you all here to photograph my ass." Jamal turned and dropped his pants for the assembled media. The red welts on his buttocks had turned to blue, purple, and green. "It was like a painting," Jamal said. The journalists dutifully raised their cameras.

Jamal told the assembled media the story of his arrest. "I want this published tomorrow," he said. His friends obliged. Photos of Jamal's bruised ass appeared alongside the story of his beating on blogs and news sites in several languages all around the world. "In Japan, China, Italy, Morocco, Sweden. Even on porn sites you would find photos of my ass." (I tried, but, alas, Hamas blocks porn sites in Gaza.) Jamal's activist friends, some with Human Rights Watch, called Hamas officials and demanded to know why Jamal had been arrested and flogged.

When he returned to the police station the following morning, his interrogators were furious. They'd seen the photos of Jamal's bruises online. Even Hamas leader Ismail Haniya had seen the photos. "How could you do this and show your ass to the world? It is *haram*! Forbidden!" The policemen let Jamal go, and Hamas eventually fired the officer who'd beaten him. Soon afterward, another pair of Hamas security agents showed up at Gallery, this time with their wives in tow, just to sit and smoke nargileh. "They told me that they were for freedom and that I could do whatever I wanted, as long as I didn't serve whiskey."

This détente did not last. In 2011, PA leader Mahmoud Abbas was scheduled to give a speech at the United Nations demanding UN recognition of the State of Palestine. Many of Jamal's regular clientele wanted to watch the declaration on the television at Gallery. On the afternoon of the speech, Jamal went to the café with his family. Security agents appeared just as Jamal was about to turn on the television. They told Jamal to come with them to the police station. When Jamal asked why, the men told him it was because he was about to show Abbas's UN speech. "So what?" Jamal said. "I am not going to show a porno movie."

The officers took Jamal to jail. Again. When they walked in, the prison's television was showing Abbas's speech while a local news scroll at the bottom of the screen read, "Theater director Jamal Abu al-Qumsan has been arrested. . . ." The prison director was enraged, but not at Jamal. "Why did you bring him here?" he shouted at the officers. "I told you never to bring him here!" He pointed to the television. "You see that everyone is talking about him now!" Then he cursed Hamas out loud.

The prison director feared that once news of Jamal's detention spread, especially considering he hadn't been charged with anything, dozens of journalists and human rights activists would invade the prison. But he had to save face and couldn't simply let Jamal go. So the director decided to play nice. "He let me choose my own cell," Jamal said. "And he recommended I share a cell with a friendly businessman with money problems." The director then instructed his staff to clean all the cells quickly and invited Jamal and his fellow inmates to choose what they wanted to eat for dinner that night. "They treated me, and the other prisoners, very well because they knew the journalists were coming."

They came in droves. Reporters, activists, and dozens of Jamal's supporters filled the jailhouse the next morning and demanded Hamas explain Jamal's imprisonment. "It was like Gallery moved to the prison," Jamal joked. The protestors transformed the prison into a place where all his friends came to meet and socialize. The authorities were desperate to invent a justification for Jamal's imprisonment. They accused him of holding a jazz concert at Gallery without a permit, which was not true. They accused him of being a member of Fatah, which was also false, and not illegal anyway. They kept Jamal in prison for four days without formally charging him with anything. Then they let him go.

Jamal won most of his battles with Hamas, but he eventually lost the war. In 2012, Hamas declared that they intended to build a cancer hospital on the land where Gallery stood. Even though Jamal was paying his lease, the site was government land and Hamas argued that a hospital was more important than Jamal's troublesome café. Bulldozers rumbled through and destroyed half of Gallery. Jamal operated the shrunken café until the following year when Hamas declared they needed the entire lot. I visited the site. There are sheep grazing on the land now, and piles of trash. There is no hospital.

Gallery, though, is not dead. Jamal and his wife recently purchased a plot of land along Gaza's beach and have procured the necessary building permits. The new Gallery will eventually feature a café, cinema, a hall for art exhibitions, and a mobile stage. I asked Jamal if he would have to renew his fight with Hamas to keep the new Gallery open. He doesn't think so. "I've learned how to be diplomatic," he said. And the café will be built on land that belongs to him and his wife. "They will have no legal way to shut the place down."

I asked Jamal why the place is so important to him. He told me Gaza's creative and intellectual communities need a place of comfort and release, especially in the face of Hamas oppression and the Israeli blockade. They need a place to gather and exchange ideas. "There is no other place like Gallery," he said. "You don't have to call someone and tell him to meet you there. You just go and find him there already."

Lara invited me to celebrate a friend's birthday at her parents' apartment. "There will be music," she said. Sixteen people crammed onto the chairs and sofas in the salon. Lara's mother and sister laid out bowls of popcorn and nuts and served trays of sweet fruit juice and tea flavored with sage. Lara tended to a pair of nargileh pipes we all shared. Lara periodically lifted the coals off the smoldering tobacco and dropped them on the tray to jar loose the cool white ash and expose their red interiors. Then she'd perch the coals back on top of the foil-wrapped bowl. The great clouds of fruity smoke that rolled out of everyone's mouths testified to the skill of Lara's tinkering.

While the pipes rumbled on the floor, and before the birthday cake was served, a man leaned forward on the sofa, lifted a violin from the table, and began to play songs by the legendary Egyptian singer Umm Kulthum. Another joined him on an oud. Then, like some exquisite miracle, Lara started to sing. A voice I'd only ever heard in whispers soared above the strings, the bubbling rumble of the pipes, and the occasional chime from someone's cell phone. I was the only one who didn't know these songs. Everyone else nodded their heads and mouthed the words, content to listen to Lara's solo singing.

Gaza does not possess a broad beauty. The wide view is too full of broken things, the vistas too craggy, and this is all we see from a distance. Gaza's beauty does not wave an easy flag of gloss. It demands more from us. To find it, we have to look close. Focus tight on the pleasure of a thirty-cent pomegranate bought from a donkey cart. On a café waiter's *habibi* and a baba reading to his child. On the sweetness of oranges. On Lara singing through smoke.

6

She Is Oranges That Explode

Mahmoud Darwish used the feminine pronoun when he wrote of
Gaza.

And Gaza is not the most polished of cities, or the largest. But she is
equivalent to the history of a nation, because she is the most repulsive
among us in the eyes of the enemy—the poorest, the most desperate,
and the most ferocious. Because she is a nightmare. Because she is
oranges that explode, children without a childhood, aged men without
an old age, and women without desire.

I, too, quickly came to regard Gaza in feminine terms. I passed
many of my Gazan hours in the company of women. This surprised me.
I thought that Gaza's inherent religious conservatism, further hardened
under Hamas, would stand between me and the women I wanted to meet.
I felt tremendously grateful to be wrong. No one taught me more about
life in Gaza than the women I encountered there. They felt the pressures
of war, occupation, and conservatism most acutely. The women writers
of Gaza craft themselves a life on the page that Gaza itself denies them.
If all Palestinian writing is, in some way, an expression of resistance, the

poems and stories of Gaza's women are acts of heroism. They transform longing and trauma into art.

Author Mona Abu Sharekh guided me through the clean side streets of Shati refugee camp. Eighty-five thousand refugees live in the half-kilometer shantytown, making the camp one of the most crowded places on earth. Some of the alleyways were too narrow for us to walk side by side. We turned one corner and found a bedsheet hanging across one of the lanes, blocking our way. A young girl, her hair a chaos of curls, explained that her family had draped the sheet to make an impromptu extension to their home. She told us adorably but firmly that we could not pass.

We wandered instead through the market, past carts of vegetables and herbs and the horrid stink of chickens, before returning to the warren of streets that wind through most of the camp. Mona translated the graffiti adorning the cement walls. Graffiti along the main roads usually bears political or religious messages—calls for people to support Hamas, for example, or to remember their prayers—but messages in the residential side streets are usually more intimate. Long lines of spray-painted script announced weddings, new jobs, or the birth of children. Mona pointed to a message written by a man congratulating his brother for graduating from university. I asked her if the messages stay on the walls forever. "Maybe another brother will graduate, and they will paint it over," she said.

I would have gotten hopelessly lost in Shati's maze were it not for Mona. She was born in the camp and spent much of her childhood in these streets, but she hesitates to call Shati home. Her father's family comes from Asqalan and fled to Gaza during the Nakba. "You know this story," Mona said. "It is boring."

The notion of home is complicated for second- and third-generation Palestinian refugees. Mona must consider Asqalan her home. To do otherwise would be to concede defeat to the occupation and admit that where she now resides is where she belongs. But she has never even been to Asqalan. "I don't feel it is my home," she admitted. Mona can see Asqalan from the top of Gaza's tallest buildings, but it remains unreachable, both physically and emotionally. Asqalan exists in her father's memory—

he disapproved of Mona's choice of husband because his family was not Asqalani—but not in her own. "I don't have my life there," Mona said. "My life is here. All the streets. All the corners of Gaza. My family are here. All my experiences. The first person I fell in love with was here. I was married here. This is the place that lives inside me." This is the refugee's dilemma: to long for somewhere you do not know, and demand a return to a place you've never been.

Mona attended primary and secondary school during the First Intifada, when education ranked low on Gaza's list of priorities. Young masked militants often shut down schools in the middle of the day in advance of afternoon clashes with the IDF. They insisted students either join their cadres of stone-throwers or return to the safety of their homes. As a school subject, creative writing was especially devalued. Mona remembers that every lesson in her textbooks ended with a list of questions, the last of which always asked students to express their feelings or opinions about what they'd just learned in a short piece of fiction or poetry. Mona's teacher told his students to ignore these exercises. He said they were not important.

Mona completed them anyway. She remembers writing a story, at the end of an Arabic lesson, about a woman battling cancer. The next day, her teacher stood at the front of the class with the pile of exams in her arms and asked where was Mona. "She didn't know me," Mona explained. "I was a very quiet student." When Mona meekly raised her hand, the teacher told her she would be a great writer someday. The compliment inspired Mona, and she began to write more often. She won first prize in a creative writing contest the following year. "That was also the year I read *Wuthering Heights*," Mona recalled. "It was the first time I cried from a book." Her mother did not like Mona reading such melodramatic novels. "She thought these books keep you sad and thinking about death," Mona said. "They were not good for a thirteen-year-old kid."

The masked boys stopped disrupting classes during the brief period of calm between Intifadas. "There was a break," Mona said. "A good life." New schools opened with new curricula and new libraries. "We were expecting Gaza to become a great city," Mona said. "Yasser Arafat told us Gaza would be the new Singapore. We believed him because we always believed him."

The Israelis shut the Erez border crossing at the beginning of the Second Intifada in 2000. The closure was an economic disaster for workers like Mona's father, who worked as a day laborer in Israel for decades and relied on employment on the other side of the line. Rather than despairing, Mona's father regarded the closure as an opportunity to change careers. He became a merchant and opened a distribution center for various goods. The family earned more money than they did when the border was open and eventually moved out of Shati and into a new home in Gaza City.

After graduating from high school, Mona enrolled in an English literature program at the Islamic University of Gaza. In addition to her course syllabus of English novels, Mona started reading Mahmoud Darwish and the authors he published in *Al-Karmel*. She read great Arabic novels, too, like Abdul Rahman Munif's *Cities of Salt* trilogy. Instead of inspiring her, though, the high quality of the writing she read made her dismissive of her own work. "Sometimes I felt like my writing did not reflect the truth. Sometimes I felt there was no value to it. Sometimes I asked myself why I am writing if the work will not change my life. What is the benefit?"

Mona set fire to any of her work that didn't satisfy her. She also burned stories her university professors particularly enjoyed; she trusted their judgment even less than her own talent. "I felt like I could give more. Something better." She incinerated her diaries, too. "I don't know why. Maybe I didn't like my life at that time. I don't know." One day, Mona's neighbor spotted flames in her backyard and called to make sure her building wasn't burning down. These days, Mona is more forgiving of her own limitations as a writer. There are no more backyard bonfires. "Now I just delete it like everyone else," she said.

After completing her English literature degree, Mona earned a master's in business administration and worked as a project manager for various NGOs. This is one of the only reliable sources of employment in Gaza, where development and charitable organizations from around the world run programs and maintain offices. She eventually landed a position at the United Nations Relief and Works Agency for Palestinian refugees. The United Nations founded UNRWA in 1949 to provide the residents of the refugee camps with education, health care, relief services, and camp infrastructure, among other services. UNRWA maintains camps in Lebanon, Syria, Jordan, and Palestine—including eight camps in Gaza.

Raja Shehadeh wrote about UNRWA in *Language of War, Language of Peace*, a book that examines the politics of words in the conflict. For Raja, UNRWA represents "the first twist in terminology." Israel refused to identify Palestinians displaced by the Nakba as "refugees," as the word implies a homeland to which they should be allowed to return. The United Nations, then, did not place these Palestinians under the auspices of the United Nations High Commissioner for Refugees (UNHCR). Instead, the UN granted them a "special status" and their own agency, UNRWA—whose title does not include the word *refugee*. This status excludes Palestinians from international refugee laws and all but eliminates the five million Palestinian refugees UNRWA serves from global refugee statistics. The only Palestinians who appear on official UNHCR counts are the approximately ninety-five thousand who live in places where UNRWA doesn't operate.

The eight UNRWA camps in Gaza employ almost 12,500 staff to tend to the Strip's 1.3 million registered refugees with schools, health centers, and social services offices. The agency also distributes food to the camps four times a year. Criteria for receiving food rations are strict. I told Mona I'd seen UNRWA-labeled sunflower oil for sale at the grocery store near my flat, in direct defiance of labels reading NOT FOR SALE and FOR FREE DISTRIBUTION TO PALESTINE REFUGEES. Mona shrugged. "Sometimes families need money more than food."

Working with UNRWA gave Mona an opportunity to meet people with experiences far different from her own. For a writer, this is a great gift. "I heard many stories from very poor families. Violated families. Families under great pressure of violence, poverty, and illness." She learned that the pressures of everyday life supersede the slogans of nationalist politics, especially with women. Mona recalled a mother she'd met after the 2014 war. Many UNRWA-run schools sheltered internally displaced families whose homes were destroyed during the bombing. The populations of the shelters steadily decreased once the war ended as people repaired their homes or found other places to live, so UNRWA started shutting down the shelters. A distraught mother told Mona that if

UNRWA forced her to leave the shelter, Mona had better give her three bullets: She planned on shooting her two daughters, and then herself.

"Then she told me a horrible story about her life," Mona said. The woman's husband had sexually abused her and her daughters many times. When they finally divorced, the woman's family threw her into the street. The woman wanted to kill her own daughters to save them from this misery. "How can you think about politics while this woman is living like this here in Gaza?" Mona asked me. "These are the stories I am used to hearing. Don't talk to me about going back to Asqalan while there are hungry people here."

When we passed through the camp's market, Mona pointed out the unemployed young men sitting idle in front of shops. I asked her if she ever grows numb to the poverty she sees every day. "No," she said. "I always see it. I am inspired by it." These people fuel both her UNRWA work and her fiction. Mona often walks alone through the camp to quietly observe how life is lived there. "I become more sensitive," she said. "Sometimes it is more important to watch and read than it is to write. You don't want to write down everything in your head."

Mona believes a writer must be able to embrace Gaza and its strange contradictions. "You need to love Gaza before you are able to write about it," she said. "Here you can find the most beautiful places at the same time as the most ugly places." Cleanliness rubs up against filth. Wealth occupies the same streets as great poverty. "Gaza has never been at peace," Mona said. "I need to understand this place. I need to know the feeling of what it means to be destroyed and rebuilt. Over and over. You cannot find yourself here. You are underneath layers and layers of experiences. You cannot find your original self."

"Do you love Gaza, then?"

She answered without hesitation. "No. I hate Gaza. Life is difficult here. There is no electricity. And there is no future. And in 2020, Gaza will no longer be fit for humans." Mona was referring to a 2012 UNRWA report that declared Gaza would soon be uninhabitable. By 2020, pollution will irreversibly damage the aquifer Gazans rely on, and Gazans will have nowhere to access safe drinking water. Standards of education and health care will continue to fall as the population climbs, and more

Gazans than ever will depend on food assistance. According to the report, Gazans need hundreds more schools and hospital beds, thousands more doctors and nurses, and tens of thousands more places to live. They need to more than double their electricity capacity. The report concluded that only "herculean efforts" by Palestinians and their partners could ensure that Gaza is still a livable place by 2020.

The report is remarkable in its pessimism. How could a territory that has hosted human life since the Bronze Age be so abruptly and irrevocably poisoned? Even the most dire climate-change predictions are measured in generations. I couldn't imagine being literally days away from the abyss. I asked Mona if Gazans take the UN report seriously. "No. My father, mother, and brother don't even know about it. We will live. We will continue. This is what we, as Palestinians, are used to saying."

Mona admits she would also disregard the report if she wasn't a parent. "Before becoming a mother, I said, 'I will live alone and I will die alone. And it is okay.' Now I say, 'What will happen to this kid?'" Mona fears for all the children in Gaza, not just her own. "I lived a little bit of a good life. I know I didn't have the chance to play and run, because it was dangerous when I was a kid. And during the Second Intifada, it was horrible. But I always had good water to drink. Good places to go. Many good things. In the end, I got good work with NGOs and with UNRWA." But today's children of Gaza will not have the same opportunities. The universities here are some of the lowest ranked in the region in terms of the quality of education. Students graduate with useless degrees. They cannot find work in Gaza.

And they cannot leave. Gazans must apply to Israeli authorities for permission to exit through the Erez Crossing. Such permits are usually granted only to traders or medical patients seeking treatment in Israel. According to Gisha, an Israeli NGO that advocates for Palestinian freedom of movement, Israel approves an "exceedingly low" percentage of exit permit applications. In the first half of 2000—before the Second Intifada, the Hamas takeover of Gaza, and the resulting blockade—more than eighty thousand Gazans exited through Erez every month. By 2016, that number had dwindled to fourteen thousand. Only sixty-three hundred Gazans passed through the checkpoint each month in the first half of 2017. The border with Egypt at Rafah is hardly an alternate escape route. Since the fall of the Morsi regime in Egypt in 2013, and the new Egyptian government's animosity toward Hamas, Egypt keeps the Rafah crossing shut tight. More Gazans passed through Rafah every month under Morsi—around twelve thousand—than left during the entire first six months of 2017, a period in which the crossing was open for only eleven days.

As a result, most Gazans are trapped. They cannot pursue employment opportunities outside the territory. They can rarely accept scholarships to foreign universities. They cannot travel. Few are as fortunate as Khaled Juma to attend family weddings in the West Bank, or to pray at al-Aqsa Mosque in Jerusalem. Instead, they sit and wait for change or the next war. For most of Gaza's two million residents, the Strip is a prison without a roof.

Mona published her first book, a collection of short stories called *What the Madman Said*, in 2008. The stories center on life in Gaza after the Second Intifada. "I was psychologically destroyed at the time," Mona said. In 2004 and 2005, in the midst of the ongoing conflict with Israel, fighting between Fatah and Hamas peaked. "I used to see people shooting and killing each other on the street," she said. "It was like a civil war." One gunfight broke out in front of her apartment and kept her trapped at home. Another started just outside the UNRWA walls. "I felt like I was destroyed internally," she said. "We are an occupied people. We have our land occupied. We have to be more civilized. The parties—Fatah and Hamas—are no longer working for the rights of the Palestinians, they are interested only in their own advantage. Their main purpose is not fighting the occupation. Their purpose is fighting each other."

The stories in *What the Madman Said* paint intimate portraits of the struggle. In the title story, a mentally disturbed man reflects on the condition of Gaza City. In another, a mother worries for her sons—one of whom was injured in the conflict and had his legs amputated. Another story revolves around a young man who has to give up his room to a cousin whose house was destroyed. All he wants is the conflict to end so he can get his room back. In Mona's favorite story, the stench of garbage in the streets of Gaza wakes the dead in a city cemetery. The corpses scold the living for the mess they've made.

Another story focuses on the life of a divorced woman. "I wasn't divorced at the time," Mona said. "Maybe I was anticipating it." A year after Mona married, her husband, also a published author, admitted he'd fallen in love with another woman. He told Mona they could remain married and go on living together if that's what she wanted, or they could divorce, but he refused to end the affair. "He said he would respect my choice if I wanted to leave him and start another life. He said he would give me anything I wanted." Mona opted for a divorce and insisted she keep custody of their infant son. Her husband agreed. "He respected my feelings as a mother," Mona said.

In spite of his infidelities, Mona still considers him a good man. "It is bad to fall in love with someone else while you are married," she said, "but you have to respect it." Mona laughed at the incredulous look on my face. "Divorce is not an ugly thing," she said. "It gave me a chance to be independent. To be stronger. To live the stories of my own life." Through her divorce, Mona earned a new affection for the women she had worked with at the NGOs whose husbands had left their families for one reason or another. "I knew what it meant to be abandoned. To have a husband who loves another woman. To have a child you want to protect. If you recover from this experience, nothing can break you again."

"What about war?" I asked.

"War is not more dangerous than divorce," Mona said.

Still, the wars have taken a toll. "I've lived through the 2008 war, the 2012 war, and the 2014 war. I am too young to have lived through three wars," she said. "You can never imagine what it is like here during the war times, especially the last one." Mona spent the fifty days of Operation Protective Edge feeling she could be killed at any time. Even some of the UNRWA-run schools and hospitals were bombed. Mona remembers wondering what her last thought would be before she died. She debated with herself if she'd rather die in her sleep, say, or while watching a movie or listening to music. "I decided that I'd prefer to die while listening to Beethoven," Mona said. "His Ninth Symphony."

Her first priority, of course, was to protect her son. Little Mohammed is only six years old and has already lived both the 2012 and 2014 wars. He remembers little from 2012, Mona said. He was only a year old and "slept most of the time." In 2014, Mohammed was old enough to realize he was in danger, but too young to understand why. "He thought that the danger came from the windows," Mona said. "So he told me to please close the windows. He was crying all day long." Mohammed hasn't forgotten that burning summer. "He is afraid now," Mona said. "Every day he asks me, 'Mommy, is there another war coming?'"

Mona currently works as a donor visibility officer in the UNWRA's communication department. She writes impact statements about the beneficiaries of UNRWA programming to raise the visibility of the organization's successes. "Our donors always want to hear that a project positively affects the life of Palestinians," Mona said. She has qualms about the work. She knows UNRWA improves life for refugee families in Gaza, but to emphasize only their accomplishments rarely reveals the whole story. People still struggle. Mona met with a family a month earlier to write about how UNRWA's food assistance program improved their lives. She learned that the father and two of his children suffered from kidney disease. The father underwent dialysis treatment three times a day and could not work. The mother was also unemployed. A fifteen-year-old son was the family's sole breadwinner. They felt grateful for the food donations from UNRWA, but writing about this family as a success story felt dishonest and propagandistic to Mona.

The job also leaves Mona with little time for her own writing. She works slowly, mostly on Saturdays while she is off work and Mohammed is in kindergarten. "I lock myself in my apartment. If I don't write, I brainstorm. Or I read. I do the things I like. It is good to be alone sometimes." Mona has spent her recent Saturdays working on a novel about a foundling—a child born to an unwed mother and abandoned. Before Mona became a mother herself, she worked for an NGO that ministered to such children. Mona comes from a large and prestigious Gaza family—one of her uncles, for example, was appointed the first sheriff of Gaza by Egyptian president Gamal Abdel Nasser—and she could not relate to these abandoned children. "What does it mean that you don't have a family? Who will protect you when you can't tell stories about your grandfather?"

After Mohammed was born, Mona began to think even more about Gaza's foundlings. She could not imagine a child who, in his first moments of life, is discarded rather than embraced. Then Mona met a woman who discovered late in her life that she had been a foundling. Her husband divorced her, and she had to fight for custody of her children.

Mona decided to write a fictionalized account of this woman who struggles to protect her children and her rights as a woman "in a city that can't even protect itself."

The father character in the story goes missing, so Mona set the novel in the 1980s and had the father shot by the IDF for throwing stones. "The perfect solution for him to be killed or disappear was to put him into the Intifada." Mona laughed at how the conflict granted her such a convenient narrative device. Characters are easily eliminated in fictionalized Palestine.

Mona resists writing about politics. "It is not attractive for me," she said, and she rejects any reader expectations that she take up the cause in her writing. "It is ugly that someone can tell you what to write about, especially in fiction, because a writer already has something in her mind. Maybe a character knocking around her head." The politics that occasionally appears in her work emerges organically. "I will include politics smoothly, and only as the story requires. But I will not sit to write about the man throwing stones." Mona believes that fiction should not preach or advocate for one set of values over another. "Fiction is for fiction," she said. "I want to produce a beautiful piece of fiction. That is all."

She concedes, though, that politics is unavoidable for Palestinian writers, especially in Gaza. Mona cannot escape the fact that her grandfather was killed in 1948 while escaping Asqalan with his family. She cannot escape the truth that, in 2009, an Israeli missile killed one of her cousins, leaving his wife a widow and his children fatherless. And, especially, she cannot forget that her thirteen-year-old brother, Amer, was killed for throwing a stone. Their mother had sent Amer to fetch falafel one morning in 1992. Amer joined the boys throwing rocks at soldiers in the market. "He was shot by a soldier in the heart." Mona was eleven years old and had to confront death for the first time. "Do you know what it means to be a child and cry because someone beloved, someone who used to sleep next to you in the same bed and crawl all over you every morning, dies? It is awful. We cannot escape these experiences."

After only a few days in Gaza's landscape of hijab and niqab, Asmaa al-Ghul's loose hair and blue jeans startled me. Asmaa is well known for rebellion. Her stories about such sensitive topics as "honor killings," domestic abuse, and government corruption have earned her scorn from Gaza's authorities and an enduring notoriety from readers. Each time I mentioned Asmaa's name to my friends in Gaza, their eyes widened. Her bravery, though universally admired, made people uncomfortable. People considered her dangerous. She was fierce, and I felt intimidated meeting her.

At another café on Omar al-Mukhtar Street, Asmaa told me she was born to parents who didn't want her. Her mother and father, both from Rafah refugee camp, had married while they were studying at a university in Alexandria. Her mother became pregnant soon afterward, but her father did not have a salary and could hardly afford a child. Asmaa's father brought his wife to a doctor for an abortion, but they had waited too long. "The baby is strong inside the mother," the doctor told them. Asmaa was born six months later, the first of nine children.

Asmaa started to read at a young age, discovering her father's library when she was six years old. By the time she was ten, every birthday brought a new stack of books from her father. She also began to write, and a local literary journal published some of her childhood poems. Asmaa placed her first article in a newspaper called *Women's Voice* when she was a teenager, and was awarded the Palestine Youth Literature Award in 2000 for a short story she'd written. After high school, Asmaa studied journalism at a university in Gaza then worked as a reporter for *Al-Ayyam*—the same newspaper where Ghassan Zaqtan worked as culture editor. In 2003, Asmaa met and married an Egyptian poet and moved to Abu Dhabi, where they had a son, Naser. The marriage lasted only eighteen months. Asmaa and Naser returned to Gaza after the divorce and moved into her parents' home in Gaza City. She published her first book of short stories in 2006.

Asmaa's blue jeans, uncovered head, and affection for Henry Miller novels drew criticism from her extended family, who are renowned Hamas supporters. The friction between Asmaa and the conservative members of her family peaked in 2007 when, while taking a journalism class in South Korea, Asmaa published an article titled "Dear Uncle, Is This the Homeland We Want?" Asmaa addressed the story to one of her own uncles, a senior Hamas military operative, and recalled how he used to interrogate and torture Fatah activists in the Rafah house she grew up in. The story savaged the Hamas government for inflicting their oppressive religious rules on the people of Gaza. Her uncle was enraged. He disowned Asmaa and threatened to kill her if she ever came back to Gaza. Asmaa was unbowed and returned. Gaza was her home, after all. The uncle never made good on his threats.

In 2009, three policemen accosted Asmaa for walking along the beach with male friends who were not relatives. The officers took Asmaa's ID card and demanded she go with them to the police station. Asmaa refused, but her male friends were detained and beaten. Two years later, police roughed up Asmaa herself after arresting her at a rally encouraging reconciliation between Hamas and Fatah. She was arrested again at another demonstration expressing solidarity with the Egyptian protestors in Tahrir Square. "I cannot be just a writer and sit at home. I cannot be a hypocrite. So I went to protest in the street." In addition to problems with the authorities, Asmaa's actions both on and off the page spawned a wave of cruel criticism online. Few Palestinian writers have endured as much social media abuse and as many death threats.

Asmaa married again, in 2011, to another Egyptian poet. They had a child, a daughter named Zeina, but were divorced three years later. (When I joked that she needs to stay away from poets, Asmaa replied, "Yes. And also Egyptians.") The marriage collapsed just before 2014's Operation Protective Edge, and Asmaa found herself mourning her personal loss in the midst of the communal trauma inflicted by the war. "I felt like all the funerals in Gaza were not just for the people who died in the war, but for my own wounds." She diluted her singular grief in the wash of Gaza's shared suffering. In a strange and perverse way, the horrors of the 2014 war aided her recovery. "The sadness was bigger than me. I forgot all the things inside me."

I'd long admired the craft and sensitivity of Asmaa's journalism from the 2014 war. They were the stories that first compelled me to seek her out. During the fighting, Asmaa accompanied a group of *New York Times* journalists to a hospital morgue in Rafah. Asmaa watched a doctor bring in one-year-old Riziq Abu Taher. His was the smallest body in the morgue, and clad in pink trousers. Asmaa wrote about Riziq in a story for *Al-Monitor*:

I observed him at length. He looked alive. One could see that he had been playing when he died, dressed in his pink pants. How could he be at such peace? The bodies of war victims look so different from how they appear on television. They are so real, so substantial, suddenly there before you, without any newscast introductions, music or slogans.

When Asmaa and the other journalists exited the room, a frantic woman rushed up to them and asked if her son was among the dead. She described her boy to Asmaa, and when she mentioned his pink pants, Asmaa said, "Yes, I saw him." The woman shrieked. She gripped Asmaa's throat with one hand and thrust her other hand down the front of her own dress. She grabbed at her breast, full of milk for Riziq. "Who will drink my milk now?" she cried. Doctors pulled the two women apart and dragged Asmaa away. The other journalists scolded Asmaa for telling the mother about her dead son. "I should have kept silent," she said.

Rafah was under siege at the time, and the IDF warned that they would shoot at anyone in the street. Asmaa did not fear the Israeli guns. "I knew in that moment nothing would happen to me," she said.

"Why not?" I asked.

"I was a bad person for what I'd done. For saying what I'd said to the mother. And bad people do not die in war."

Asmaa didn't die, but many in her family did. The next day, two missiles struck the household in Rafah refugee camp where Asmaa grew up—the same house Asmaa had written about in her notorious open letter to her uncle seven years earlier. The blasts killed nine members of Asmaa's family: three men, three women, and three children. Among them was Mustafa, who had been born alongside his identical twin brother, Ibrahim, the day before. "Who identified them when their father died and their mother lay wounded in intensive care?" Asmaa later wrote in a painfully personal story about the attack. "Who was Mustafa, and who was Ibrahim? It was as if they had merged upon one twin's death."

Asmaa insisted that while none of the nine dead were militants, their death and the death of other innocents in Gaza would create millions of Hamas loyalists. "For we all become Hamas if Hamas, to you, is women, children, and innocent families. If Hamas, in your eyes, is ordinary civilians and families, then I am Hamas, they are Hamas, and we are all

Hamas." Asmaa ended her story with the sentence: "Never ask me about peace again."

In the wake of the deaths of her family in Rafah, as the war continued to boom around her, Asmaa stood in brief solidarity with the militants who launched attacks against Israel. "When you are under the war for fifty-one days, and you've lost children, you will be with the rockets," she told me. I'd heard this from other Gazans, too: While they resent and reject Hamas's peacetime excesses, they will support the resistance in times of war, regardless of which flag they fight under. But this feeling passes, just as it did for Asmaa, who believes that, in the end, a writer cannot advocate war or violence. Regardless of the horrors one endures, a true writer always values humanity over revenge and peace over war. "If a writer says that he wants to kill others, then he is not a writer," Asmaa said.

Asmaa finds Gaza difficult to write about. She believes Gazan writers too often end up trapped in their collective experience and become part of what she calls "the factory." Instead of writing intimate fiction that examines the humanity of an individual, writers trade in external symbols. Gaza's "issues"—war, occupation, women's rights, Hamas—all wrest control of a writer's narratives like hijackers. "Gaza is stronger than us," Asmaa said. "Nobody can write Gaza."

The international media celebrates Asmaa as a feminist and a secularist. Even a right-wing Israeli newspaper lauded her for being "a thorn in the side of Hamas," and organizations around the world have praised her advocacy for human rights. In 2010, Human Rights Watch awarded Asmaa the Hellman/Hammett Grant for her "commitment to free expression and courage in the face of political prosecution." Two years later, she won the Courage in Journalism Award from the International Women's Media Foundation. Regardless of these accolades—which mean nothing to her, she says—Asmaa is a reluctant activist. "I always wanted to be a writer. And now I am known as a fighter. I don't want to be a fighter. I don't want to be a political woman. I never wanted that at all."

I didn't believe her. Everything I'd read by and about Asmaa suggested she relished challenging oppressive structures in Gaza. I reminded her about the time in 2010 when she rode a bicycle with an American journalist and three Italian human rights workers. While not strictly illegal, it is not socially acceptable for a woman to ride a bicycle in Gaza, especially not in the face of Hamas's fierce grip on female behavior. Asmaa flouted this rule and rode for thirty kilometers up the beach road from Rafah to Gaza City—almost the entire length of the Strip.

"Surely you knew, when you got on that bicycle with those foreign activists, that it was a political action," I said.

Asmaa glared at me. "No. It was a human action. It was the action of someone who has not been on a bike since she was fourteen," she said. "But the world gives names for everything. This is activism. This is politics. This is feminism. But I am not a feminist. I am not political. I am doing what I feel I want to do." The memory loosened her scowl, and her eyes cast downward. "I felt like I was flying," she said. "It was the first time since I was fourteen years old that I had the wind in my face." Then she looked back up at me. Her face hardened again. "I want to be a writer," she said. "I don't want to be a topic."

I learned long ago that the easiest way to procure a dinner invitation in the Arab world is to feign ignorance about the local cuisine. So when my friend Haneen asked me if I'd ever eaten *maftoul*, I shrugged. Thirty-six hours later, Haneen picked me up to bring me to her apartment for dinner. Her four-year-old daughter, Habiba, slept in the backseat. "I have a surprise for you," Haneen said. "I cooked the *maftoul*, but my neighbor Wisam has prepared the rest of the meal. And she is famous." Haneen told me Wisam hosts a weekly cooking show on one of the local television stations and is one of Gaza's celebrity chefs.

I followed Haneen, her daughters Habiba and Hala, and her son, Omar, into Wisam's apartment. Wisam was clearly thrilled to host us. A string of tiny Christmas lights hung on the wall of her dining room, and the table had already been set. Each plate bore a serving of *musakhan*, sumac-spiced chicken on a bed of thin *taboon* bread and baked onions. The rest of the table was crowded with cured black olives shining in a shallow dish of oil, bowls of garlicky yogurt, and a plate of fresh arugula leaves. At the center of the table sat a platter of Haneen's promised *maftoul*: Palestinian couscous flavored with the typically Gazan marriage of hot peppers and dill seed.

Wisam's daughter, Wadees, joined us at the table, but neither Haneen's nor Wisam's husband was there. "Don't worry," Haneen said. "We asked our husbands' permission for you to come over." I feigned relief. Then we ate. Wisam lifted olives from their oil and onto my plate. I cooled the unexpected scorch of the *maftoul* with spoonfuls of yogurt. After Haneen scolded me for using my fork to eat the *musakhan*, I pulled at the chicken with my fingers and followed Haneen and Wisam's lead by chasing each bite with a pinch of arugula. "This is good for men," Haneen said. "You know what I mean? For sex." She relayed a bit of Palestinian folk wisdom that says a wife should keep arugula under her pillow for her husband. I blushed each time I took another leaf.

After dinner, I scandalized the women when I rose to help clear the table. Haneen and Wisam bellowed at me to stop and ordered me into the salon, where they served sage tea, tiny cups of coffee, and a chocolate ice cream cake, which, Wisam explained, had partially melted due to a power cut earlier in the day.

"Now the children will perform for you," Haneen said. Hala and Wadees pulled Palestinian embroidered dresses over their clothes. Hala hung a key around her neck, the symbol of the Palestinian demand for the right of return, and gave a fiery nationalist speech she wrote. "The whole world knows Palestine," she insisted. She recited a poem after the speech, and then she and Wadees performed a Palestinian folk dance. Afterward, Omar heaved his heavy Arab dulcimer onto his lap to play the Palestinian national anthem and a couple of other songs while Hala and Wadees changed back into their regular clothes. The girls danced again, this time to some contemporary Arab pop music. Hala, serious and self-assured, led the dancing while Wadees tried to mimic her steps. Little Habiba, feeling left out of the show, did somersaults on the couch.

After the performance, Haneen and Wisam told me their neighborhood, Tel al-Hawa, was the scene of fierce fighting during both the 2008 and 2014 wars. Haneen's kitchen was the safest place on the floor, since it was the farthest room from any street-facing windows and the least vulnerable to tank shells and gunfire. During the burning summer of 2014, all the families on Haneen and Wisam's floor, thirty-five people in all, crowded into Haneen's kitchen. They huddled together in the dark on the linoleum for two days, without power or water, and waited out the fighting raging in the streets outside.

The women told me, too, how they stockpile foodstuffs in preparation for future wars. Sacks of dried beans and peas, jars of olives, and packets of dried pasta stand ready in cupboards for when bullets and bombs keep the families trapped at home. "We eat a lot of *mujadara* during the war," she said, referring to the popular Arab dish of rice, lentils, and fried onions. The women also stock emergency supplies of gasoline and cooking gas to deal with shortages and curfews.

What saddened me the most was how Haneen and Wisam spoke of war the way Canadians speak of winter storms. We never know exactly when they will arrive, but we are certain they will, so we'd best be ready. Gazans know the fighter jets will return to carve the sky like blades, and this place will blister again into war. Preparing for inevitable conflict is as much a part of Gaza's culture as short stories, dill seed, and chilies.

Mayy Ziyadeh was an Arab feminist when there was no such thing. Born in Nazareth in 1886 to a Palestinian mother and Lebanese father, Mayy attended a French convent school in Lebanon before emigrating to Cairo with her parents in 1911. She published her first of more than fifteen books that same year: a volume of French poetry written under the fabulous pseudonym of Isis Copia. Ziyadeh lived in a time and place that regarded notions of women's identity and liberation as an outrage, but she became a compelling voice for Arab women's emancipation nonetheless. "We should free the woman, so that her children won't grow up to become slaves," Ziyadeh wrote. "And we should remove the veil of illusions from her eyes, so that by looking into them, her husband, brother and son will discover that there is a greater meaning to life."

Mayy fell in love with Lebanese poet Khalil Gibran, though she would never meet him. Their romance endured for nineteen years, sustained solely through the love letters they sent back and forth from Cairo to New York, where Gibran lived. This was the most literary love affair I'd ever heard of. His death in 1931 shattered her.

Mayy ran the most famous and one of the most enduring literary salons in the Arab world. Beginning in 1913 and continuing every Tuesday evening for twenty-three years, she welcomed leading writers, activists, and intellectuals—men and women both—into the warmth of her father's apartment, where they debated culture and politics over cups of tea and rosewater. Mayy's salon became known as a place of serious learning, friendly but not frivolous. She expected her guests to arrive on time, and those invitees who dared to miss a gathering were obligated to apologize by phone or in writing. From her salon blossomed the ideas that fueled the Arab Nahdah, or awakening, a renaissance movement that challenged the then prevailing traditions of literature, gender, language, and culture.

In 2002, more than sixty years after her death in 1941, Mayy Ziyadeh's famed Tuesday salon inspired another Mayy, Mayy Nayef, to create her own literary salon in Gaza. Mayy named the salon Nuun after the letter in the Arabic alphabet that indicates the feminine. On the fifteenth of each month, between fifty and a hundred people gather in a meeting room in central Gaza City to "examine culture from a woman's point of view." They discuss the work of female writers and artists, the portrayal of women in the arts, and women's contributions to Palestinian cultural life. Men are welcome to attend, Mayy says, as long as they know they are there to talk about women.

"At first, we had to go to the authors and invite them to come and speak about their books," Mayy told me in the leafy courtyard of Gaza's Marna House Hotel. "Now they come to us." Authors plead with Mayy to include them in Nuun's program.

For writers living under blockade, the salon provides a rare opportunity to meet with an audience of engaged and intelligent readers. Nearly all of Gaza's writers, male and female both, have been invited to speak at Nuun. So have authors visiting from the West Bank and abroad. Professors from the English department in Gaza's universities have given talks about female writers from the United Kingdom, the United States, and Africa. The salon hosts musicians and visual artists, too, who come to speak about their work.

But they don't talk about politics. This is Mayy's rule. "We talk only about books and about culture. I think culture is more powerful than anything anyway." Because politics invades the daily life of Gazans in so many pervasive ways, Nuun's attendees appreciate the rare reprieve the salon offers. "We are very proud of this," Mayy said.

Nuun may avoid politics, but politics does not avoid Nuun. The Ministry of Culture has started to notice the salon since the Hamas takeover. Nuun never had links to government agencies, and Hamas's conservative officials tend to distrust any organization they do not oversee. Nuun's independence, this unmonitored exchange of ideas, worries the ministry. They also don't like women and men gathering together, especially to discuss women's issues. "They think we are dangerous," Mayy said. "We talk about freedom at Nuun. We try to open minds. This is terrible to them."

A couple of weeks before I sat with Mayy, a newly assigned deputy minister of culture called her and demanded a meeting. She tried to ignore him, but the deputy minister persisted. Mayy finally relented. In his office, the deputy told her he wanted her to relocate the salon from its current venue to a room at the ministry itself. Mayy refused. "I told him that we've been operating without any relationship to the government and that I want to keep it that way."

"Either you hold the salon under our wing or we close you down," the official said.

"But you have no wings," Mayy responded. "You've only had this job for two months. We've been here for fourteen years."

"Then we will send someone to the salon to see what you are doing."

"You can send anyone you want. We don't talk about politics. We talk about culture."

"Culture is very powerful," he said. "We want to know what you are talking about." Then the deputy told Mayy that the ministry had published a book of poetry written by four young Gazan women. "If we gave you the book, would you invite the poets to the salon?"

"If the poems are by women, then yes," Mayy told him. "I don't care if the poets are Hamas or Fatah. If they are women, then they are welcome. We can talk about the poems, and people who are listening can say whether they like the poems or not." The official agreed.

"And how were the Hamas poems?" I wondered.

Mayy shrugged. "They were all nationalist poems. They were not bad."

Mayy's acceptance of the government-sanctioned poets earned Nuun a reprieve from the ministry, but I wondered if Mayy feared for Nuun's future. She didn't. "They keep changing the minister," she said. "And they keep forgetting about us." She figures that even if this particular deputy remains suspicious of the salon, he and the minister of culture will be reassigned before they have the chance to shut Nuun down. Still, Mayy holds no illusions. She knows that the government could, if they really wanted to, kill the salon. "And maybe not just Nuun," Mayy said. "Maybe every cultural meeting place. Remember what they did to Gallery Café."

In her roles both as a scholar of Arab literature and as the fourteen-year *salonnière* of Nuun, Mayy has borne witness to the changes in Gaza's literary culture—especially in regard to women's writing. She told me that while many male poets still adhere to the strict poetic forms indigenous to the Islamic world, like ghazals and qasidas, female poets have embraced new poetry styles that more resemble prose. They have grown bored of the complicated verse structures of the venerable Arab masters, most of whom were men. "The old style is heavy," Mayy said.

Female writers in the Arab world have embraced free verse because it allows them to express themselves outside the restraints of traditional forms. They can break the rules of rhythm the old masculine structures imposed. The new poetry styles offer a freedom on the page that Palestinian women, especially in Gaza, often do not enjoy in their own society. Restricted by both politics and patriarchy, the female poets of Gaza snatch at freedom wherever they can, granting their pens an emancipation their bodies are too often denied.

Sumaiya al-Susi lived an accelerated girlhood. She started school when she was only four years old because one of her relatives was a teacher who allowed Sumaiya to register early. She enrolled in an education degree program after graduating from high school. She didn't want to be a teacher, but the Islamic University of Gaza had been closed due to First Intifada violence, and Sumaiya's sole option for a post-secondary education was at the newly opened al-Azhar University, which only offered degrees in education at the time. By the time Sumaiya finished university, she was married and the mother of a one-year-old daughter.

For a year after graduation, Sumaiya lived at home and cared for her daughter, but she bristled at the idea of remaining a stay-at-home mom. She found work teaching English at a secondary school in Deir al-Balah, but she didn't like this, either. Her teaching career lasted three days. "I spent the first two days doing some games and songs in English, but when the real work started, I said no." She found work in a Fatah government planning office a few months later and still works there now.

Sumaiya started writing short fiction and poetry in her mid-teens and continued writing while in university. She entered one of her short stories in a writing contest and won the opportunity to attend a women's writing workshop. Sumaiya and the other writers were supposed to meet with workshop mentors, Khaled Juma among them, twice a week for about four months. But Khaled lived in southern Gaza and frequent military curfews often hindered his commute. What was supposed to be a four-month workshop took nearly two years to complete. "It was good for us," Sumaiya said. "We grew up like a family." Each time Khaled published a new book he would bring copies to the workshop participants. Khaled and the other mentors introduced Sumaiya to the life and writings of other Palestinian writers, especially Mahmoud Darwish, whom she'd heard of but hardly read.

Sumaiya's husband did not support her poetry at first. "It is hard to be a woman and a writer in Gaza," Sumaiya said. Her family members saw little value in poetry and feared ridicule from friends and neighbors who considered writing a waste of time. Working as a writer also meant attending conferences and festivals abroad, and conservative families refused to let their daughters travel. Sumaiya found an ally in her mother-in-law. She was a keen reader who gave Sumaiya books to read and encouraged her to keep writing. Eventually she finished writing a book of poems she'd started in university.

Sumaiya writes what she calls "prose poetry," which resembles long descriptive essays rather than structured verse. In them, she reveals a particularly Gazan brand of ennui I'd witnessed over and over during my time in the Strip. Before my travels, I'd only ever thought of Gaza when something dramatic happened there. But my weeks living in Gaza revealed that often nothing happens at all. Israel's blockade and Hamas's oppressive rule have robbed Gazan society of forward momentum. Sumaiya's poetry reveals the weariness and tedium of life in Gaza—a tragedy less acute than the blood and bombs of war, but continual and all encompassing. Sumaiya writes:

> In Gaza, there is a great surplus of time, which you must know how to use up, how to get rid of, in every possible way, as there are no important appointments binding you to your schedule, and no particularly sacred or respected times. Everything is possible at any time, and it's up to you to kill time as you see fit. So you either remain a prisoner in your own home, workplace, or wherever it is that you know and that knows you, or you think of other ways to kill time. Whatever you do will lead you to the same result in the end: you will make it as far as your pillow, at night, with a sense of absolute futility.

The vast killing fields of time—online chatrooms and Facebook walls—are as authentically Gazan locales as Nedal's citrus fields and the wobbly tabletops at Karawan. The internet is another Palestinian territory. Gazans live online, especially during the blacked-out hours of night when the wireless router's flickering lights, powered by battery, stand in for stars. The internet also grants Palestinian writers, many of whom lack access to traditional publishing houses, a space to share their work. Blogs often take the place of books.

But I wondered if the internet, for all the virtual escapes it offers to these shackled citizens, is just another type of prison. Gazans are trapped in an online illusion of freedom, the confines of digital artifice. Is the internet just another jailer? In Sumaiya's work, this virtual space "teems with bored friends" and offers little respite. In a poem called "Night, Net, Gaza," Sumaiya writes of a typical late-night gathering of the faceless avatars on her screen:

> You observe them all, so as to add new details of relationships that only you believe in to your imprecise and sparse memory. You begin keeping track of who enters when, connecting times and people, searching for what relationships (illusionary ones, of course) lie behind the green icons on the screen. You are also here to discover whether one or another of your friends have taken advantage of your departure from the

forum to start a slanderous new discussion thread, along with the other people there, of course, about you. You might even be thinking about deleting them from your contact list, for failure to uphold the Microsoft Messenger terms of use—which no one ever signs.

In her poem "The City," Sumaiya insists that in order to live in Gaza, Palestinians must create their own "secret world," a place hidden from disapproving eyes. "My secret world is my family," she said. Sumaiya had two daughters by her early twenties. Then, eleven years later, she started having children again. In addition to her two adult daughters, Sumaiya now has a seven-year-old daughter, a five-year-old son, and a five-month-old baby girl. "My eldest daughter and I were pregnant at the same time," Sumaiya said, laughing. She credits her second wave of motherhood for easing the darkness of Gaza's recent history. Her meetings with other writers at places like Gallery Café inevitably led to depressing conversations about being denied exit visas or the abuses of Hamas. Her children gave her an excuse to avoid such conversations. "When I had those small children, I didn't have to go out and meet people. I can create my own mood at home with my children," she said. "It creates balance for me somehow."

For Sumaiya, being a mother often means having to protect her youngest children from what they learn in kindergarten. She fears her kids are being taught to venerate Hamas and celebrate the actions of the al-Qassam Brigades, Hamas's military wing. "They have the idea of war instead of the idea of peace. They don't think about Palestinian independence at all." I was surprised children that age were taught such things. "There are kindergartens for Hamas and for Islamic Jihad," Sumaiya said. "You can imagine what they are teaching the children. If you are a girl, you cannot sit next to a boy." These children will also learn to judge everyone by the depth of their faith. "They will learn to ask, 'Are you a Muslim or an infidel?'"

Sumaiya does her best to counter what her children learn in school, but she cannot shield them from war. Her daughter was four and her son three during the war in 2008. Sumaiya told them the bombs were fireworks, but by 2014 they would not be fooled. Her children knew the clamor of drones and bombs and fighter jets. They could tell the difference between a Qassam rocket and an Israeli missile by the sound each one made. In this curriculum of violence, Gazan children develop an ear for bomb blasts. They become unwitting connoisseurs of shock waves and weaponry. This horrible education conducts an interrogation in reverse: forcing these children, through violence, to learn what they don't want to know.

"I don't know what will happen, but at least I can teach my children a sense of how to deal with everything," Sumaiya said. "How to deal with war. To deal with peace. How to deal with each other. And to let them be strong. Somehow, they should be strong. This society does not allow weak people to continue."

My friend Haneen insisted I meet her mother, Um Abdallah, and urged me to join her family's regular Thursday gathering at her mother's home. I was the only male invited—the men were smoking and watching television elsewhere—and I had to wait behind a curtain in a darkened room until all the women fetched their headscarves. Someone drew the curtain back, and I entered a room filled with smiling women. Um Abdallah welcomed me with typical Palestinian warmth. As is the custom of devout Muslim women, she did not shake my hand but patted the couch next to her to invite me to sit. She occasionally tapped me on the leg as she spoke, and I appreciated this casual and tactile intimacy. The innocent subversion of traditional decorum felt like another sort of welcome.

Um Abdallah's daughters, granddaughters, and daughters-in-law continued to arrive until women and girls occupied every chair and cushion. Each woman kissed Um Abdallah's hand as she arrived before joining the others as they passed around glasses of Orange Fanta, date-stuffed pastries, crackers, coffee, and fruit. "This comes from the tree in my garden," Um Abdallah said of a plate of sliced guava as she tapped my leg again. One of the women had just preserved a batch of red chilies and handed out jars to her sisters.

All of Um Abdallah's daughters are well educated and do important work for women's organizations in Gaza that engage with issues such as women's health, women's agriculture, and domestic abuse. At seventy-four years old, Um Abdallah is as busy as any of her daughters. She rises at four each morning to pray before tending to her garden. She volunteers with the elderly in her community and teaches religion at the neighborhood mosque. "Not doctrine," she is quick to clarify, "but the role of faith in everyday life." She rarely returns home before seven o'clock. Thursday is her only free night, hence the weekly gathering, but the women all know to call ahead just in case she is busy. Several times during my visit, Um Abdallah lifted her cell phone from the table to check her Facebook page.

The women talked about how much they missed my friend Hadeel, Haneen's sister, since she moved to Canada, and how their children love speaking to her on Skype. They told me about a sister-in-law, absent that night, whom everyone likes. "In Gaza, we don't usually like the sisters-in-law," someone said. (This made me smile; I'd already learned about warring female in-laws from Sharif Kanaana's book of folktales.) I showed photos of my wife and son on my cell phone and scandalized Um Abdallah when I told her we would not have another child. She has ten children and forty-six grandchildren already and is not yet satisfied.

Before I left Um Abdallah's salon, we all took group pictures with our cell phones. The image of me surrounded by a dozen beaming *hijabis* is my favorite photo from Gaza. Then Haneen drove me back to my flat. Wedding musicians played in the back of pickup trucks that plied up and down the beachfront road. In each, a lone videographer pointed a camera back at the bride and groom following in the car behind them. Wedding guests jammed the sidewalks in front of each hotel and wedding hall. Street vendors sold brined lupin beans and paper bowls of chili-dusted corn kernels. "People are happy," Haneen said as we drove past the melee. "There is power tonight, and the streetlights are on."

Like teenagers everywhere, Rana Mourtaja always has her earphones on. And like parents everywhere, hers warn she'll lose her hearing if she doesn't turn the volume down. "That day is coming soon," Rana admits. I found her SoundCloud page online. Her playlist includes scratchy recordings of Arab singers from the 1950s and '60s, beat-heavy contemporary Lebanese pop, and a few sugary Western love songs—including an unforgivable Nickelback ballad. Rana told me she listened to these songs during the 2014 war. She drowned out the buzzing drones, bomb blasts, and gruesome news reports with the music she loves.

But Rana felt guilty listening to her favorite music "as if nothing was going on." In an essay published during the war by *New Internationalist* magazine, Rana wrote:

> An undertaker on the radio won't stop ranting about the rising number of martyrs, each one adding insult to injury. I wonder what would happen if I listened to music instead of accompanying him in this endless counting of martyrs, airstrikes, aircrafts, prayers of the elderly, screams of infants. Would turning him off make me a traitor? . . . I hope the devil knows that, in this, I do not betray those who booked their tickets to God, or those awaiting their turn in the long line. I only betray the war.

Rana titled the essay "Is 53 Seconds Long Enough to Gather My Soul?" in reference to the IDF's practice of "roof knocking." During all three Gaza wars, Israeli aircraft dropped small explosive charges onto the rooftops of buildings the IDF suspected were used by militants. The charges were often strong enough to shatter windows and rattle walls, but not usually powerful enough to cause severe damage. Residents knew this was only a prelude—a cordial message from the IDF that fire would soon come down from the sky. After the roof knock, panicked residents had a short amount of time to flee the building before a missile struck. Gazan families devised intricate escape plans. An eldest daughter would be assigned to gather the passports and family jewelry, say, and the sisters-in-law would rouse the children from their beds. A pair of brothers might be tasked to carry an infirm grandmother out on a mattress. Many Gazans I met told me they keep a bag containing money, important documents, and their most treasured family photos ready near their doors.

Residents usually had ten or fifteen minutes to leave their homes before the missile came, but in 2014 a family in Rana's neighborhood had only fifty-three seconds to flee before the airstrike demolished their home. Rana wrote:

At the beginning of the war, I packed up a few of my favorite clothes, plus a few books that I initially struggled to pick out (finally selecting only those that contained signatures and personalized dedications, plus a few other "must-reads"). I didn't forget to pack my certificates of excellence from school, minor awards for minor accomplishments, and the keffiyeh I was given by my friend in Jerusalem on my sole visit to that city. Nor did I forget the souvenir my friend Rima gave me a few days before her departure, notes I exchanged with my classmates, and a few letters from other friends. After quite a tussle my bag managed to accommodate these, plus some greeting cards, photo albums and other presents. . . . I try not to think about the fact that I might not be able to gather up my soul from all the places it's scattered in this spacious universe, should I be struck by a missile in the midst of fleeing, or if the pilot decides not to pause for his usual 53 seconds between the "warning missile" and my one.

The IDF considers the roof knocking evidence of its efforts to spare civilian lives. But even when this works, the practice can feel like punishment. I heard stories of families who heeded numerous warning calls and roof knocks, each time scrambling terrified from their homes, but no missile ever struck. These false alarms impose their own acute cruelty on families who are forced, over and over, to flee missiles that may never come, each time wondering if this time the warnings will hold true.

Rana was born in Minsk in 1997 to a Belarusian mother and a *Ghazzawi* father. The two met in Belarus, where her father was studying law. Many Gazan men traveled to former Eastern Bloc countries for university in the open days between Intifadas, and many returned with new wives and children. "You will find here a lot of people my age who are half Belarusian, half Russian, or half Ukrainian." Rana came to Gaza with her parents when she was five years old and her father found work as a lawyer for the PA.

Tania, Rana's mother, studied English literature in Belarus and gave Rana books about Cinderella and Pippi Longstocking. She started writing her own stories in the third grade. "In my stories, Pippi Longstocking would come to my house and have dinner with me," Rana said. Her parents enrolled her in workshops at the Tamer Institute, where she worked with Khaled Juma and Atef Abu Saif. "I was lucky to be in a family that gave me the space to be myself," she said.

Rana most enjoys creating lives for the characters she invents in her stories. "If I had to choose a job, I would choose the job of God," Rana said. She paused, then added, "I am sorry. I am not religious." Most of the time, Rana publishes her stories on her Facebook page, but one piece, titled "The Bus Mirror," earned inclusion in a Swedish-produced anthology of writing by Gazan youth called *Novell Gaza*. In 2015, Rana was among thirty-five young writers chosen from Arabic-speaking countries, Russia, China, and the United States to attend the two-week Between the Lines program at the University of Iowa. She was the only Palestinian from the West Bank or Gaza to be accepted into the program.

Unlike the other Palestinian writers I met, in Gaza and elsewhere, Rana does not craft Palestinian lives on the page. "I am trying to create my own world," Rana said. "To escape what I see in Gaza." Rana sets her often romantic short stories in locales that are vaguely European, and she rarely gives her characters Arab-sounding names. "Atef said I should try writing something from my reality. But I can't. I can't imagine anything from here. When it comes to writing a story, I will never write about Gaza."

If Gharib Asqalani represents the first generation of Palestinian writers, who wrote in the service of the nationalist cause, and Atef represents the second generation, who traded nationalist symbols for the details of a regular Palestinian life, then perhaps Rana represents the next generation: men and women who are not compelled to portray Palestine at all. I asked her if she feels any responsibility to write Palestinian stories. "I feel a responsibility to the people," she said. "Not to the cause." Rana bristles at those who talk about Palestine solely in relation to borders and territory. "When they say 'land,' I say, 'Go fuck yourself with your land. This is not about the land. It is about the people.'" She also resents the Palestinian tendency to neglect the future in favor of the past. Rana sees little value in simply enumerating lost lives and stolen villages. Palestinians need forward momentum. "The point is not what happened. The point is what's next."

More than anything, though, Rana wants her writings to reveal that

Gazans are normal. "I am under occupation. I lost a lot of my friends and family members during the wars," Rana said. "But I also think about good-looking guys. Like teenagers all over the world, I have my crazy stuff. You can find me dancing at midnight every night. It is normal. I am trying to act like a normal human being." She resents the fact that much of the world looks at Gazans as if they are "mentally sick" and in need of help. "Don't help me," Rana said. "Understand that I am human."

After she graduated from high school, Rana enrolled at Gaza's al-Azhar University. She was two months into a law program when we met, and things were not going well. "It is not for me. I am dying," she said, with typical teenage melodrama. She especially despises waking early for lectures and holds particular disdain for her Islamic studies class. "The professor's voice is really loud, and he keeps shouting the whole lecture. And he just reads from the textbook. So I sit in the back and read Dan Brown." Rana appreciates the irony of surreptitiously reading *The Da Vinci Code* during a lecture on religious history in an Islamic university. "I know I am not the ideal university student."

Rana would switch from law to psychology the following semester, but her affection for post-secondary education would not increase. "University sucks!" she wrote to tell me a few months later. "I hate mornings and I hate morning people."

Najlaa Ataallah wore a blue headscarf with pink stars and a pink sweater when I met her in her living room. She was three months pregnant at the time and her husband, Raghab, served us sage tea and date-filled cookies as we talked about war.

During the wars of 2008 and 2010, Najlaa felt a distance between herself and the danger. The Israelis launched attacks on specific targets, and there were places in Gaza where she could feel safe. But like I'd been told over and over again, nowhere felt safe in 2014. Najlaa's family lived on Jal'aa Street in the city center. The safest neighborhood in Gaza, they thought. And yet her cousin was killed by an airstrike only a hundred meters from her front door. "I felt it so close. The sounds of the war happened inside me," Najlaa said. "From the first minute of the war, I thought these were our last moments in this life; every Gazan will die sooner or later. And when they targeted the towers, I totally believed they would also target our house."

In the final week of the war, warplanes attacked three multistory apartment towers in Gaza City. On Saturday, they completely demolished the twelve-story Zafer 4 Tower in Tel al-Hawa and rendered forty-four families homeless. The following Monday, three missiles from an F-16 sheared a side off the sixteen-story Italian Complex, which included fifty residential apartments. And before the sun rose on Tuesday, the last day of the war, Israel bombed the al-Basha Tower. All thirteen floors came crashing down in a heap of rubble. The IDF took care to ensure that the residents of these towers had evacuated before the attacks, and no one died when the buildings came down. But aside from vague suggestions that the towers "housed facilities linked to Palestinian militants," Israel never explained why it chose to level entire buildings rather than launch more directed attacks on individual apartments. An Amnesty International report suggested that the destruction of the towers was wanton, unjustified, and "intended as a form of collective punishment against the people of Gaza." It called the attacks a war crime. I've heard Gazans refer to them as Gaza's 9/11.

As the bombs and buildings fell around her, Najlaa started to write. She posted daily on her blog about her experiences during the bombing. In one entry, Najlaa imagines a boy who, after surviving a night of bombing, vows to reveal his feelings to the girl he fancies:

> After surviving each aggression, you always make a promise to yourself. The promise that if you were to stay alive, you will live and embrace life with more joy than ever before. You will tell the carefree girl in your neighborhood as you observe her walking in and out of her house that you really admire her. In fact, you will tell her that you love her. You will not hold back in reluctance, not even for once. You feel this love exploding inside you as did the explosions that took all the houses in the airstrikes.

In another post, from the fifth day of the war, Najlaa wrote:

Shook out of bed from the all the deafening sounds that reached your ears, yet mostly from the vivid scenes of war in your own head. You reach out to feel your body parts, making sure every piece is still in its place. Your head still sits above your neck. You rush to the mirror and examine every detail of your face; you confirm and reassure yourself, "These are my two eyes . . . My nose . . . My mouth . . ." They are still intact, where they all should be. Neither part is lost nor shattered into remains. You are still in one complete piece, the way your mother had given birth to you.

Taken as a whole, Najlaa's blogged diary of the war reveals what it means to be in constant terror. The same fears echo over and over in her work, and the repetition has a cumulative effect. Days of dread piled on Najlaa's psyche like bodies in a morgue. The scale of her horror is striking and inescapable.

This writing gave Najlaa no comfort. "When I write, I feel the conflict more. I don't feel better. I feel the danger so close to my house. So close to my heart. So close to my room." Najlaa wrote through the war because she knew no other way to express what was happening around her. As a writer, she felt a responsibility to make people outside Gaza understand.

Najlaa was raised to be a writer. Her mother started giving Najlaa Agatha Christie mysteries to read when she was seven years old and rewarded her good behavior with Russian novels. "I remember reading *Crime and Punishment* for the first time when I was eleven," Najlaa said. She started writing her own short stories when she was ten years old and joined the Tamer Institute in her teens to work with writers like Atef Abu Saif and Gharib Asqalani. "They encouraged us to keep this talent inside us," she said. Her first novel, *A Cup of Coffee*, followed the life of a girl about Najlaa's own age who rebelled against the rules and customs of Gazan society. Tamer published Najlaa's second novel, *The Picture*, when she was twenty years old. The book focused on the struggles of an overweight teenage boy in Gaza and was named as one of the best 101 books for adolescents in the Arab world.

Her current novel should have been finished by now. Tamer expected it last year. "I am a little lazy," Najlaa admitted. The book follows a teen-age refugee who dreams of leaving Gaza and continuing his studies else-where. "He sees Gaza as a jail," Najlaa said. "Throughout the novel he asks himself, 'Why was I born here?' 'Why am I in this camp?' 'Why is my mother my mother, and my father my father?'" After the split be-tween Fatah and Hamas, many young people in Gaza have these ques-tions and yearn to leave.

Much of Najlaa's writing focuses on the intimate physicality of her characters, often with a vivid sensuality that reminded me of Raji Bathish's work. In a story called "Midnight," the narrator is a weight-obsessed young woman who describes the feeling of her body after a workout:

> I lie on my irritating bed, remembering to flex my torso and hold my-self in a good posture—my thigh, my hands, my flat stomach, and a little bit of love . . . I'll wash myself, I'll strain to get my body's weight over there and get rid of the last few drops of sweat with a little purify-ing water. My clothes are wet; as I take them off I focus for a moment, trance-like, on my breathing, my increasingly rapid panting. A beau-tiful body, and a loving power that has grown with each of the twenty years I've lived in it for.

The corporeal evolves into the erotic in Najlaa's "The Whore of Gaza," which appeared in *The Book of Gaza*. The story brings readers into the bedroom of a woman named Azza who works as an escort for men but is still technically a virgin. The story is remarkable for its descriptive scenes of female eroticism rarely seen in the writing of Palestinian women. In one section, Azza lies masturbating on her bed. She fondles her own breasts, "receiving them with her lips, moistening them" before "reaching out for her heavenly center." The scene ends as she "rubs vigorously, to the point of burning up, feeling the liquid coming out of her, the thrill subsiding."

The inner landscape of Azza's lonely bedroom reflects the claustro-phobia of Gaza itself, especially for women, whom Gazan society pres-sures to conform and behave. Her sexual fantasies aside, Azza most longs for a cigarette, but Gaza denies her even this tiny, physical pleasure. For women, cigarettes are "carved in stone as forbidden." Azza rages:

It is not for stupidity that even past the age of thirty I'm afraid of everything! Of the hymen. Of walking accompanied by one of them in public. Of letting a strand of my hair show in case one of them should stop me in the street, scared of my very eyes, and scream at me to cover up. Or of simply being seen with a male friend in a public place where we might talk about things: What will happen to this little place called Gaza? More to the point, what will happen to us? How we have lost or are wasting our lives, draping ourselves in sins we haven't committed or that we fear committing!

Najlaa wanted to reveal the inner social lives of women in Gaza, "but people don't read as you want them to read," she said. All her critics saw was the sex. "I broke some taboos in Gaza, and wrote about things you are not supposed to talk about." To desire is normal, Najlaa said, but to express desire, like Azza does in her bedroom, is forbidden. "It is not good for an Oriental girl to write a story like that. It is not good for her reputation." Najlaa regrets writing the story. She was only twenty-one years old when she wrote it and at a stage in her life when she had "this enthusiasm of youth that wanted to break everything, even religious things."

Now Najlaa is older. And married. "And in six months I will have a baby," she said. "The world changed, and my thoughts changed. Now it is better to be conservative in my writing. To respect my country and my country's traditions." Raghab agrees. He supports and encourages her writing but vets all her stories before she shows them to anyone else. He makes sure she doesn't put out anything that can be seen as critical of the government or will cause her trouble. "He is afraid for me," Najlaa said.

"The Whore of Gaza" was not the only story in *The Book of Gaza* to draw criticism. Readers wanted more stories about war, politics, and the blockade—issues of larger import than what Raghab called "small problems not worth writing about." Raghab feels that writers should tackle bigger issues in their work that increase awareness of the struggle, especially when they publish in English for an international audience. He sees little value in writing about internal issues like Palestinian cultural heritage or domestic violence. Najlaa disagrees. She doesn't believe every Palestinian writer should "carry the cause." Besides, everything she writes will be seen through the lens of politics anyway.

After they were married, Najlaa and Raghab obtained exit visas to leave Gaza for their honeymoon. They dreamed of traveling to Istanbul, but decided not to. They couldn't rely on the Erez checkpoint being open when they returned from their honeymoon and didn't want to risk losing their jobs in Gaza. Najlaa and Raghab also briefly considered buying an apartment but decided against this, too. They did not want to spend their savings on a home that might not survive the next war.

Gazans lack certainty more than anything else. They cannot rely on anything or take anything for granted. In a 2009 interview, Atef Abu Saif said, "I think nothing in Gaza is regular. Everything is irregular. You cannot expect anything. You cannot say I want to do this tomorrow and I want to do that the day after. I think even you cannot promise to do anything." A mother in Gaza does not know if her *musakhan* will finish baking before the power goes out on her electric oven. A fisherman does not know how far he can sail on any given morning, and a farmer does not know if there will be a market for the strawberries he plants today. The fresh university grad smiles for selfies in her graduation robes but knows the degree in her hand cannot guarantee her a job. Gazans don't know if the border will ever open, whether they will be permitted to visit their cousins in Ramallah or pray in Jerusalem. Only war is reliable. It's as certain as the seasons.

One day at noon, as the Friday sermon boomed out from the Fisherman's Mosque, I went for a walk along the seafront road. The November air felt warm to me but evidently too cold for Gazans, as the beach was completely deserted. I stepped off the sidewalk and across a white sand beach littered with plastic bottles, take-out containers, and the carcasses of ketchup packets. Fried chicken bones were picked clean by seabirds and bleached white by the sun.

Down at the water's edge, where the sea smooths the sand, human litter gives way to what a sea leaves behind. A scattering of clamshells— orange, blue, and brown—spreads across the packed sand. They crunch beneath my sandals along with the occasional claw from an unfortunate crab. The sea here smells like a sea should. On the edge of the water, at least, the beach is beautiful the way all beaches are.

I remember walking with Mona after our tour through Shati. She wanted to bring me to Kazem, one of Gaza City's famous ice cream parlors, for a morning sundae, and we walked along the seafront road a few kilometers north of this stretch of beach. There, open trash bins stunk of rot and buzzed with flies next to leaning shacks built of wood scraps and rusting sheet metal. "It is not a very nice walk," Mona said, but then her gaze lifted over the stench and squalor to the Mediterranean beyond. "I don't know how people can live without the sea," she said.

The sea grants Gaza its only visible horizon and its only open space. Every other vantage point reminds Gazans of closure and incarceration. Mona said that the seaside is the only place she can imagine being out of Gaza. The sea offers no actual escape, of course; Gazans are not allowed a port along this coastline. No ships carry Gazans away from here. But the sea is a window, at least, if not a door.

Her Name Is Maram

I wanted to find the girl in the green dress. The girl who plucked books from rubble during the 2014 war. The girl who first inspired me to seek out Palestine's books and writers.

I contacted the Palestinian media agency that first published the photos. It connected me to the photographer, Mo'men Faiz. He remembered the girl. "She had very beautiful eyes," he said. "I thought her family might be from Afghanistan." He agreed to meet with me one morning and to help me find her.

Mo'men's body tells its own narrative of war and resilience. Ten days before the outbreak of the 2008 war, on the Eid al-Adha holiday, Mo'men and two other journalists traveled to the border to cover a story about the closing of the Karni checkpoint in northern Gaza. An Israeli rocket struck the neighborhood and blasted Mo'men into a coma. He woke up in a hospital bed days later surrounded by weeping relatives. Mo'men's legs felt heavy. "As if they were tied to a tank," he said. When he pulled away the blanket he saw that both of his legs were gone.

The Saudi king flew Mo'men and other injured Gazans to Riyadh for treatment. There he met Deema Aydieh, a young journalist and Palestinian refugee living in Saudi Arabia who was sent to interview Mo'men in the hospital. Deema wore a niqab and Mo'men never saw her face, but he was drawn to her obvious intelligence and education. They were married a month later and returned to Gaza together. Now they have two daughters.

Mo'men's disability has hardly slowed his work. His photography, especially his compelling and often beautiful images of Gaza's children, appears in newspapers and on media websites around the Middle East and Europe. The sight of Mo'men wheeling his chair through Gaza's shattered streets, perched on a folded keffiyeh with his camera on his lap, has made him a celebrity. But Mo'men winced when I mentioned I'd like to write about him. He doesn't want to be pitied. Besides, he'd rather tell his own stories of Gaza through his photography than be a foreign writer's subject.

Mo'men picked Lara and me up in a modified SUV with hand levers rigged to the brake and gas pedals. We drove south along the seaside road toward the Nuseirat refugee camp. Just before we reached the point along the shoreline where a sewage outlet pipe dumps raw filth into the sea, Mo'men signaled I should roll up my windows. Then he squirted cologne from a small glass bottle onto the dashboard air vents to mask the stench coming from the outside. The sewage smeared a great brown stain in the seawater that stretched to the horizon. Mo'men told me that a fish-monger once sold him a fish caught in the polluted water. When Mo'men cut into it he found it was black on the inside. Once we safely passed through the stench, Mo'men asked me to roll down the windows again.

We pulled off the highway and into the camp. Mo'men drove to the site of the Farouk Mosque, which had been destroyed by an air strike during the 2014 war. "I photographed the girl here," he said. By now, most of the rubble had been cleared. Only a couple of concrete pillars and a clot of twisted rebar stood where the mosque used to be.

Mo'men parked in front of a nearby shop and summoned the shop-keeper to the driver's side window. I showed him the photos of the girl on my phone. The man did not recognize her. We moved ahead to a bar-bershop, but the barber did not know her, either. We kept driving, from shop to shop, showing the photos to shopkeepers and customers until one young man in a chin-strap beard said he recognized the girl and knew her neighborhood. He got into the SUV with us and guided Mo'men to the street where he thought the girl's family lived. While our chin-strapped friend knocked on a few doors, Mo'men waved to a young girl in a black dress and a frilly white collar. When he showed her the photos, the girl said, "She goes to my school, but I don't know where she lives."

Chin-strap returned with another man. Mo'men held out my phone to him. "Do you know this girl?" he asked.

"Is she a martyr?" the man asked reflexively. Then he looked closer and said, "I know her. She is my cousin." He led us to a house a little farther down the street.

We knocked on the door. The girl answered. Our arrival must have startled her—she could not have expected a visit from a foreign man, a young Gazan woman, and a legless photographer in a wheelchair. Yet her wide greenish-brown eyes, the same eyes that first drew Mo'men's camera lens, betrayed no alarm. She called for her mother, who quickly welcomed us into her home while a group of young men rushed to set up some plastic chairs for us to sit on. Another man brought coffee. In the commotion, the girl went inside to doff her headscarf and change into a blue floral-print shirt. She'd seen Mo'men's camera and wanted to wear something pretty.

Her name is Maram. She is twelve years old and the youngest of nine children. Like most Gazans her age, Maram is a third-generation refugee. In 1948, her family fled Joolis, a village in the southern district of Palestine—a different village than the Joolis where Abu Ahmed settled after fleeing al-Birwa. Maram's family sought safety in central Gaza, where a former British military prison was set up to house refugees. UNRWA soon formed the Nuseirat refugee camp nearby. The camp's population swelled over the years, and Maram's family now lives among sixty-six thousand registered refugees.

Maram told me about the books in the photographs. She had taken advantage of one of the cease-fires during the 2014 war to finally leave her house and go for a walk. She noticed torn book pages blowing on the street. "I saw they were from the Holy Koran," she said. Some young boys were stepping on the pages as they played in the road, so Maram decided to gather them up. She followed the trail of pages, stooping to collect each one, until she reached the ruins of the mosque where she found the rest of the tattered Koran. Then she climbed the pile of rubble that once stood as the mosque's library and rescued whatever books she could pull from beneath the broken concrete.

"I loved going to the library," Maram said. "My mother does not read very well. She would take me there so I could help her read and memorize verses from the Koran." Maram used to visit the library by herself, too, to study the Koran and read other books. Sometimes a local *sheikha* taught biology and English classes there. "I also want to be a *sheikha*," she said. "To sit and talk to people."

Near the end of our visit, just before she posed beside me for Mo'men's camera, Maram recited a few lines of poetry. In a self-assured voice and rolling cadence, Maram said:

Beloved Palestine, how can I live
Far away from your plains and hills?
The mountain slopes, red with anemones, call out to me
And traces of the hills on the horizon.

The lines come from a famous poem by Abu Salma called "We Shall Return," written in the years following 1948. Elsewhere in the poem, Abu Salma asks, then answers, the central question for Palestinians:

Will there be a return, my comrades ask,
A return after such long absence?
Yes, we'll return and kiss the moist ground,
love flowering on our lips.

Maram's family will never return to Joolis. Nothing is left to return to; the Israeli army reduced the village to stones after 1948. But the end of Joolis is not the end of Maram's Nakba story. For Palestinians, the Nakba is not a historical event that happened seventy years ago. In 2008, three months before he died, Darwish wrote: "The Nakba is not a memory, it is a continuous uprooting that makes Palestinians more worried about their existence. The Nakba continues because the occupation continues. Continuing occupation means the continuation of the war." The Nakba is an unfinished novel—three generations long, and counting, with no denouement. It is the poem that never ends, persisting and pressing forward. Of all the things I learned in Palestine, this felt among the most important.

During my time among the readers and writers of Palestine, I found no life undarkened by the Nakba and the conflict it continues to bear. Yet I found no life wholly defined by the conflict, either. Palestinians may long for a justice long denied them, but they also long to marry, and to see their children marry. Palestinians want to see Paris. Teenagers blast their ears with pop music. Boys kick footballs on beaches with their cousins and try to catch the eye of the pretty girl in their Arabic literature class. Palestinians star in cell phone commercials and on cooking shows. They coach basketball. Sometimes they write poems. The Palestinians live complete lives in their disputed space, regardless of all they've lost and continue to lose.

I also learned that beauty flashes brighter in the blackness of this loss. Cruelty's shadow amplifies Palestinian humanity, like the green of a girl's dress against a background of gray. As I left Gaza—and Palestine—by passing back through Erez's cold steel, I thought about how much I will miss the brightened beauty of this place. The way the fragrance of jasmine intensifies at dusk. The bloodred sunsets. The green neon on the minarets, and the calls to prayer they radiate over the hills. The smell of sage in every cup of tea. The way every Palestinian who enters the café bids everyone inside *As-salaam-alaikum*—"Peace be unto you." The wedding bands that play from the back of moving flatbed trucks. Falafel for breakfast. Walking beneath the mulberry trees and mashing the fruit beneath my sandals. *Za'atar* and labneh and paying a single shekel for six warm rounds of pita. The gratitude Palestinians express for my willingness to come and see this place for myself.

I found a story in every crack of this place. Stories about how taxi drivers who ply the Ramallah–Jericho road die young. They spend years traveling back and forth from the heights of Palestine's hills to the depths of the Jordan Rift Valley near the Dead Sea, and the constant altitude change stresses their hearts. About professors in a Gazan medical college who began to worry when too many students were recognizing the cadavers provided for their anatomy classes. The college arranged for the students to study anatomy at a school in Cairo, where they were less likely to face their own relatives on the dissecting table. About a cobbler in Hebron who adds a pinch of dirt from the nearby hills to the soles of the shoes he makes. That way, no matter where his customers go, they will always walk upon the soil of their homeland.

READING LIST

The following is a partial list of books, journals, and online sources where English-translated material from the writers I profile can be found, organized alphabetically by author.

A selection of **Maya Abu-Alhayyat**'s poems, including "Children," translated by Liz Lochhead, can be found in *A Bird Is Not a Stone: An Anthology of Contemporary Palestinian Poetry*, edited by Henry Bell and Sarah Irving (Glasgow: Freight Books, 2014). "Secrets," a chapter from her forthcoming novel, *Bloodtype*, appeared in the magazine *Banipal* 45 (Winter 2012), translated by Nancy Roberts.

I referred to **Gish Amit**'s article "Salvage or Plunder? Israel's 'Collection' of Private Palestinian Libraries in West Jerusalem," *Journal of Palestinian Studies* 40 (4) (Summer 2011).

Atef Abu Saif's memoir is *The Drone Eats with Me: Diaries from a City Under Fire* (Manchester: Comma Press, 2015).

Mona Abu Sharekh's short story "When I Cut Off Gaza's Head," translated by Katharine Halls, appears in *The Book of Gaza: A City in Short Fiction*, edited by Atef Abu Saif (Manchester: Comma Press, 2014).

Asmaa al-Ghul's short story "You and I," translated by Alexa Firat, appears in *The Book of Gaza: A City in Short Fiction*, edited by Atef Abu Saif (Manchester: Comma Press, 2014).

Gharib Asqalani's short story "A White Flower for David" appears in *The Book of Gaza: A City in Short Fiction*, edited by Atef Abu Saif (Manchester: Comma Press, 2014).

Najlaa Ataallah's short story "The Whore of Gaza," translated by Sarah Irving, appears in *The Book of Gaza: A City in Short Fiction*, edited by Atef Abu Saif (Manchester: Comma Press, 2014). "Midnight," translated by Alice Guthrie, can be found in *Transcript* 33 at www.transcript-review .org/en/issue/transcript-33-gaza/najlaa-ataallah. Ataallah's writings from Operation Protection Edge appear in the July and August 2014 postings on her blog, nataallh.wordpress.com.

Asmaa Azaizeh's poem "Do Not Believe Me If I Talked to You of War," translated by Sani Meo, can be found in the March 2017 issue of *This Week in Palestine*.

A selection of poems by **Moheeb Barghouti**, translated by John Peate, can be found in *Banipal* 45 (Winter 2012).

Mourid Barghouti's books in translation include *I Saw Ramallah*, translated by Ahdaf Soueif (New York: Anchor Books, 2003), and *I Was Born There, I Was Born Here*, translated by Humphrey Davies (New York: Bloomsbury, 2011).

Raji Bathish's short story "Nakba Lite," translated by Suneela Mubayi, can be found in *Banipal* 45 (Winter 2012).

I referred to the following books by **Mahmoud Darwish**: *Memory for Forgetfulness: August, Beirut, 1982*, translated by Ibrahim Muhawi, foreword by Sinan Antoon (Berkeley: University of California Press, 1995); *Unfortunately, It Was Paradise: Selected Poems*, translated and edited by Munir Akash and Carolyn Forché with Sinan Antoon and Amira El-Zein (Berkeley: University of California Press, 2003); *A River Dies of Thirst*, translated by Catherine Cobham (London: Saqi Books, 2009); *Journal of an Ordinary Grief*, translated by Ibrahim Muhawi (New York: Archipelago Books, 2010); *In the Presence of Absence*, translated by Sinan Antoon (New York: Archipelago Books, 2011). Interviews with Darwish include one in *Bomb* 81 (Fall 2002) and one by Maya Jaggi, "Poet of the Arab world," *Guardian*, June 8, 2002, www.theguardian.com /books/2002/jun/08/featuresreviews.guardianreview19.

I referred to **Salha Hamdeen**'s fairy tale *Hantoush*, illustrated by Ahmed al-Khalidi (Ramallah: Tamer Institute for Community Education, 2014).

Ala Hlehel's essay "I Would Like to Apologize to the World," translated by Iyad Maalouf, can be found on his blog at hlehel.blogspot.ca/2014/07 /i-would-like-to-apologize-to-world.html.

Khaled Juma's "Oh Rascal Children of Gaza" can be found at Nerdalicious, nerdalicious.com.au/poets-stage/khaled-juma-oh-rascal-children-of -gaza. "Unseen Aspects of War," translated by Kevin Moore, can be found on the Edinburgh Arabic Initiative at edinburgharabicinitiative.wordpress .com/2014/07/17/unseen-aspects-of-war-by-khaled-juma. Juma's website, www.khaledjuma.net, contains English translations of some of his poems.

I referred to **Sharif Kanaana**'s collection *Speak Bird, Speak Again*: *Palestinian Arab Folktales*, co-authored by Ibrahim Muhawi (Berkeley: University of California Press, 1989).

Ghassan Kanafani's books include *Men in the Sun and Other Palestinian Stories*, translated by Hilary Kilpatrick (Boulder: Lynne Rienner Publishers, 1999), and *Palestine's Children: Returning to Haifa and Other Sto-*

ries, translated by Barbara Harlow and Karen E. Riley (Boulder: Lynne Rienner Publishers, 1999).

Walid Khalidi edited the book *All That Remains: The Palestinian Villages Occupied and Depopulated by Israel in 1948* (Washington: Institute for Palestine Studies, 1992).

I referred to **khulud khamis**'s novel *Haifa Fragments* (Oxford: New Internationalist Publications, 2015).

Much of **Mohammed el-Kurd**'s writing can be found online at his *Medium* page medium.com/@mohammedelkurd.

"Is 53 Seconds Long Enough to Gather My Soul?" by **Rana Mourtaja**, translated by Ibtihal Mahmood, appears in *New Internationalist*, newint .org/features/web-exclusive/2014/08/26/gaza-53-seconds. The story "The Bus Mirror" appears in *Novell Gaza: Ten Short Stories from the Youth of Gaza* (Sweden: Novell Gaza, 2013).

Wisam Rafeedi's letters from prison and testimony from his mother can be found in *Homeland: Oral Histories of Palestine and Palestinians*, edited by Staughton Lynd, Sam Bahour, and Alice Lynd (New York: Olive Branch Press, 1994).

I referred to **Sandrine Dumas Roy**'s children's book *Jour de vote à Sabana* (the original French edition of *Election Day in the Savanna*), illustrated by Bruno Robert (Nice: Les Editions du Ricochet, 2006).

Raja Shehadeh's books include: *Strangers in the House* (London: Profile Books, 2002); *Palestinian Walks: Forays into a Vanishing Landscape* (London: Profile Books, 2007); *Occupation Diaries* (London: Profile Books, 2012); and *Language of War, Language of Peace: Palestine, Israel and the Search for Justice* (London: Profile Books, 2015).

Translations of **Sumaiya al-Susi**'s poems can be found online at the English PEN World Atlas website penatlas.blogspot.ca/search/label

/Soumaya%20Susi. The poems "Night, Net, Gaza" and "The Art of Living in Gaza," translated by Alice Guthrie, can be found in *Transcript* 33 at www.transcript-review.org/en/issue/transcript-33-gaza/somaya-el-sousi. A selection of poems, translated by Charlotte Runcie, are included in *A Bird Is Not a Stone: An Anthology of Contemporary Palestinian Poetry*, edited by Henry Bell and Sarah Irving (Glasgow: Freight Books, 2014).

I referred to the following works by **Ghassan Zaqtan**: *Like a Straw Bird It Follows Me and Other Poems*, translated by Fady Joudah (New Haven: Yale University Press, 2012); *The Silence That Remains: Selected Poems*, translated by Fady Joudah (Port Townsend, WA: Copper Canyon Press, 2017); and his essay "We Were Born in the Houses of Storytellers," translated by Sam Wilder, *World Literature Today*, March 2016, www.worldliteraturetoday .org/2016/march/we-were-born-houses-storytellers-ghassan-zaqtan.

ACKNOWLEDGMENTS

I am grateful to everyone everywhere who supported this book in any way—either by generously sharing their stories, by helping me navigate the complicated logistics of such a project, by extending welcome to a traveling Canadian, or by simply offering encouragement and friendship. They are:

In the West Bank: Mahmoud Abu Hashhash, Maya Abu-Alhayyat, Moheeb Barghouti, Ghassan Zaqtan, Abbad Yahya, Murad Sudani, Raja Shehadeh, Penny Johnson, Salha Hamdeen, Mohammed Hamdeen, Wisam Rafeedi, Sharif Kanaana, Khaled Juma, Beesan and Zeina Ramadan, Morgan Cooper and the staff at Café La Vie, the A. M. Qattan Foundation, Haya Naja, the Palestine Writing Workshop, Omar Robert Hamilton, Nora Lester Murad, Ruba Totah, Ibtisam Alzoghayyer, the Ghirass Cultural Center, Suhail Hijazi, Nabil Al Raee, and Yara Saqfalhait.

In Gaza: Atef Abu Saif, Dr. Refaat Alareer, Wisam Shath and her daughter Wadees, Newrose Qarmout, Othman Hussein, Ziyad Fahed Bakr, Abdusalam al-Manasrah, Gharib Asqalani, the Tamer Institute for Community Education, Jamal Abu al-Qumsan, Mona Abu Sharekh, Asmaa al-Ghul, Mayy Nayef, Donia Al Amal Ismail and her family, Sumaiya al-Susi, Rana Mourtaja, Salim al-Nafar, Najlaa Ataallah and her husband, Raghab, Mo'men Faiz, Ahmed Shehada, and Maram Al-Assar.

In Jerusalem: Mahmoud Muna, Rachel Ukeles, Gish Amit, Mohammed El-Kurd, Ali Jiddah, Haifa and Asem Khalidi, and David Ehrlich.

In Israel: Abu Ahmed Sa'ad, Mohammed Kaial, Najwan Darwish, Ala Hlehel, Raji Bathish, Zochrot (especially Raneen Jeries), Bashar Murkus, khulud khamis, Usama Mohammed Ali, Asmaa Azaizeh, Jennifer Attallah, and Evan Fallenberg.

In Beirut: Anni Kanafani, Nahla Ghandour, Ryma Hady, and Farouk Ghandour.

In France: Sandrine Dumas Roy.

In Canada and the United States: John Vigna, Anahid Melikian, Anahid Helewa, Ghada Ageel, Ilene Prusher, Fady Joudah, Adina Hoffman, Julia Hurley, Hadeel Qazzaz, Mike Crawford, Filomena Gomes, Cathy Ostlere, Harold Knight, Hala Alyan, Sharif Elmusa, Jonathan Garfinkel, Chris Turner, the Calgary Public Library, and everyone at WordsWorth—especially all the young writers.

A few people deserve a special mention. Thanks to my wonderful Gaza fixers, Nedal Samir Hamdouna and Lara Aburamadan, who taught me more about Gaza than anyone else; to Haneen Rizq El-Sammak, her children, Hala, Habiba, and Omar, and her mother, Um Abdallah, for making me feel a part of their beautiful family; to Marcia Lynx Qualey, who I pestered constantly to put me in touch with Palestinian writers; to Edmée Van Rijn for offering to kill the snake in my bathroom; to special agents Jackie Kaiser, Liz Culotti, Meg Wheeler, and Hilary McMahon at Westwood Creative Artists for waving this book in the face of publishers around the world; to the keen eye of my editor Linda Pruessen, who liked this manuscript long before I did; and to Susanne Alexander, Karen

Pinchin, Martin Ainsley, and the rest of the crew at Goose Lane for their continuing enthusiasm for my work.

This project could not have been accomplished without the support of the Alberta Foundation for the Arts and the Canada Council for the Arts.

Lastly, thank you to Moonira Rampuri and Amedeo Di Cintio for your patience, encouragement, and love.

Author photograph by James May

MARCELLO DI CINTIO is the author of four books, including the critically acclaimed *Walls: Travels Along the Barricades*, winner of the 2013 Shaughnessy Cohen Prize for Political Writing and the City of Calgary W.O. Mitchell Book Prize. Di Cintio's essays have been published in *The Walrus*, *Canadian Geographic*, *The New York Times*, *Condé Nast Traveler*, and *Afar*. He lives in Calgary. Find more at marcellodicintio.com.